A Time of Respair

A Time of Respair
Beyond COVID, Volcanic Eruptions, Hurricane Elsa,
and Global Turmoil — Fresh Hope for
St. Vincent and the Grenadines

© 2022 Ralph E. Gonsalves

Printed in the United States

ISBN #9798849318677

Published by Strategy Forum, Inc.
Kingstown, St. Vincent and the Grenadines

A Time of Respair

Beyond COVID, Volcanic Eruptions, Hurricane Elsa,
and Global Turmoil — Fresh Hope
for St. Vincent and the Grenadines

by

Dr. The Hon. Ralph E. Gonsalves
Prime Minister, St. Vincent and the Grenadines

Contents

Dedication

To the families who have endured the pain,
suffering and hardship of the COVID pandemic,
the volcanic eruptions, and Hurricane Elsa
in St. Vincent and the Grenadines.

Poetic Reflections

We are all time,
Yet only the future is ours
To desecrate.

The present is the past,
And the past
Our fathers' mischief.

We are the Cenotaphs, by Daniel Williams
Poet of St. Vincent and the Grenadines

"Beneath the rain of drums
The flute's black stalk
Grew, withered, and sprouted again.
Things cast off from their names
I flowed
At my body's edge
Among the unbounded elements."

Release by Octavio Paz,
Mexican Nobel Laureate In Literature

"Morning by morning new mercies I see
All I have needed thy hand hath provided
Great is thy faithfulness, Lord, unto me."

Great is thy Faithfulness by William Runyan,
Thomas Chisholm, and Eric Schrotenboer

Preface

I started to write this book in my head in November 2021; I usually write in my head before I "put pen to paper". I began working on the first draft of the manuscript on January 1, 2022; I felt an urgency to do it for our government, our people of St. Vincent and the Grenadines whom I love dearly, and for the wider Caribbean.

The urgency is compelling given the challenges before us. On January 1, 2022, the immediacy of the socio-economic and physical ravages of the volcanic eruptions of April 1, 2021 were still with us. There were then 82 COVID-related deaths. In early July 2021, Hurricane Elsa — the first of the 2021 hurricane season — struck. By the end of February 2022, there were 106 such deaths and by February 24, 2022, Russia and Ukraine were at war with knock-on, adverse economic and security impacts for the world, including St. Vincent and the Grenadines. There is an unprecedented urgency about all matters of public policy, programmes, and project implementation in Budget 2022, and for the indicative years of 2023 and 2024.

The book is designed to assist greatly with the understanding of the government's people-centred vision; its philosophy of advanced social democracy applied to our circumstances; its encompassing socio-cultural framework for the further ennoblement of our Caribbean civilisation, inclusive of its magnificent Vincentian component and the genius of our people; our quest to build a modern, competitive, many-sided post-colonial economy that is at once local, national, regional, and global; our economic approach in shaping an integrated, mixed economy with the private, cooperative, and State sectors; the desirable socio-economic outcomes embedded in the 17 Sustainable Development Goals, arising from the post-colonial economy and our economic approach; the place of targeted strategic interventions in our economy at the time of a paradigm shift to a modern, post-colonial economy; the special measures necessary and desirable to tackle the fall-out from the pandemic, the volcanic eruptions, the convulsions of monopoly capitalism globally, the geo-political uncertainties, and climate change; the fashioning of a mature regionalism within CARICOM and the OECS; the building of internationalist solidarity; the immediate overarching thrust of respairing as we recover and rebuild in the aftermath of the pandemic, the volcanic eruptions, and Hurricane Elsa; and our commitment to an alive constitutionalism and the praxis of good governance.

Strategically, during the two-year period, and continuing, of the pandemic, exacerbated by the volcanic eruptions of April 2021, and Hurricane Elsa of early July 2021, our government ensured that the planning and preparation necessary to emerge from this metaphoric valley of immense dislocation was being done methodically; this requirement was substantially achieved so that the climb out from the valley of dislocation to the veritable mountaintop of a recovery and beyond, would be focused, durable, swift, and sustainable. Accordingly, we had to survive and thrive in "the valley" while preparing for an immediate ascent. This was not, and cannot be, achieved through serendipity.

All these central themes connect to, and are interconnected with, Budget 2022 that was presented to Parliament in January 2022; it is, too, offered herein through a sketching of its essentials and its developmental thrust. Important raw data are thus summarised about our economy and Budget 2022.

The book consists of six chapters, plus the Introduction that maps the broad context of the publication. Chapter One addresses the historical backdrop of relevance in our quest to respair, inclusive of a discourse on the ideational ferment in the Caribbean regarding socio-economic development. Chapter Two details the paradigm shift in the construction of a modern, competitive, diversified, post-colonial economy and its central features, and the twin related issues of sustainable development and economic growth. Chapter Three is about Budget 2022 in all its relevance for our current push to respair and recover. Chapter Four addresses a range of miscellaneous issues arising from Budget 2022, especially the critical issues of good governance and institution-building for now and the future. Chapter Five presents the framework and details of the mixed economy, including an analysis of the private, cooperative, and State sectors. Chapter Six concludes with vital considerations of managing the paradigm shift, our Caribbean civilisation, leadership, the summation of the process of respairing and the outpourings of the genius of our people. An Appendix provides the details of the capital projects by Ministry in the Budget 2022.

Although I am the author of the book, and I take full responsibility for its contents, it is essentially a collaborative work between my Cabinet colleagues, professionals in the public service, the various stakeholders in our economy, and me. In some places I have relied heavily on others. For example, Chapter Three on Budget 2022 is largely due to the preparatory work of Edmond Jackson, Director General of Finance and Planning, and Ken Morris, the Budget Director of the government of St. Vincent and the Grenadines. Similarly, sections on the Bank of St. Vincent and the Grenadines, the National Insurance Services, the St. Vincent Electricity Services, the Central Water and Sewerage Authority, and the National Telecommunications Regulatory Commission, are drawn copiously from the briefing notes of their respective Chief The Minister of Finance, Camillo Gonsalves, read the draft manuscript to do fact-checking and make useful suggestions for textual improvements. I thank him.

Thanks also to Mrs. Angie Williams-Jackson who kindly typed the manuscript, on her own time, outside her usual hectic schedule as Permanent Secretary at the Office of the Prime Minister.

I am grateful, too, for the kind assistance of Inga Rhonda King of Strategy Forum Incorporated for bringing the book to publication. My wife Eloise has been extremely supportive as I near-obsessively wrote the pages at home at Gorse or Kingstown, and on the road, at late nights in London, Dubai, and Qatar. I owe much to her.

I dedicate this book to the families who have endured the pain, suffering, and hardship of the COVID pandemic, the volcanic eruptions, and Hurricane Elsa in St. Vincent and the Grenadines.

Ralph E. Gonsalves, Prime Minister
St. Vincent and the Grenadines
July 31, 2022

Introduction

The year 2022 in St. Vincent and the Grenadines began with the immediacy of the ongoing consequences of the COVID pandemic that has been raging since March 2020, and continuing; the volcanic eruptions of April 2021; and Hurricane Elsa of July 2, 2021. This bundle of debilitating external shocks to the socio-economic system constitutes a continuation, and exacerbation, of exogenous health, climatic, economic, social, and security threats to the well-being of this small, multi-island developing State with a landscape of 150 square miles and a seascape of some 11,000 square nautical miles, populated by 110,000 persons but possessed of a large, inter-linked diaspora of over twice that number.

This near-perfect metaphoric storm of pandemic, volcanic eruptions, and a tropical hurricane has descended upon a small, developing Caribbean nation with inherent vulnerabilities, inclusive of those resident in adverse climate change; scarce material resources; an historical legacy of underdevelopment arising from native genocide, the enslavement of Africans, the indentureship of Madeirans and Indians, and a destructive process of colonisation of some 200 years; the contemporary challenges emerging from the global political economy of monopoly capitalism, inclusive of its oppressive contradictions; and an array of unfinished business, internally, of our young nation, which commemorated on October 27, 2021, the forty-second anniversary of its reclamation of independence from Britain.

The unvarnished facts, in *summary form*, as at December 31, 2021, tell the tale of the damage and loss caused by the pandemic, the volcanic eruptions, and the hurricane.

COVID. Some 6,000 cases; nearly 600 active cases; 82 COVID-related deaths, 70 of which occurred subsequent to the first week in August 2021; some 62,000 vaccines administered (35,000 first doses and 27,000 second doses); economic contraction of 3.5 percent in 2020 and minimal economic growth (0.7 percent or thereabouts) in 2021;

over 3,000 local employees laid off; 3,500 hospitality workers either sent home or reduced to part-time employment; some 1,500 seafarers returned home when cruise tourism fell apart globally; in all approximately 20 percent of the employed labour force were thus initially affected adversely; 400 businesses either closed temporarily or laid-off workers; thousands more persons, particularly in the informal sector, had incomes reduced sharply or lost completely due to fewer tourists, limited foot traffic, and restricted outdoor gatherings; schools were closed or only partially opened; classes were held online; the usual main drivers of government revenue fell significantly; public debt increased; and at the peak of the pandemic's economic impact in January – March 2021, local borrowers numbering 1,340 received forbearance on EC $268 million worth of loans from the banks. (EC $2.70 = US $1.00).

In late 2021 I caused to be published a monograph I wrote entitled *The Atomised Individual, The Social Individual, and the COVID Vaccine*; in this publication I discussed, at some length, all these inter-connected issues of the pandemic, and more.

VOLCANIC ERUPTIONS. Thirty-two explosive eruptions occurred between April 9th and April 22nd, 2021, category 4 on the Volcanic Explosivity Index or 10 times more explosive than the category 3 eruptions of April 1979; 500,000 metric tonnes of emitted ash, coating roads, homes, and public infrastructure across St. Vincent; one-fifth or 20,000 of the population were evacuated; lahars and pyroclastic flows destroyed or damaged buildings and farms across the northern third of St. Vincent; over 700 homes were damaged or destroyed; preliminary, incomplete analysis from the United Nations Development Programme estimates loss and damage in excess of EC $635 million or nearly one-third of Gross Domestic Product (GDP); one-third of agriculture was devastated; much of fishing badly affected; students were to return to face-to-face classes on April 12, 2021, in a trial run during the pendency of the pandemic, but the eruption of April 9th put paid to that; the suitable schools were all used as shelters for evacuees. Thankfully, neither the eruptions nor the evacuation process resulted in anyone dead or injured.

HURRICANE ELSA. First hurricane of the 2021 Atlantic Hurricane Season: it damaged scores of homes, public buildings, infrastructure, and the coastline, and displaced over 200 persons; it affected mainly the north-east of St. Vincent that was already battered by the volcanic eruptions; *preliminary* estimates of damage and loss amount to some $50 million.

The triple shocks (pandemic, volcanic eruptions, hurricane) have severely tested the resilience of our people, our strengths, and possibilities. Prior to these shocks, St. Vincent and the Grenadines had a GDP in 2019 of approximately EC $2.2 billion and an average annual per capita GDP of some EC $20,000. Unemployment hovered at just under 20 percent of the labour force; general poverty was assessed at 30 percent (assessment in 2009) and indigence at some 3 percent.

At the same time, St. Vincent and the Grenadines was listed by the United Nations Development Programme on its Human Development Index as a country with a High Level of Human Development, above "medium", but below "very high". St. Vincent and the Grenadines is a thriving multi-party, highly competitive, liberal democracy with very high scores accorded to it by all reputable international agencies for civil and political freedoms, freedom of the press, economic freedoms, free and fair elections, and political democracy generally.

Debates on public policy and governance are robust in parliament, in the media (independent newspapers, online publications, radio stations, and television channels). The online global networking is also done through cellphones (more active cellphones than the population size), computers, tablets or other electronic devices on various Internet platforms. Accordingly, the misuse and abuse of information technologies to spread misinformation and falsehoods often exceed their proper use for the dissemination of truthful information or factual representations.

In responding to the immediate disasters of the pandemic, the volcanic eruptions, and the hurricane, the government mobilised all the relevant institutions of State in concert with the people and civil society, the regional family of nations, and the international community to forge an appropriate strategic path forward to address efficaciously the short-term humanitarian concerns, the relief efforts, and the medium-term recovery and rebuilding exercise.

The financial year, January to December 2020, had run a mere ten weeks when the World Health Organisation (WHO), on March 11, 2020, declared a worldwide outbreak of COVID-19 (Coronavirus Disease). On that very day, St. Vincent and the Grenadines recorded its first COVID case — an imported one — by way of a citizen who had returned from the United Kingdom. A national budget had already been passed in the Parliament for the 2020 financial year amounting to EC $1.186 billion: Recurrent Spending of $875.58 million, inclusive of $197 million for Amortization of the national debt and the Sinking Fund Contribution; and Capital Expenditure of $310.77 million.

The immediacy of COVID's devastating impact was so swiftly felt that by March 25, 2020 — two weeks after the first case — I made a national address outlining a package of measures, fiscal and otherwise that I was proposing to take to Parliament. Thus, in early April 2020, Parliament approved several measures, including substantial amendments to the Public Health Act of 1977, specially-targeted and Supplementary Estimates and a Supplementary Appropriation Bill, to tackle the pandemic.

The upshot of all this, and more, was to revise upwards the initial 2020 Estimates of Expenditure from $1.1864 billion to $1.3434 billion, a hefty increase of $157 million or 13.2 percent. The increased expenditures were almost all related to COVID: spending on health-related aspects of the pandemic; extensive social safety net supports for displaced workers; short-term job creation initiatives; and production supports, mainly to farmers, fisherfolk, and small businesses.

For the financial year 2021, Parliament approved a national budget through its Estimates of Expenditure amounting to EC $1.2 billion: Recurrent Spending of $895.2 million, inclusive of Amortization and Sinking Fund Contribution of $197 million; and Capital Expenditure of $317.4 million. These sums were more than the Approved Estimates of 2020 but less than the Revised Estimates of that very year.

Thirteen weeks after the commencement of the 2021 financial year, for which Estimates and Appropriation Bill Parliament had already granted approval, the La Soufriere Volcano erupted on the morning of April 9, 2021. Yet again my government had to go to Parliament to revise upwards its budgeted expenditures to meet the exigencies of the volcanic eruptions.

Thus, on May 7, 2021, Parliament approved Supplementary Estimates and a Supplementary Appropriation Bill to address the multiple fall-outs from the volcanic eruptions and the further spread of the COVID pandemic. Parliament, over the next few months, approved, too, further amendments to the Public Health Act and passed other relevant legislative measures designed to improve the handling of the pandemic. A number of statutory rules and orders — subsidiary legislation — were also put in place to tackle more effectively the pandemic, including among frontline and strategic employees in the State sector.

The revision of the Approved Estimates for 2021 accordingly rose to $1.365 billion, an increase of $149 million or 12.3 percent more than the Approved Estimates for 2021 of $1.2126 billion.

Between the start of the pandemic on March 11, 2020, and the Declaration of a Public Health Emergency accordingly, and the commencement of the financial year 2022, there were Supplementary Estimates and a Supplementary Appropriation Bill in 2020, Special Warrants for other urgent and unforeseen expenditure, and substantive Estimates and an Appropriation Bill for 2021 during that time of COVID, and an additional set of supplementaries to address the consequences of the volcanic eruptions of April 2021, which measures also dealt with additional COVID-related matters. In these respects, and more, the State administration and Parliament performed mighty deeds.

By the start of the financial year for January 1st to December 31st, 2022, Parliament had already approved, in December 2021, the Estimates of Expenditure and Revenue for 2022 in the aggregate sum of EC $1.3293 billion: Recurrent spending of $931.88, inclusive of Amortization and the Sinking Fund Contribution of $204 million; and Capital Expenditure of $397.46 million. Overall, these sums are less than the Revised Estimates for 2021, but more than the Approved Estimates of 2021. The Appropriation Bill for 2022 went before Parliament and was approved after much parliamentary maneuvering due to COVID infections among Parliamentarians, on January 14, 2022.

During the very testing period of March 11, 2020, to January 2022 — a period of 22 months — and continuing, there have been immense dislocations and disruptions touching and concerning lives, livelihoods, and production, as reflected particularly in the areas of health, the economy, the society (including education), and security.

In his Budget Address for the fiscal year 2022, delivered on January 10, 2022, and entitled "Rising from the Ashes to the Challenges", Minister of Finance Camillo Gonsalves summarised the adverse impacts and the core responses of the government thus:

> Between April 2020 and June 2021, the Government and the National Insurance Services spent $14 million in income support to 6,000 persons economically-impacted by the pandemic. A further $15 million in income support was provided to vendors, entertainers, farmers, taxi, minibus and handcart operators. Millions more were spent on sickness benefits, funeral grants, medical care, and other measures to combat the astronomical health effects of the disease.

Our country is neither large nor wealthy. We are defined by our vulnerabilities as much as our strengths. Yet we met the enormity of the 2021 challenges with compassion and creativity. Our Government was never going to be able to single-handedly shield all citizens from the full impact of 2021's triple threats. Our people have suffered tremendously. However, the work of all branches of the State apparatus has been extraordinary in markedly easing the burden on Vincentians.

In spite of these monumental challenges, 2021 was also a year of enviable accomplishment. Let us list some:

- For the first time in our history, we welcomed direct flights from the United Kingdom, via the acclaimed Virgin Atlantic airways.

- We ensured that every student in this country, from kindergarten to Community College, received a tablet computer, to help navigate the challenges of online education.

- We secured 55 scholarships to the University of Wales Trinity St. David and 40 additional Taiwanese university scholarships over a five-year period. We also granted over 500 Tuition Scholarships to various universities; and allocated 61 National Scholarships, National Exhibitions, Special Awards and Bursaries to our outstanding young students.

- We constructed and opened four modern temporary schools at Bequia, Black Point and Arnos Vale, to allow for massive rehabilitative works on our education facilities.

- We completed multimillion dollar coastal protection projects in Georgetown and Sans Souci, and river defences in Buccament and Carriere, to safeguard vulnerable villages and infrastructure.

- We built bridges from Grand Sable to Chateaubelair, new roads in Belle Isle and Long Line, and commenced a comprehensive road repair programme through BRAGSA.

- We awarded 138 PRYME grants to young entrepreneurs and constructed the first PRYME Community market in Glen.

- We constructed or expanded more than 50 Lives to Live homes, completed houses for 49 families to be relocated from Rose Place, and built 27 volcano-replacement homes in Orange Hill thus far to ensure safety and security to vulnerable families.

- We constructed and refurbished hard courts in Lowmans Hill and Green Hill, built a playing field in Evesham, and secured World Athletics' certification for the athletic track at Diamond.

- We massively expanded our social protection architecture to directly touch the lives of over 40,000 Vincentians who were vulnerable, displaced by the volcano or affected by the pandemic.

• We fully or partially vaccinated roughly 35,000 Vincentians against the worst effects of COVID, making them, their families, and our country more resilient against the pandemic.

• In a year of massive temporary increases in unemployment, we nonetheless saw the creation of close to 1,200 jobs by the private and public sectors, helping to lessen the impact of our challenges, and will position us for stronger growth once the immediacy of our current challenges has passed.

• And we enrolled over 800 students in technical and vocational courses, adding crucial skills and certifications to our workforce, particularly among young people.

• In the private sector, 2021 saw numerous initiatives, in concert with proclaimed public policy and the Government's practical incentives, including the following:

• The opening of the La Vue Hotel and the continued construction of the Royal Mill Resort, by the same developers;

• The accelerated construction of Myah's Luxury Suites that will open this year;

• The significant progress made on the construction of the $10 million Coreas Distribution Centre that will be completed this year

• The completion of the $10 million Rainforest Seafoods Processing Facility;

• The further development of the Medicinal Cannabis industry, including preparations for the first exports of medicinal cannabis from St. Vincent and the Grenadines;

• The rapid expansion of the Clear Harbor Call Centre, now employing over 600 workers; and

• The recruitment by Sandals Resorts of the first 150 Vincentian workers – out of a planned 500 workers – to staff Sandals and Beaches Resorts across the Caribbean.

The pandemic and the volcano demanded the Government's focussed attention, but they did not consume us. Beyond those challenges, the work of nation building was unceasing. Project by project – including the ongoing preparatory work on major ones such as the Modern Port, the Acute Referral Hospital, and the Marriott Resort at Mt. Wynne – we continued to lay the foundation for transformative development and people-centred progress."

In summation, the government's specific, COVID-related recurrent and capital expenditure in 2020 amounted to over $50 million, and slightly less in 2021. The government's expenditure in 2021 of volcano relief, specifically, approximated $100 million. In 2022, the budget, recurrent and capital, show similar huge expenditure sums on these two items — the pandemic and the recovery after the volcanic eruptions.

The supply chain challenges, inclusive of price rises and critical shortages, during the global pandemic, have been exacerbated as a result of Russia's military activity in Ukraine. A few examples will suffice, evidentially: the cost, insurance, and freight (CIF) price of a tonne of wheat to St. Vincent and the Grenadines increased from US $347 in 2020 to US $575 in April 2022; crude oil prices per barrel jumped from US $20.86 in April 2020 to US $100 in April 2022; and the global container freight rate rose by 551 percent from April 2020 to January 2022.

The price of fertilizer to the farmers has skyrocketed over the early months of 2022. Accordingly, the government has had to increase sharply the usual subsidies for fertilizer purchased through the State-owned Agricultural Input Warehouse Limited. Thus, for example, in April 2022, on a purchase of a shipment of 7,520 sacks of (100 lbs.) of various fertiliser (NPK, 4,600; Sulphate of Ammonia, 460; vegetable fertilizer, 460; and urea, 2,000 sacks) costing approximately EC $0.8 million, the government has had to provide a subsidy of EC $0.42 million so as to keep the prices for the farmers at a level close to the pre-February 2022 prices. The subsidy per sack ranged from EC $21 for sulphate of ammonia to EC $73 for urea; the popular NPK is subsidised at EC $55 per sack.

In the case of fuel, the rapidly increasing price prompted the government to cut the excise tax on a gallon of gasoline by EC $1.50 and on diesel by EC $1.05. The cost to the revenue is approximately EC $1 million per month; this measure is slated to be a short-term one for three months. Similarly, in respect of the electricity bill issued to all consumers in mid-June 2022, both the government and the State-owned St. Vincent and the Grenadines Electricity Services Limited (VIN-LEC) provided a subsidy towards one-half of the increase in the fuel surcharge amounting to EC $800,000, due to the increase in the price of imported diesel, and the fall in the electricity output from the three hydro-electricity plants due to drought.

Additionally, the government has waived the customs service charge of 6 percent on the price of a cylinder of liquified petroleum gas (LPG — cooking gas). Other supportive measures for some 4,000 farmers, 1,000 fisherfolk, and vulnerable social groups, inclusive of some 5,000 families, have also been further strengthened. It is a most challenging time; but there is a fresh hope.

The government has had to ensure that the pain on our people, occasioned by exogenous factors, not of our making, is eased as far as is humanly possible while at the same time advancing the agenda to build a modern, competitive, many-sided post-colonial economy in our quest for overall sustainable development. And we are making progress!

The International Monetary Fund (IMF) projects that in 2022, given the public and private sector investment initiatives in train, the economy of St. Vincent and the Grenadines is slated to grow at near 3 percent; our own experts in the Ministry of Finance and Economic Planning, more conservatively, project economic growth slightly less. Real economic growth of this magnitude may return the size of the economy to about the pre-COVID level, taking into consideration the economic contraction of 3.5 percent in 2020, and the modest growth of 0.7 percent in 2021 in the year of massive natural disasters and the further spread of COVID.

So, barring the realisation of downside risks such as a prolongation or deterioration of the pandemic, further natural disasters, knock-on turbulences from the global political economy, and sub-optimal performance of capital investments, the prospects of recovery and rebuilding stronger are at hand. The extent of the adverse knock-on effects of the Russia-Ukraine war of February 24, 2022, and continuing, is not yet fully known, but already price hikes in imported commodities such as fuel, fertiliser, flour, sugar, animal feeds, and cooking oils have shaken the recovery and rebuilding process. The government, from its slender resources, has been providing time-bound subsidies for fuel, fertiliser, flour, and animal feeds to meet the harsh exigencies of price rises.

From the current vantage point, I speak more of respair, rather than recovery, rebuilding, or rehabilitation only. RESPAIR is a beautiful word in the English Language that, sadly, has fallen into disuse; it is both a verb and a noun; it means fresh hope, and a recovery from a period or condition of setbacks, dislocations, disruptions, uncertainties, despondency, and despair; it goes to our existential beings. Respair is more compelling and comprehensive a concept or idea than its synonyms; it is an uplifting idea which, as "fresh hope", embraces faith and love, the trilogy of which are resident in our people's consciousness as core essences of our Judeo-Christian socialisation and our Caribbean experiences, grounded in social solidarity.

Even before the full extent of the COVID-19 pandemic had been felt by the people of St. Vincent and the Grenadines, and one year before the volcanic eruptions, I had already sensed that an extraordinary set of circumstances was unfolding, demanding an especial existential response of a united people.

Indeed, on April 5, 2020, three weeks after the global and national declaration of the pandemic on March 11th, I launched on behalf of the government and people of St. Vincent and the Grenadines a **GOOD NEIGHBOUR PARTNERSHIP** to fight COVID-19. In a brief one-page document on this Partnership I stated:

> "Each of us is a neighbour to each other. Each of us has a responsibility to look after ourselves, our families, our neighbours, our communities, our nation. This responsibility resides, too, in our churches, our NGOs, our various organisations, businesses, and workplaces.
>
> The **GOOD NEIGHBOUR PARTNERSHIP** is a broad-based national family initiative to which everyone of us is entitled to belong. You join immediately by your actions, not mere words, in fighting COVID-19.
>
> Here are the TEN PRINCIPLES for action as a GOOD NEIGHBOUR:
>
> • Be a good neighbour and citizen. Practice best personal hygiene: washing hands, wearing protective masks.
>
> • Observe personal and physical distancing; avoid or reduce gatherings.
>
> • Stay in quarantine if advised or ordered to do so.
>
> • Show especial love to the afflicted, the elderly, and children.

- Care for your immediate community in every way.
- Be nice to nurses, doctors, and other frontline employees, including the police.
- Be disciplined, focused, resourceful, and creative in all we do; do not panic.
- Listen and follow the advice of the authorities.

All these principles are inter-connected. Let us in each of these ways: BE THE BEST WE CAN!

These simple verities, derived from the tried and tested, uplifting values of our Caribbean civilisation were fortified on an ongoing basis as the pandemic unfolded, through actions by the State and the people's social solidarity. At the time of the launch of the **GOOD NEIGHBOUR PARTNERSHIP**, vaccines to fight COVID-19 were not yet available in St. Vincent and the Grenadines; later when they became available, they were incorporated as vital to the Partnership and social solidarity.

The volcanic eruptions of April 2021 and their socio-economic and physical aftermath required, too, even greater social solidarity, and a deepening Good Neighbour Partnership, and efficacious actions by the State. In our nation's rebuilding and recovery, we must go beyond the ordinary. We must embrace FRESH HOPE at this our existential time of RESPAIR.

Unfortunately, over the period since March 11, 2020, up to the present time, political factionalism and other forms of divisiveness have racked our society, undermining the greater requisite of social solidarity. Over this period, general elections were held in November 2020; in keeping with competitive electoral contests in our multi-party, liberal democracy there was intense political campaigning. After the return of the Unity Labour Party (ULP) for its fifth consecutive five-year term in government since March 2001, the political competition and divisiveness have not ceased or abated; indeed, forces opposed to the government, including the opposition New Democratic Party (NDP), have been in a veritable state of permanent campaigning, ignoring completely the existential challenges at hand. More than ever, though, this very opposition intransigence and factionalism make it an imperative of the highest socio-political order to hold aloft the banner of enhanced social solidarity, a Good Neighbour Partnership, and national unity to go beyond rebuilding and recovery, and to respair in quest of a many-sided sustainable development. Those who prioritise political divisiveness, factionalism, and anti-social behaviour at a time of urgent respair must be pushed back on all fronts as we Lift SVG Higher!

Parallels exist in our history and the history of other nations to assist in guiding us as we go forward. I shall shortly survey the period in our own history from 1881 to 1931 to aid us in our efforts. But first, let us reflect on the manner in which the young American Revolution in the late 18th century addressed the malaise of political factionalism/divisiveness.

I take as our inspirational text in this regard *The Federalist Papers*, No. 10 of November 22, 1787, by James Madison on "the tendency", "the propensity" of "the dangerous vice" of factionalism in the body politic.

Madison tells us:

> By a faction I understand a number of citizens, whether amounting to a majority or minority of the whole, who are united and actuated by some common impulse of passion, or of interest, adverse to the rights of other citizens, or to the permanent and aggregate interests of the community."

With incisive logic and sparing language, James Madison gets to the heart of the matter:

> There are two methods of curing the mischiefs of faction: The one, by removing its causes; the other, by controlling its effects.

> There are again two methods of removing the causes of faction: The one by destroying the liberty which is essential to its existence; the other, by giving to every citizen the same opinions, the same passions, and the same interests.

> It could never be more truly said than of the first remedy, that it is worse than the disease. Liberty is to faction, what air is to fire, an aliment without which it instantly expires. But it could not be a less folly to abolish liberty, which is essential to political life, because it nourishes faction, than it would be to wish the annihilation of air, which is essential to animal life because it imparts to fire its destructive agency.

> The second expedient is as impracticable, as the first would be unwise. As long as the reason of man continues fallible, and he is at liberty to exercise it, different opinions will be formed....

> So strong is this propensity of mankind to fall into mutual animosities, that where no substantial occasion presents itself, the

most frivolous and fanciful distinctions have been sufficient to kindle their unfriendly passions, and excite their most violent conflicts. But the most common and durable source of factions, has been the various and unequal distribution of property."

In St. Vincent and the Grenadines, additionally, we note that political factions, and divisiveness have been engendered by the thirst or hunger of many persons for status, office, position, patronage, or some such personal or material gain.

So, since the causes of faction are unlikely to be, or are not easily removed, and in a context of liberal democratic freedoms, factions to one degree or another will continue to exist and to be fuelled, the remaining issue is the managing or controlling of factions and their divisiveness.

In this regard, the overwhelming majority of the people of St. Vincent and the Grenadines broadly recognise, first, that political factions or divisiveness ought not to degenerate into an intolerance that may breed violence. Secondly, that violence in the pursuit of factionalism or political divisiveness be eschewed; that peaceful and orderly ventilation and/or resolution of disputes is the only way to good governance order and progress. Thirdly, constitutionalism and the rule of law provide the avenues for legitimate expression of political factionalism, divisiveness or differences. And fourthly, there are free and fair elections, held at regular, periodic intervals, to resolve the issue as to which political party holds the reins of government. These are among the foundational precepts to which the Unity Labour Party (ULP) is committed; they, too, guide our government.

In short, in this period of respair and building back better and stronger, let those who oppose practice their lawful, peaceful oppositional factionalism. Those who are elected to govern, do so wisely, maturely, and as inclusively as is humanly practicable in the public interest; and continue to win elections in the interest of the public good and sustainable development.

At this time of respair, more than ever, good governance demands not only the greatest practicable manifestations of national unity, but also an especial focus on those who are, for one objective reason or another, marginalised, disadvantaged, possessed of disabilities, suffering injustice or material hardship. These considerations have defined, historically, and currently, the governance of, and by, the Unity Labour Party.

It is a truism that if the wage-earner in every form of economic activity, the farmer, the fisherfolk, the trader, own-account worker, and the business person do well or are comparatively comfortable, it is absolutely sure that all others and the nation will be well off, too. The reverse is also true. Good times and bad times affect us all, though not in equal measure.

In his first State of the Union address in 1901, at the time of fresh hope at the turn of the American century, despite the pall of the recent assassination of President William McKinley, President Theodore Roosevelt spoke relevant home truths, thus:

> The fundamental rule in our national life — the rule which underlies all others — is that, on the whole, and in the long run, we shall go up or down together. There are exceptions; and in times of prosperity some will prosper far more, and in times of adversity, some will suffer far more, than others; but speaking generally, a period of good times means that all share more or less in them, and in a period of hard times all feel the stress to a greater or less degree. It surely ought not to be necessary to enter into any proof of this statement; the memory of the lean years which began in 1893 is still vivid, and we can contrast them with the conditions in this very year which is now closing. Disaster to great business enterprises can never have its effects limited to the men at the top. It spreads throughout, and while it is bad for everybody, it is worst for those farthest down. The capitalist may be shorn of his luxuries; but the wage-worker may be deprived of even bare necessities."

As we traverse together the journey beyond the COVID pandemic, the volcanic eruptions and Hurricane Elsa, and as we embrace fresh hope, uphold the faith made manifest in works, and act humanly in love, the government and people must shape the public policy responses with all these truths in mind. Like one of the esteemed leaders of the twelve tribes of Israel, Issachar, we must know the times and act accordingly. Those who are driven to factionalism and divisiveness for whatever reason, let them not detain us as we do our mighty deeds for our families, our communities, our nation.

One central systemic or strategic question that arises theoretically and practically in the good governance of St. Vincent and the Grenadines, generally, and especially at this time of respair concerns the relationship between labour and capital. I have written extensively on this matter, most recently and comprehensively in my book, *The Political Economy of the Labour Movement in St. Vincent and the Grenadines*, published in 2019. The published documents of the ULP, including its

Election Manifestos, and the relevant publications of the ULP government address this issue, too.

For our purposes here, in the spirit of our times, and in the aftermath of the convulsions, dislocations and extraordinary challenges caused by the pandemic, the volcanic eruptions and climate-change events, the sage advice of the revered 19th century President of the USA, Abraham Lincoln, are perhaps appropriate on the linkage between labour and capital:

> Labor is prior to, and independent of, capital. Capital is only the fruit of labor, and could never have existed if labor had not first existed. Labor is the superior of capital, and deserves much the higher consideration....
>
> Capital has its rights, which are as worthy of protection as any other rights.... Nor should this lead to a war upon owners of property. Property is the fruit of labor.... Property is desirable, is a positive good in the world....
>
> "Let not him who is homeless pull down the house of another, but let him work diligently and build one for himself, thus by example assuring that his own shall be safe from violence when built."

Additionally, in our context in St. Vincent and the Grenadines, the ULP says that by sound public policy, the State will facilitate or assist the homeless in securing or building a home for himself/herself!

Central to our respairing, the embracing of fresh hope, it is vital that we protect our environment, our physical resources; conserve the bounty of nature, and cause it to be restored, where it has been damaged or despoiled, in a condition better than before.

These elemental tenets we hold dear as we respair.

At this time of respair *beyond* the COVID pandemic, the volcanic eruptions and Hurricane Elsa, we must of necessity explore our historical legacies of underdevelopment and the challenges arising from the contemporary global political economy.

St. Vincent and the Grenadines will not be able to do it alone. To be sure, we possess enormous strengths and possibilities but we are constrained immensely by our weaknesses and limitations. We are required ourselves to do the creative thinking, the smart working, and the heavy lifting. But we have to do so in concert with our regional partners, and our international friends and allies.

In addressing the pandemic, we have been well-supported by several organisations: the Caribbean Public Health Agency (CARPHA); the Pan-American Health Organisation (PAHO); the World Health Organisation (WHO) and its affiliate agencies, such as COVAX; the Regional Security System (RSS); the Mustique Charitable Trust; private benefactors and other charitable bodies.

On matters touching and concerning the volcanic eruptions and climate change, including Hurricane Elsa, other regional and global entities came to our aid and comfort, including the United Nations and its various agencies (WFP, UNEP, UNICEF); the Caribbean Disaster Emergency Management Agency (CDEMA); Seismic Research Centre of the University of the West Indies; Red Cross International; World Central Kitchen; the Commonwealth; the World Bank, and the International Monetary Fund (IMF).

Regional and hemispheric organisations proved most helpful, with both the pandemic and the volcanic eruptions, including: the Caribbean Community (CARICOM), the Organisation of Eastern Caribbean States (OECS); the Association of Caribbean States (ACS); the Community of States of Latin America and the Caribbean (CELAC); and the Organisation of American States (OAS).

Governments from the Caribbean and internationally came to our support, including: every member-State and associate member-State of CARICOM, and the OECS; most of CELAC, especially Venezuela and Cuba; Taiwan, the USA, Canada, the United Kingdom, Australia, New Zealand, the European Union and states within the EU, the United Arab Emirates, Qatar, Morocco, several countries in the African Union, Japan, India and Russia.

And, of course, tremendous support, during the natural disaster emergency consequent upon the volcanic eruptions, came from Vincentians overseas, and non-Vincentians from across other CARICOM countries, and elsewhere. There still remains tremendous goodwill towards St. Vincent and the Grenadines from all our friends and allies all over our region, our hemisphere, and the world. This social solidarity and internationalism are sources of inestimable strength and possibilities in our quest to respair!

To respair our lives, livelihoods and production is a many-sided process awash with multiple contradictions. It is not a linear process; it has its ups and downs, setbacks and advances, its zigs and zags; it is both a process and a destination; it culminates not in a dead end. Its many-sided quest is to achieve sustainable development in accord with the seventeen Sustainable Development Goals (SDGs) and attendant actions and targets as universally-endorsed by the member-states of the United Nations, including St. Vincent and the Grenadines, in September 2015.

Hitherto, at the turn of the Millennium, there were the Millennium Development Goals (MDGs) that gave way to the SDGs. The SDGs were integral to the Election Manifestos of the Unity Labour Party (ULP) in December 2015 and November 2020. The ULP government, which I have headed continuously since March 2001 for 21 years, thus far, has been pursuing first the MDGs and thereafter the SDGs as the bedrocks of our public policies.

In life, living and production, in their inter-connectedness and dialectical progression, there are always obstacles, dislocations, disruptions, and varied challenges to overcome. In the last two years or so since March 11, 2020, St. Vincent and the Grenadines has, I reiterate, experienced, unprecedentedly, the debilitating pandemic, the volcanic eruptions, and a hurricane, among other exogenous shocks. Respairing the condition in St. Vincent and the Grenadines demands, centrally, a completion of the humanitarian relief, and corrective tasks arising from the triple shocks, while at the same time pursuing the longer-term strategic initiatives embedded in the SDGs and the practical policies and programmes on the agenda of a people-centred government. Essentially, we are in the process of deepening, broadening, consolidating our social democratic revolution in a new period of extraordinary challenges.

In pursuance of this many-sided respairing, it is necessary and desirable to grasp the following: first, the historical legacies of our country's underdevelopment; second, the setbacks and advances, broadly, of the country's political economy during the 50-year period between universal adult suffrage in 1951 and the arrival of the Millennium; third, the central developmental accomplishments and challenges of the ULP government since March 29, 2001, and continuing; fourth, a more detailed survey of the achievements, tribulations and lamentations of the last two years; fifth, the policy and programmatic matrices of Budget 2022 in its quest of respairing, inclusive of, but beyond, recovery and rebuilding; and sixth, the vision ahead in addressing the collection of unfinished tasks in our ongoing social democratic revolution, and in the quest of peace, security and prosperity for all.

The "Introduction" to this book ends with an encouraging and apt quotation from Thomas Piketty's *Time for Socialism: Dispatches from a World on Fire, 2016 – 2021* (Yale University Press, 2021):

> Let's start with a statement that some may find surprising. If we take a long-term perspective, then the long march toward equality and participatory socialism is already well under way. No technical impossibility prevents us from continuing along this already open path, as long as we all get on with it. History shows that inequality is essentially ideological and political, not economic or technological.
>
> This optimistic point of view may seem paradoxical in these times of gloom. Yet it corresponds to reality.... Much remains to be done, but the fact is that it is possible to go much further by drawing on the lessons of history.

Piketty was writing specifically of France, and generally of Europe; but he could have been commenting on our march over the past 21 years in St. Vincent and the Grenadines under the banner of advanced social democracy applied to our own circumstances and in quest of, among other things, the building of a modern, competitive, many-sided post-colonial economy that is at once national, regional, and global so as to achieve, overall, sustainable development.

We in St. Vincent and the Grenadines have done much under the ULP government, and much more remains to be done. To do more, we must, among other things, draw on the lessons of our history and that of our regional and global political economy.

Chapter One

Historical Backdrop of Relevance to Our Quest to Respair

British Colonialism to Reclamation of Independence: 1763-1979

In 1763, some 206 years before the formal restoration of "self-government" in 1969, and 216 years before the formal reclamation of our country's independence in 1979, the British colonialists assumed suzerainty of the nation which, since 1979, we call St. Vincent and the Grenadines. The indigenous people, the Callinago and the Garifuna, referred to our nation variously as Yurumein, Youlou and the Begos, or Hairouna; the Europeans named it St. Vincent until we added "the Grenadines" upon our reclamation of independence.

Britain took possession of St. Vincent and the Grenadines in 1763 at the end of the Seven Years' War, through the Treaty of Paris, in a general carve-up of territories in the Eastern Caribbean between France and Britain. Save and except for a brief retake of St. Vincent and the Grenadines by the French between 1779 and 1783, Britain remained the colonising power until October 27, 1979.

Central to Britain's conquest, settlement, and craven exploitation of St. Vincent and the Grenadines for its own material benefits and political purposes, were the following: the forcible deprivation of the indigenous people of their lands (150 square miles or 96,000 acres); genocide and forcible deportation of over three-quarters of the 1795 indigenous population, estimated in 1795 to have been approximately 9,000 (some 2,500 were killed wantonly by the British and in the guerrilla war against them between 1764 and 1796; 2,445 died from maltreatment and disease on the nearby inhospitable island of Balliceaux to which they were marooned; 222 died on the way to forcible exile to Roatan Island in the Bay of Honduras, they having left St. Vincent and the Grenadines from Balliceaux, on March 9, 1797; 2,206 arrived at Roatan on April 12, 1797); the enslavement of 55,562 Africans who were forcibly transported by the British colonialists between 1764 and 1808 — 6,614 or nearly 11 percent of the 62,176 who were embarked for St. Vincent and the Grenadines, died during the horrendous Middle Passage; the indentureship, in the aggregate, between 1845 and 1881, of 5,575 persons: Madeiran Portuguese (2,100), Liberated Africans (1,036), and East Indians (2,429); the establishment of a slave mode of production (1764 to 1838) with European, largely British, slave-owners/owners of sugar plantations, but with trading links to mercantile capitalism and an expanding industrial capitalism in Britain; the imposition of a colonial State apparatus with various unrepresentative political forms over time, backed always by force (internally and externally), and buttressed by an imposed Anglo-centric value system of presumed white racial superiority; the establishment of a plural society of rigidity in which race and class were intertwined in such a manner that each racial, ethnic or cultural section had its own relatively distinct pattern of socio-cultural integration, with the whites at the narrow top of a socio-economic pyramid and the enslaved Africans at the bottom of a broad base; and the propagation of a starched, and oft-times hypocritical, Anglicanism as the religion of State, and the suppression of indigenous forms of worship practised by the Callinago, Garifuna and Africans.

The British slave trade was abolished in 1807, but slavery continued until 1838, with a transitional "apprenticeship" period from 1834. At slavery's end, there were 22,997 enslaved Africans, including those born in St. Vincent and the Grenadines: 69 percent were field slaves; 13 percent were non-field slaves; 13 percent were children under 6 years of age; and five percent were aged and infirm. The slave-owners were paid an aggregate of £592,509 in compensation for their slaves, their "property". How much money is that worth in today's currency?

The answer to this query, and other related ones, has been provided by a team of professionals at the Centre for the Study of the Legacies of British Slavery at the University College, London, and other academics, who have concluded, persuasively, after considerable research, that "the compensated value" of the slaves is to be assessed by utilizing a factor of up to 829 to calculate the present-day monetary value of compensation required, inclusive of the sum paid in 1833-1834 to the slave-owners. A higher factor is surely necessary to be applied for any reparatory justice for native genocide, for forced deportations of the indigenous people (an estimated aggregate of 7,193 persons), and for lands "stolen" prior to the 1833-1834 period.

What about lands the British "stole" from the indigenous people?

Let us itemise the parcels of land in St. Vincent and the Grenadines the British colonialists sold or granted that clearly did not belong to them:

In 1764, the British government granted to General Monckton, a "hero" of the Seven Years' War, 4,000 acres of land on the Windward side of St. Vincent. Monckton never settled the land but sold it instead for £30,000 at an average of £7.10 shillings per acre. These lands between Biabou and Stubbs are very valuable today, including where the Argyle International Airport is located.

In 1764, too, the British government auctioned off 20,538 acres. This sale earned the British Treasury £162,854, an average of £7.10 per acre.

Between 1776 and 1779, a further 2,156 acres were disposed of by the British government through Governor Valentine Morris. Some of these were newly-opened up "Carib" lands, north of the Yambou River.

In 1807, a domestic "land crisis" erupted. British occupiers (largely former soldiers) of lands between Byera River in the south to Cayo River in the north ("Carib country" lands) found out that 6,000 acres of these lands had been granted to an American Royalist from Georgia (USA), Colonel Thomas Brown. In a resolution of "the crisis", Brown was allowed to keep 1,600 acres plus an indemnity of £25,000, part of the Treasury's earnings from the eventual sale of the occupied lands (the remaining 4,400 acres) to their occupiers at an average price per acre of £22.10 shillings. These lands included some of the best sugar cane lands on St. Vincent. They included the following seven estates: Tourama, Orange Hill, Waterloo, Lot No. 14, Rabacca, Langley Park and Mt. Bentinck. Colonel Brown's estate of 1,600 acres was Grand Sable Estate. The 4,400 acres sold to the said "occupiers" earned the Treasury £99,000 (4,400 x £22.5 per acre).

Pricing Colonel Brown's 1,600 acres similarly, the 1807 value is £36,000 (1,600 x £22.5 per acre).

For a more detailed analysis of the value comparables for the lands "stolen" by the British, for the compensation paid to the slave-owners for the slaves, and for native genocide, please refer to my book *The Case for Caribbean Reparatory Justice* (2014), in particular the essay that addresses this very question.

These four land transactions, together amounting to 32,694 acres, would have been sufficient, at today's value, to finance the entire recurrent and capital Estimates of Expenditure in St. Vincent and the Grenadines in 2019, the year before COVID! The aggregate, even a conservative estimation, of "compensation" for the freed slaves and Britain's genocidal acts against the indigenous people would certainly exceed the total budget of the government of St. Vincent and the Grenadines for the year 2022. This sum, too, is in excess of the disbursed public debt of St. Vincent and the Grenadines at the end of 2021. Reparations is connected not only to the broad issue of the legacies of underdevelopment; it is also intricately linked to fiscal policy and debt relief.

Two other large parcels of land were disposed of in the early years of colonisation for which more details are to be researched. First, on the northwest coast of St. Vincent, a large tract of land was granted to Lt. Colonel George Etherington. The actual size of the grant was not specified but it was north of, and bounded on the south by, the Wallilabou River. Secondly, between 1779 and 1784, when St. Vincent and the Grenadines was under French over-rule, a "Dame d' honneur" in the French Palace, Martha Swinburne, was granted 20,000 acres of largely unoccupied land, but belonging to the indigenous people. I am yet to ascertain the exact location of all these lands that reverted to the British after they reconquered and re-occupied St. Vincent.

The British government sold most of these lands to private owners. These monies accrued to the British Treasury. They are to be put in the reparations pool! Together these lands, and other parcels, excluding those hitherto identified, amounted to another 32,000 acres or so. It is to be noted that one-third of the lands overall, in St. Vincent and the Grenadines have been in forests or other land reserves above the 1,000 feet contour.

By 1777, within 14 years of British conquest and the start-up of its settlement of exploitation, the Land Surveyor, Mr. Byers, described the general state and disposition of lands on St. Vincent (not the Grenadines) as follows: lands sold at public sale, leased, and appropriated for public uses: 20,392 acres; lands "granted" by the British to "friendly Caribs", 1,210 acres; lands "granted" to General Monckton, 4,000 acres;

lands "granted" to the Caribs by Treaty in 1775, 27,628 acres; cultivated lands undisposed of, 9,777; "impractical" (uncultivated) land, 21,074 acres. The aggregate total of all this was 84,286 acres of the 85,120 acres on St. Vincent. It is to be noted, importantly, that the so-called "grants" to the "Caribs" listed above were later revoked, in war, by the British; in fact, by 1805 "the Caribs" (Callinago and Garifuna) were *legally prohibited* from owning lands.

It is to be noted further, that in 1777, Byers reported that 34,000 acres of land were already in plantation-estate hands. And by 1827, 44,798 acres of land in the whole of St. Vincent and the Grenadines were in 110 estates, most of which were owned by one person or family. Before emancipation in 1838, the gross inequality in the distribution of land had already been put in train by extractive British colonialism. It doomed generations of the off-spring of the indigenous Callinago/Garifuna, the enslaved Africans, the indentured Madeirans, so-called "free" Africans, and indentured Indians to poverty and indigence. All this is part of the legacy of colonialism's under-development of our country. The respairing in 2022 and beyond cannot be complete without reparations for all these legacies of underdevelopment.

Britain's extractive colonialism in its own interest in St. Vincent and the Grenadines was merciless, draconian, cruel, and executed with urgency. The indigenous people had never seen anything like this before. Within one year of Britain's occupation of St. Vincent and the Grenadines, it declared that all the land belonged to the British Crown. It moved swiftly to establish sugar cane plantations, grounded in the slave labour of imported Africans; by 1775, it had forcibly disembarked 11,895 Africans and enslaved them on 34,908 acres of land on St. Vincent, organised as sugar plantations in Charlotte Parish (11,849 acres, from Yambou to Fancy); in St. George's Parish (9,337 acres, from Redemption ("Sharpes") to Diamond up to Akers); in St. Andrew's Parish (4,096 acres, from Montrose to Peniston); in St. David's Parish (4,198 acres, from Aker's Layou to Westwood); and in St. Patrick's Parish (5,426 acres, from Belmont to FitzHughes to Wallibou).

Britain dispossessed the Callinago and Garifuna people of their land. Naturally, the indigenous people resisted in a protracted guerrilla war from 1764 to 1795 when Paramount Chief of the Garifuna people, The Right Excellent Joseph Chatoyer, our first and thus far only National Hero, was ambushed and killed by the British. Over that period, the British engaged in duplicitous peace-making and treaty-making, only to break the peace and the treaties willy-nilly, until they finally subjugated the Callinago and Garifuna. As I detailed earlier, a brutal genocide was carried out against the Garifuna.

The British, in introducing the sugar industry in St. Vincent and the Grenadines, applied all their knowledge and experiences gained from the mature, West Indian sugar economies, especially those of Jamaica, Barbados, Antigua, and St. Kitts.

Sugar production in St. Vincent and the Grenadines amounted to a mere 35 tons in 1766; by 1770, it rose to 1,930 tons; then 3,130 tons in 1774 only to fall away to 2,049 tons in 1779. The French recapture of St. Vincent and the Grenadines (1779 – 1783) affected adversely sugar production. The return of Britain in 1783 and the defeat of the indigenous people's resistance in 1795 paved the way for the consolidation of Britain's colonial conquest and the achievement of an enforced "ordered" settlement by 1800. Thus, after 1800, sugar production was stabilised, reaching its peak in 1828 of 14,403 tons. Then it declined over the next five years. The period 1839 to 1902 witnessed a further decline in the sugar industry until its veritable collapse in 1902. In 1840, sugar production was 6,900 tons; it increased to 8,829 tons in 1852 and dropped sharply to 4,908 tons in 1855; there was a resurgence between 1865 and 1878; thereafter a terminal decline set in; between 1883 and 1892 sugar production declined by 58 percent; in 1902, sugar production fell to a paltry 262 tons.

By 1892, arrowroot had already outpaced sugar as the main export commodity. In the early 20th century, cotton became the major export, temporarily. Sugar was restored in the late 1920s and continued until its closure in 1962. It was revived briefly between 1979 and 1984, then closed forever.

During the Second World War, ground provisions and coconut products gained export prominence, mainly to Barbados and Trinidad. In the late 1940s, arrowroot resumed its dominance. The introduction of a commercial banana industry in the mid-1950s had it jostling with arrowroot for export pre-eminence in the 1960s; by the 1970s until the declining years of the twentieth century, banana production and banana exports dominated the economy; thereafter, it declined markedly as the market preferences for our bananas in the United Kingdom were eroded to the point of extinction. Services, especially tourism services, became central to the economy from the late 1990s onwards.

Several issues of relevance arise in our current discourse. For roughly 120 years between 1763 and 1881 (the latter year from which the sugar industry in St. Vincent and the Grenadines declined sharply),

Britain exploited our country's material resources (the land and agricultural production), slave labour (1764 to 1838), post-emancipation labour (freed slaves and indentured labourers from Madeira and India). It invested very little in infrastructure, health, education, and housing for the people whom it exploited. Between 1838 and 1969 (internal self-government), Britain still profited from St. Vincent and the Grenadines through trade, investments, and the exploitation of labour and land, and within the wider Caribbean context; and politically, our country still mattered to Britain's declining Empire. In these years, too, Britain hardly placed much public investment in infrastructure and the people. It was quite stingy compared to the French, American or Dutch colonialists in the Caribbean. Between 1969 and 1979, Britain provided very little financial aid to the internally-self-governed St. Vincent and the Grenadines. Over the sweep of history from 1763 onwards, most progress has been achieved by St. Vincent and the Grenadines in the post-independence years, 1979 to the present day.

The Demand for Reparations and the Unfolding of Social Democracy

The first issue that emerges is that of reparations from Britain for the legacy of underdevelopment arising from lands "stolen" for colonialism's profit, native genocide and the enslavement of Africans. At every turn, Britain has opposed reparations, but an adequate recompense is a just demand in terms of public morality and a justifiable, and justiciable one, in international law. At the initiative of my government, CARICOM adopted, in 2014, as regional public policy, the demand of reparations from the former colonising powers (Britain, France, Holland) in CARICOM member-countries. There is established, too, a CARICOM Reparations Commission. A ten-point Reparations Plan has also been approved.

From the 1920s onwards to the current era, Caribbean intellectuals and political leaders have been making the demand for reparations in one form or another from Britain. Early out of the blocks in this regard, in the 1920s, was Marcus Mosiah Garvey of the Universal Negro Improvement Association (UNIA) with the demand for reparations from colonial/imperial powers in the Caribbean and Africa in order for our people to repair appropriately on account of the Europeans' colonial policy and practice, native genocide, the enslavement of Africans, and the rapacious exploitation of the peoples and countries of the Caribbean and Africa.

In 1939, a twenty-three year old Caribbean economist from St. Lucia, but working and researching in Britain, W. Arthur Lewis, addressed precisely the same issue, among others, in his *Labour in the West Indies: The Birth of the Workers' Movement.* , did the nationalist and trade union leaders throughout the Caribbean who gave testimony in 1939 before the West India Royal Commission chaired by Lord Moyne.

None of this reparations demand impressed Lord Moyne and his British Commissioners who had arrived in the West Indies in the midst of an unfolding social democratic revolution with mass anti-colonial uprisings between 1935 and 1938 across numerous territories in the region, including St. Kitts, St. Vincent, Jamaica, Trinidad, and Barbados. The Moyne Commission advanced a bundle of piece-meal legislative reforms, minimalist social welfarism, and snail's pace constitutional devolution of authority to "native peoples".

Derisively, the Moyne Commission ignored or down-played a chorus of voices, including some progressive ones in Britain itself such as William M. Mac Millan's 1936 *Warning from the West Indies: A Tract for Africa and the Empire*, calling for significant capital sums to finance a genuine developmental plan to tackle the misery and underdevelopment in the West Indies after centuries of extractive British colonialism, in partnership with a white planter-merchant elite exploiting for themselves cheap labour (unfree and free), natural resources and cheap raw materials.

The Moyne Commission also ignored the advice of the British trade unionist and Labour Party parliamentarian (and subsequent Colonial Secretary in 1945), Arthur Creech Jones, who as a member of the Parliamentary Colonial Advisory Committee on Education on April 5, 1939, asserted thus:

> We carry a grave responsibility for a colonial policy based on cheap labour and cheap raw materials. The facts are out, and we can no longer plead ignorance and indifference. Of course, there has been official irresponsibility and the dominance of narrow calculating colonial interests. We can point to years of criminal neglect when official ineptitude and sloth have permitted affairs to drift and the islands to sink with unpardonable misery. Now a point has been reached when action is desperately urgent and British concern must be *paid in hard cash*. The hopeless squalor of today is in a real way the measure of the shortcomings of our colonial policy and of our economic neglect.

The Moyne Commission proposed itself, in the telling words of Professor Hilary Beckles, a "petty reparations fund" of £1 million per year for 20 years for the entirety of British colonial territories in the Caribbean. The trade unionists and anti-colonial leaders heard this with dismay, and rejected this miniscule amount of cash for developmental purposes.

This "petty reparations fund" fitted well in the Moyne Commission's central narrative:

> While the United Kingdom must play an important part in the improvement of conditions by providing financial assistance for social service and markets to foster West Indian economy, it is equally important that an emergence of a spirit of self-help, thrift and independence should come about among the West Indian people themselves. ...some small increase in industrial employment may be afforded by the development of secondary industries; but these can at best be dependent for their prosperity on that of the main industry of the whole area, namely agriculture. A new economic policy for the West Indies must therefore be an agricultural policy.

Thus, 100 years after the abolition of slavery, British colonial policy was still: no reparations or recompense for native genocide, enslavement of Africans, indentureship of Madeirans and Indians, continued extractive colonialism, and imperial dispossession. No industrialisation (*"no nails or horseshoe manufacture to be done in the West Indies"*) or meaningful diversification: only a continuation of agriculture based on cheap labour. No social development; only minimalist social welfarism and hypocritical lectures from colonialists and planters about self-help by the poor, who worked so hard to make these very persons rich. No popular democracy; only a continuation with slight modification of undemocratic colonial, gubernatorial over-rule in concert with the planter-merchant elite.

But twenty years before the Moyne Commission, Marcus Mosiah Garvey of the UNIA was carrying an alternative compelling message to his black audience (American and Caribbean) in 1919 in New York: "We organised the Black Star Steamship Corporation three months ago for US $500,000 and it will be a capitalised corporation of ten million dollars."

Two months later in December 1919, Garvey wrote:

> There is a world of opportunity awaiting us, and it is for us, through unity and will and of purpose, to say we shall and we will play our part upon the great human stage of activity. We shall

start steamship lines, factories and banks. ...we shall cause men to regard us as equals in achievements, in industry, in commerce, in politics, in science, art and education. We shall make Ethiopia a mighty nation and we of this generation shall cause our children to call us blessed.

The ULP government shares these large aspirations and uplifting vision of Garvey; these perspectives are necessary and desirable for our respairing; and they are reflected concretely in Budget 2022.

In 1938-1939, Arthur Lewis was articulating a broad strategic framework for Caribbean development drawing, in appropriate measure, from the working people's demands arising from the anti-colonial uprising, Garveyism, his theoretical knowledge of political economy, the specific Caribbean experiences and condition, and comparative political economy of Britain, the developing world, especially Africa and Asia. Lewis was later to enlarge his perspectives and authoritativeness in his hugely influential article in the Manchester School of Economic and Social Studies (May 1954), entitled "Economic Development with Unlimited Supplies of Labour", and several books, including *The Principles of Economic Planning* (1949), his magisterial *Theory of Economic Growth* (1955), *Development Planning* (1956), *Tropical Development, 1880-1913* (1971), and *Growth and Fluctuations, 1870-1913* (1978). In 1979, Sir Arthur Lewis was awarded the Nobel Prize for Economics on account of his seminal contribution to development economics.

In his 1939 publication, in contrast to colonial apologies, incorrect prognoses, and racist, monopoly capitalist, and dead-end prescriptions of a retrograde British colonialism, Arthur Lewis succinctly focused on the unfolding social democratic revolution:

The general aims are to raise the economic and cultural standards of the masses, and to secure for them conditions of freedom and equality.

...The total income of the West Indies must be considerably increased; and in the second place it must be more equitably distributed.

Let all of this ring in our ears and prompt our actions as we set about to respair in 2022 and beyond!

Lewis emphasised economic growth and a more equitable distribution of income; he argued that it would be "a mistake to ignore either of these two aspects." In the process he demanded a significant infusion of the British government's capital to kick-start and assist in the pursuance of a sustainable development. He lamented Britain's gross neglect of the economic and social development and called essentially for reparatory justice.

Further, too, Lewis insisted on a fair and just external trade arrangement that involved special, market preferences for all exports from the West Indies to Britain.

In quest of the general aims of the social democratic revolution, Lewis proposed that Britain make available, too, grants or loans at low rates of interest to enterprising individuals and small businesses. He was clear that it was necessary and desirable for our region:

> (To) make a radical attack on poverty...to open up new areas and finance land settlement schemes, to improve housing conditions, to build new schools and finance the proper training of teachers, to build and equip hospitals and clinics, to drain swamps, and to supply drugs for a concerted attack on malaria, yaws, venereal disease, children's diseases, and other ailments of the people."

All of this resonates with the ULP government and are amply reflected in Budget 2022 and its predecessor budgets, after March 2001.

To do all this in 1939, and continuing, under colonialism, a package of reparatory finance, among other things, was required from Britain. But it never came then or subsequently. So, this struggle for reparations continues as our nation currently engages in the quest to respair!.

Decades of colonial neglect in the West Indies, including St. Vincent and the Grenadines, the deteriorating socio-economic conditions consequent upon the economic depression in the world capitalist system between 1929–31, the nature of colonialism's socio-political oppression of the working people and peasantry, the rampant white racism locally, and the unfavourable conditions globally for black people, provided abundant combustible material upon which the spark of anti-colonialism was lit to cause, in the 1930s, the massive anti-colonial uprisings. Both this neglect and the people's efforts at pushing for a social democratic revolution, and their consequences, are among the factors that shape the backdrop to the evolving context to our renewed quest to respair, though in altered circumstances.

We have noted the inability of colonialism to rule in any way but the old way, the resistance by the people to being ruled in the old way, the vain attempts by a Royal Commission to provide a tinkering of the old way for a possible altered path, and the rejection by the people of that programmatic tinkering. Popular demands for social democratic initiatives, new pathways, and reparations were rejected by colonialism as pie-in-the-sky propositions. The current opponents of the efforts of my Unity Labour Party government to respair and advance are the inheritors of the colonial and neo-liberal perspectives that have consistently stood in the way of people's progress, historically.

Indeed, even as colonialism had dispatched its Royal Commissioners to the West Indies, in quest of a tinkering social welfarism, the solidified, anti-developmental attitude and policy orientation of colonialism was brazenly ignorant and ill-suited to any genuine reform prospects, as was evident in the remarks of the Secretary of State for the Colonies, Malcolm Mc Donald, reported in the *Daily Gleaner* of Jamaica (November 20, 1939):

> It is true to say that the standard of living of workers in the colonies was generally low. This fact was inevitable and absolutely natural; it was even right in colonial conditions. In countries where the sun shone perpetually and nature was very beautiful and where the problems of life were comparatively few and simple, people could be content and happy with a comparatively simple manner of life and with simple standards. Indeed, incursions of expensive ideas very often destroyed happiness.

How many of the opposition New Democratic Party's expatriate friends on Bequia and passport-selling mercenaries abroad still hold these backwards ideas in today's St. Vincent and the Grenadines? And do those who pay the piper call the tune from the shadows? Have these sentiments not endured among the nasty collaborators of neo-colonialism, neo-liberalism, and imperialism? Does the minimalism of the NDP's philosophical outlook, policies and programmes not reflect today the lack of ambition and anti-people orientation of the colonialists of yesteryear and the neo-colonialists of today?

Sadly, these kinds of colonialist and neo-colonialist perspectives still find resonance among some social, political, economic, and religious elites in the Caribbean. They have a leave-it-alone thesis; they propose minimalist State intervention; they advocate *laissez-faire* economics; they proclaim "the nobility of poverty" and that God will provide for his "indolent, simplistic but happy children". It is all a load of self-serving and ignorant rubbish!

Arising from the anti-colonial and social democratic struggles in the early decades of the 20th century, were proposals to federate or integrate the region in the people's interests rather than in the interests of colonialism and monopoly capitalism. Regional integration was thus a people-centred plank to advance better governance, constitutional de-colonisation, improved and expanded common services, and an economic union of a developmental kind.

The popular, national leaders had gathered in Conference on the matter of "closer union" in 1932 in Roseau, Dominica. In September 1945, the Caribbean Labour Conference summoned a meeting in Barbados to discuss the federal idea for the West Indies as a critical path to self-government and an end to British over-rule. Of course, Britain was not opposed, in principle, to federation but it was not keen on a self-governing or independent federation. Among other things, the British insisted that they had no intention to finance a self-governing or independent federal government of the West Indies.

Interestingly, Arthur Creech Jones, who, as a British Labour Party parliamentarian, advocated in April 1939 "desperately urgent" action, "paid in hard cash", by Britain for its "indifference", "official irrespon-sibility", "official ineptitude", and "criminal negligence" in the West Indies, now sang a distinctly different song as the Labour government's Colonial Secretary in 1945.

Hilary Beckles in his recent impressive book, *How Britain Under-developed the Caribbean — A Reparation Response to Europe's Legacy of Plunder and Poverty (2021)* tells the story very well:

> The not-so-subtle threat of the British government came from Creech Jones, colonial secretary. He informed labour leaders and politicians (at the 1945 Barbados Conference) that their choice would mean a vote for financial independence, and that the Brit-ish government would continue to assist only territories already dependent on grants in aid. A federal government in the West Indies, he warned, would be cutting financial aid from Britain, and as a result should be financially independent. He walked the path during his career, leading West Indian leaders into believing in his support for development, while being unprepared to press his government to honour its financial obligations to the region."

These types still exist in the citadels of power or authority in the wealthy metropoles of today. They talk of global partnerships with developing countries but resist doggedly, in practice, to meet even their agreed obligations, whether on developmental finance or on climate change. And they resist, unreasonably, the fashioning of a multi-dimen-sional vulnerability index (MVI) to replace or supplement the narrow and grossly unfair criterion of per capita income as the basis for middle-income but vulnerable small island developing states, like the Caribbean, to access finance on concessionary terms.

The West Indies Federation collapsed for various reasons, which need not detain us here, but undoubtedly two of them related to the colonial structuring of the Federation and the connected issue of British parsimony regarding its non-funding. Britain wanted a federation on the cheap; and it got it. Indeed, Hilary Beckles argues persuasively that Britain had set out to punish the Caribbean people for their presumed effrontery in rebelling against British colonialism in the 1930s at the very time British virtue was on parade in their opposition to rising Nazism in Germany and the companion Fascism in Italy. Essentially the British attitude according to Beckles was, "How dare you black people be in open revolt against us when we are so benevolent to you? We will punish you slowly and not-so-slowly. No money for you."

Similarly, Britain granted independence of its Caribbean colonies on the cheap. There was not the slightest nod to reparatory justice on their part. It mattered not which leader or which country or which time, the story was the same: Norman Manley and Alexander Bustamante of Jamaica (1962); Dr. Eric Williams of Trinidad and Tobago (1962); Forbes Burnham of Guyana (1966); Errol Barrow of Barbados (1966); Lynden Pindling of The Bahamas (1973); Eric Gairy of Grenada (1974); Patrick John of Dominica (1978); John Compton of St. Lucia (1979); Milton Cato of St. Vincent and the Grenadines (1979); V.C. Bird of Antigua and Barbuda (1981); George Price of Belize (1981); Dr. Kennedy Simmonds of St. Kitts and Nevis (1983); there never was, and there is not now, any intention of Britain to deliver a "golden handshake" of any significance to any country in the West Indies. Our history thus invites a cynicism, and more, in this regard.

The truth is that Britain will never entertain reparations unless compelled to do so by a constellation of forces: on-going political and diplomatic pressure externally; international law through an appropriate finding by the International Court of Justice; and public support, today, within Britain for reparatory justice.

It is interesting and informative, to note that over 70 years ago, a leading British official, C.Y. Carstairs, in a letter to another colleague I.B. Watt on September 5, 1949, unburdened himself on this issue:

> The argument that self-government must be in step with financial stability is indeed relevant and can be used to a chosen audience. To some West Indians, however, such an argument is complete

anathema; they believe like the Irish, that Her Majesty's Government is perpetually in debt to the West Indies for errors of omissions of the past three hundred years. *The sum mentioned, in all seriousness, to liquefy this debt is astronomical and would undoubtedly provide financial stability for a greater or less number of years.* (My Emphasis)

In 2014, at my urging, the Heads of Government Conference of the Caribbean Community (CARICOM) placed the issue of reparations from Britain, France, and Holland (CARICOM consists of 12 former Brutish colonies, one former French — Haiti — and one former Dutch — Suriname) on account of native genocide and the enslavement of Africans. At that said Heads' Conference, a Prime Ministerial sub-committee under Barbados' chairmanship was established to drive the process for reparations. A CARICOM Reparations Commission (CRC) was also established under the chairmanship of Professor Hilary Beckles (now Vice Chancellor of the University of the West Indies) with membership from the National Reparations Commission of each member-State of CARICOM. The CRC has drawn up a Ten- Point Reparations Plan that has been endorsed by the Heads of CARICOM.

Some work has been done on the road to reparations by CARICOM and the CRC, but there is far more work to be done. Educational, political, and diplomatic work is ongoing, but it has all yielded no reparations thus far from the British, French, or Dutch governments.

To be sure, the University of the West Indies has crafted a limited "reparations agreement" with the University of Glasgow in Scotland on matters of research and educational opportunities. And one University in Wales, which has had an early 19th century financier owning slaves on a plantation in St. Vincent and the Grenadines, has provided 55 scholarships (40 undergraduate and 15 post-graduate) valued at over 4 million pounds sterling, but these scholarships at the University of Wales Trinity St. David were not framed within the context of reparations. These scholarships were granted following a request from me to Prince Charles — Prince of Wales — consequent upon the volcanic eruptions on St. Vincent in April 2021; Prince Charles approached the university and arrangements were subsequently concluded between the university and my government.

The issue of reparations is very much on the agenda globally at the United Nations, in the USA, Britain, Europe, Africa, Latin America, and the Caribbean. My government has ensured that it has formed part of political declarations by several regional and global institutions. It is open to CARICOM governments to pursue the matter, also, to the International Court of Justice under relevant international law.

In the process of respairing in St. Vincent and the Grenadines, the matter of reparations is critical! One of the planks of the CRC's plan for reparations includes debt relief; but St. Vincent and the Grenadines owes Britain very little debt; further, the debt relief proposals by the international financial institutions are of very little benefit to St. Vincent and the Grenadines since our country has almost zero commercial debts in its debt portfolio. There has to be a particular tailoring of multi-lateral debt relief for countries like St. Vincent and the Grenadines. Reparations, of course, go way beyond debt relief. Among other things, the CRC plan includes grant financing for development, and assistance in areas of health, education, science and technology, physical infrastructure, and appropriate historical memorials.

What Can We Learn from a Rough, Colonial Yesteryear for Today's Quest to Respair?

Let us now move from the generalised misery of the West Indies in the 1930s, and thereafter, and the responses provided by both colonialism and the social democratic revolution. We will return to all this later; but let us now pose another important set of queries arising from the socio-economic backdrop in our quest to address our current challenges.

Two relevant queries are: What bundle of externally-sourced or exogenous historical circumstances in the political economy of St. Vincent and the Grenadines most closely mimic or resemble, or is analogous to, the exogenous factors of the triple whammy of the COVID pandemic, the volcanic eruptions, and Hurricane Elsa, *and* the post-global recession context from 2008 to the multiple dislocations of 2022 — a 14-year period? and, How did the governing authorities and people respond then?

Perhaps the closest analogous historical period of socio-economic challenges comparatively, post-slavery, to our current circumstances, was the fifty-year period 1881 to 1931, arising from exogenous shocks, and their knock-on effects. Please note that the emphasis in the analysis is on the nature and extent of the exogenous shocks and the responses to them; to be sure the internal conditions of the country are of importance to the shaping of the responses to the exogenous challenges.

By 1881 the sugar industry, the main employer of labour and foreign exchange earner, was severely distressed and on the verge of collapse due to external market conditions from competitors of sugar and beet producers, internal weaknesses relating to managerial inefficiencies, wrong and ill-suited technologies, and issues regarding labour availability and productivity.

By the 1890s, arrowroot displaced sugar cultivation and production as the major industry but it was unable to take up fully the number of displaced sugar-cane workers; as a result, some 60 percent of the labour force was unemployed or under-employed. Land ownership was highly-skewed, predominantly in the hands of some 100 plantation owners; the Royal Commission of 1897 was yet to report on land reform, and the limited land reform programme was yet to be effected — land settlement estates on the Leeward side of St. Vincent and enhanced peasant ownership in a few other places, including the Park Hill-Three Rivers-South Rivers areas, Clare Valley-Questelles, and Arnos Vale-Belair.

In 1898, the most devastating hurricane in living memory struck, killing 298 persons, causing extensive damage and destruction to buildings, physical infrastructure, and most of the arrowroot and sugar mills. In 1902, the volcanic eruption of La Soufriere caused the death of some 2,000 persons and the further extensive destruction of buildings, physical and productive infrastructure, including agriculture.

In the early 20th century, cotton temporarily displaced arrowroot as the premier crop; between 1914 and 1917 the First World War affected colonial St. Vincent very badly; the "Spanish flu" epidemic of 1918 disrupted post-war recovery globally, including in St. Vincent; in 1926, another hurricane struck and shortly thereafter the sugar industry was reintroduced; and in 1929-31, the massive, world capitalist, economic depression caused further economic ruin to St. Vincent.

The colonial State did little or nothing to alleviate the extreme socio-economic hardship, poverty, and indigence of the overwhelming majority of the population; average life expectancy hovered just above 40 years; by 1947, average life expectancy was 46 years; the overwhelming majority of people did not have access to pipe-borne water; electricity by the 1930s was available only for a small group of upper-middle class and elite persons in the city of Kingstown and its environs; the provision of primary education was limited — the Methodists, Anglicans, and Roman Catholics ran some small primary schools, along with the highly insufficient number operated by the colonial State; the Boys'

Grammar School with a few dozen students was established in the first decade of the 20th century as the only government-operated secondary school, followed shortly thereafter by the opening of the Girls' High School. Between 1881 and 1931, life for most people in St. Vincent and the Grenadines was Hobbesian: nasty, brutish, and short! Since the colonial State was focused on coercion, law and order, and elemental State administration, the people looked elsewhere for refuge.

The people's principal avenue for survival and advancement was migration and their self-organising to make ends meet. People left St. Vincent and the Grenadines in their many thousands. Indeed, between the 20-year period, 1891 and 1911, the annual rate of net migration was a whopping minus 18.89 per thousand persons, the highest ever recorded by any official census; the actual net migration in raw numbers was minus 15,667 persons.

So, although the natural increase of the population between 1891 and 1911 amounted to 16,490, because of the size of the net migration, the actual increase in the population in that 20-year period was a mere 823 persons! Then, between 1911 and 1921, the population increased from 41,877 to 44,447. The natural increase of 8,160 was offset by a net outflow of 5,590 persons. In the 1921 to 1931 period, migration slowed somewhat and the population increased by 3,514 persons, growing from 44,447 in 1921 to 47,961 in 1931.

In the 50-year period (1881 to 1931), the total population of St. Vincent and the Grenadines increased absolutely from 40,548 to 47,961, a very modest increase of 7,413 persons. But, the natural increase of the population (births minus deaths) in that period was 40,420; so, massive outward migration in this 50-year period ensured a relatively small increase in the actual population.

In that 50-year period, where did most of the migrants from St. Vincent and the Grenadines go? Mainly to other Caribbean countries, principally the British Caribbean especially Trinidad and Guyana (then known as British Guiana), and, to a lesser extent, Barbados. Other major Caribbean destinations were the Dutch Antilles (Curacao and Aruba), and Cuba; Vincentian migrants sought work, too, in Panama, Costa Rica, and Brazil. There were no migration restrictions to the other British colonies of Trinidad, Guyana, and Barbados. In the case of Cuba, significant numbers of Vincentians, among other Caribbean nationals, were recruited to work in the sugar industry in Cuba largely as cheap field-labourers, but also as sugar factory workers. Not many

migrants went to the United States of America and the United Kingdom from St. Vincent and the Grenadines in this period.

In the 14-year period 2008-2022, the economy of St. Vincent and
the Grenadines was struck by the following exogenous challenges: the
almost complete extinction of the preferential market treatment for our
bananas consequent upon Britain's entry into the Single Market and
Economy of the European Union on January 1, 1993; a year earlier, St.
Vincent and the Grenadines exported nearly 80,000 tons of bananas
valued at nearly EC $120 million in the British market; gradually, in
stages, the market preferences were eroded through action by the World
Trade Organisation (WTO) and the European Union itself, so that by
2008 hardly any bananas were exported to Britain. In 2008-2009, a
financial crash on Wall Street, New York, USA, metamorphosed into the
worst global economic depression since the 1929-31 period; its reverberations were still being felt a decade or so later when the pandemic
struck. Between 2008 and 2020, adverse weather events repeatedly
struck: storms, hurricanes, excessively heavy rainfall, landslides, storm
surges, coastal and river erosion, and alternating drought conditions, all
connected to global warming and climate change. These hazards caused
loss of life, socio-economic dislocations, and damage to physical and
production infrastructure amounting to, in the aggregate, in excess of
EC $750 million or some 30 percent of GDP.

In 2020, the pandemic occasioned a 3.5 percent contraction of
GDP; and it continued unabated up to 2022, and continuing, causing
further socio-economic dislocation and damage. In April 2021, the volcanic eruptions devastated one-third of agriculture, caused damage and
loss of nearly $700 million; destroyed or damaged severely in excess
of 1,000 houses; damaged or destroyed other physical infrastructure;
and kept some 20,000 evacuees (one-fifth of St. Vincent's population) in
public shelters, private homes, or guest houses for some six months.

In the 2008-2022 period, and more particularly in the last two
years, the government and people, in concert with each other, have
accomplished mighty things. Indeed, since internal self-government
in 1969, and especially since independence in 1979, successive governments, though not in equal measure, have improved, markedly, the
condition of our people's lives. There is absolutely no way colonialism's
governance can be favourably compared to that of our governance since
the resumption of self-governing and independent nationhood. That is
a big difference between the 1881 to 1931 period under colonialism and
the post-independence years, especially since 2001, in tackling the ex-

ogenous shocks and structural challenges in the political economy. For example, in the latter period, advances in land reform, housing, education, health, water, electricity, transport, telecommunications, banking, financial services, airports, seaports, roads, and mobilisation of private (local and foreign) investment have made it easier to handle the contemporary exogenous challenges.

It is interesting to note the movements in the population between 1931 and 2012, and make some relevant observations.

Between 1931 and 1960, the population experienced its most rapid annual rate of growth in its census history since 1844. The rate of growth of the population was a whopping 1.72 percent per year over these 29 years. High fertility rates combined with declining mortality accounted for the growth of the population from 47,961 persons in 1931 to 79,948 in 1960, an increase of 31,987. Not even significant migration could offset sufficiently the natural increase. For example, between 1947 and 1959, the natural increase amounted to 28,000 and net migration was -11,220; net migration thus reduced the natural population increase by 40 percent. Without emigration, the population would have doubled in seventeen years.

It is to be noted, too, that between 1931 and 1957, colonialism ran the governmental affairs of St. Vincent and the Grenadines. To be sure, the introduction of universal adult suffrage in 1951 and popular representation in the legislature brought people's grievances and alternative development perspectives to the attention of the Colonial Administrator in St. Vincent and the Grenadines and the Windward Islands' Governor in Grenada, but the Executive Council of the colonial government still drove public policy despite a sprinkling of popularly-elected representatives on that body. It was not until a quasi-Ministerial system was introduced in 1957 and a Chief Minister, Ebenezer Joshua, first appointed in 1960, that there was enlarged popular input in the Executive Council's decisions, but still within a colonial straight-jacket. Internal self-government, with Milton Cato as the first Premier, was restored in October 1969; and sovereign independence was reclaimed under Cato in October 1979.

Over the 52-year period (1960 to 2012), the population increased to 109,991 or an increase of 30,043. The data show that the most rapid *average annual increase* was in the inter-censal period 1950-1960 of 1,307 persons and in the inter-censal period 1970 -1980 of 1,090 persons. Fertility rates in the 1960 to 1980 period were still quite high and declining mortality rates continued. In the two most recent inter-censal periods 1991-2001 and 2001-2012, the *average annual increases* were comparatively low, with increases in the average number of persons annually being 142 and 88 respectively. In fact, these latter twenty-one years have seen the *lowest average annual increase* since the 1891-1911 inter-censal years. Improved education, modernisation, and birth control together conspired to reduce markedly the extent of fertility. To be sure, there was emigration but it was not as large or as significant on the country's demography as in the earlier period 1881 to 1931.

From 1991, the average annual increase in the population started to diminish sharply. In 1980, the population stood at 97,845; it grew between then and 1991 to 107,598. Between 1991 and 2001, the population increased to 109,022; by 2012, the population edged up to 109,991 or by an absolute increase of 969 persons over the eleven-year period 2001-2012. The rate of increase of the population between 2001 and 2012 was the lowest since 1911. But this low population growth was not on account of huge migration.

During the most recent inter-censal period 2001-2012, a total of 4,851 persons migrated, many fewer than the years immediately prior, and far fewer than in the various inter-censal periods between 1891 to 1980, reflecting less of a desire to migrate as the local socio-economic situation improved; in recent years, too, permanent migration has been much more difficult to the USA, Canada, and Britain, three traditionally favoured locales for Vincentian migrants in the post-1950s era. Still, in the 2001-2012 period, 45 percent or 2,812 of the 4,851 who emigrated did so for employment; but more than one-half migrated for other reasons: 28.5 percent (1,380 persons) emigrated because of family reunification; and the remainder for various other reasons including as students and for medical attention. Emigration, and the remittances that flow therefrom, continue to be important to the political economy of St. Vincent and the Grenadines. But emigration flows of the earlier years (1881 to 1931) have not been replicated in the most recent years, including 2008 to 2022, as the solution to the exogenous shocks and structural weaknesses in our political economy.

The relevant historical survey shows that the colonial authorities had very little to teach us in addressing efficaciously our contemporary challenges in the people's interest.

In the very rough and difficult 50-year period (1881-1931), the Vincentians who did not migrate, those who soldiered on with their tough lives of limited opportunities, what did they do?

First, there were those — the bulk of them — who worked on the 100 or so plantations eking out a livelihood at below subsistence wages as labourers or employees at the arrowroot and sugar factories. Others, especially women, worked as poorly-paid domestics in the households of the planter-merchant elite, the estate supervisory staff, public servants, teachers, some smaller farmers and small business people.

There were also those fully or partially self-employed persons who were gainfully employed as small farmers (including animal husbandry) on rented crown lands or lands distributed after the limited post-1897 land distribution programme or on "yam-pieces" granted as tenancies-at-will by plantation owners to preferred estate employees for own-account agricultural activities. Many descendants of former enslaved or indentured persons worked, too, as skilled workers in the villages or for the planter-merchant elite as carpenters, blacksmiths, wheelwrights, shoemakers, bakers, cooks, or sawyers ("saw-men") in forestry; and there were fisherfolk who engaged in artisanal fishing.

A small section of the offspring of indentured labourers from Madeira (1845 – 1850) had by the latter part of the 19th century become small shop-keepers, small traders, small farmers, fishers, and persons involved in baking, wine-making or other skilled work. A similar trend occurred among the descendants of the indentured labourers from India (1861 – 1881), except that they were not wine-makers. Most of the offspring of both sets of indentured labourers stayed in farming either as estate labourers or as small, own-account farmers.

In the immediate post-emancipation period, a significant number of ex-slaves left the plantation barracks and lived in "free villages" they established. In time, these free villages became more or less self-sustaining communities in which there was marked solidarity between the villagers; constellations of poorer folks gathered, too, in this or that poorer section of one of the urban communities.

Communal activities of one kind or another helped people through these extremely difficult years. There was very little money available, so people fed themselves from the lands and the seas. The bulk of the houses were wattle-and-daub (wattle and clay) and the roofs were thatched with sturdy plant products, invariably with "old-man beard" grass; pillows and mattresses were stuffed with "barfleau" or a soft grassy material. Community solidarity of religion (churches), and family cohesion kept the communities together. Some remittances came through the Post Office outlets from migrants overseas. The colonial State maintained law and order, imposed taxes, and maintained minimal social services in education and health. The people's solidarity and resilience were critical for survival and limited advancement.

I was born in 1946 and much of these conditions existed into the early 1950s; I remember them well as a boy growing up in the rural village of Colonarie in the northeast of St. Vincent. More importantly, though, I recall the stories told to me by my grandparents, all four of whom were born in the latter decade of the 19th century, by my father (born 1916), by my mother (born 1919), and by the contemporaries of my grandparents and parents. My maternal grandparents had in fact migrated to Trinidad; my mother was actually born there; they returned to St. Vincent and the Grenadines in 1924-1925. My paternal grandfather migrated to Cuba in the late 1920s and spent two difficult years there during the world capitalist economic depression. My own father's primary education was cut short; he went to work on Mt. Williams Estate as a labourer before he was a teenager. Hard and smart work, resilience, family, and community solidarity, including in the churches, kept them barely afloat. Opportunities for advancement were minimal for the poor!

In the 50 years (1881-1931) of real hardship a few specific initiatives, through or by the colonial State that barely helped the poor and the marginalised to cope with the challenges, only offered, at the margin, a fragile base for possible further advance. These initiatives included:

• The purchase by the colonial government of some estates and the distribution of small plots of lands (one-to-five acres) to some of the landless in the aftermath of the Royal Commission of 1897. By the end of 1913 limited land reform occurred at Cumberland, Linley, New Adelphi, Park Hill, South Rivers, Richmond Hill, Clare Valley, Coopers Bay, Rutland Vale, Sandy Bay, Belair, and Union Island. In the aggregate, some 5,000 acres were distributed for farming and community settlement (housing). St. Vincent (including the Grenadines) had some 60,000 acres available, in total, for farming, housing, buildings (State and private business) and community purposes.

• Minimal legislative interventions to protect labourers/small farmers from summary ejection from private lands through the Labourer's Occupancy of Land Regulation Ordinance. It was rarely utilised perhaps because its effect was limited.

• The passage of the Agricultural Products Protection Ordinance to regulate the sale of cotton, cocoa, nutmegs and mace so as to safeguard cultivators from the scourge of praedial larceny; this law helped the larger planters far more than the smaller ones.

• The establishment of the St. Vincent Cocoa Growers Association and Agricultural and Commercial Society; and the Arrowroot Growers and Exporters Association. Both of these were public-private partnerships. The larger producers benefitted.

• The introduction of cotton as a commercial crop in the early 20th century.

• The establishment of the Boys' Grammar School and Girls' High School, which took in small numbers annually.

By 1959, the Grammar School admitted only 30 new students; however, through acts of commission or omission the colonial State failed to rise to the challenges of the dreadful fifty-year period, 1881 to 1931, including:

• Little or no disaster preparedness for the 1898 hurricane or the 1902 volcanic eruptions.

• Abysmally poor humanitarian relief efforts.

• Practically zero social safety net support for the poor and the infirm; widespread starvation was not addressed at all.

• Very little provision of social services (education, health, housing, sports, and water).

• Minimal infrastructural development.

• The banning of the practice of "Shakerism" (Spiritual Baptists' Faith) with the passage of the Shakerism Prohibition Ordinance of 1912.

• The banning of Carnival after the "Masquerade Riot" of 1879; it was revived in 1907, but the colonial State was wary of it; in 1917, the colonial government foolishly opposed the Carnival on the ground that it was a needless frivolity at the time of war — meanwhile there was much "frivolity" in London. Carnival was, and is, a promoter of social solidarity, a cultural expression, and a societal release from daily pressures.

- The banning of *The Negro World*, the newspaper of the Universal Negro Improvement Association.

- The consolidation of a racist, patriarchal, unrepresentative, and fascist mode of governance and society by colonialism. There was absolutely no developmental thrust. And colonialism acted in concert with the planter-merchant elite in a society marked by social oppression, extreme economic hardship, and gross inequality.

- The failure to increase labourers wages, which were a pittance.

The people themselves, however, sought to achieve mighty things in a most difficult set of circumstances. Among the highlights of the people's collective efforts were:

- The formation of numerous Agricultural and Credit Societies by small farmers/peasants. The first such society so formed was in the Clare Valley-Questelles area in 1910. In 1913, there were six such Societies with a membership of 135; by 1919, there were 21 with an aggregate membership of 1,660. The colonial government sought to regulate them with the enactment of the Agricultural Cooperative Societies Ordinance.

- The activism of three newspapers: *The Sentry* and *The Times* of St. Vincent; and *The Federalist* of Grenada in which the activist lawyer in St. Vincent, Charles Mc Leod, wrote a progressive column.

- The participation of small farmers in the Cotton Growers' Association and the Arrowroot Association.

- The establishment of a local branch of the West Indian Civil Rights Defence Union in the 1890s with George Smith, a Barrister, as Chairman, and Joseph Corea as Secretary.

- The widespread organisation of large sections of the population in Friendly and Benevolent Societies.

- The founding of the St. Vincent Representative Government Association (SVRGA) in 1917 that agitated for an end to pure crown colony government and for representative government.

- Strong participation in the Kingstown Town Board, a local government body with limited representative government.

- The formation of the local branch of Marcus Garvey's Universal Negro Improvement Association (UNIA); it was headquartered in Stubbs.

- The founding of the Agricultural Credit and Loan Bank by Joseph Burns Bonadie, the editor and owner of <u>The Times</u>.

- Repeated public protests over the 50-year period on a wide range of matters: against confederation; for representative government; for lands and improved wages; for Carnival; against this or that colonial official.

- The founding of the Intermediate High School in 1926 by J.P. Eustace.

- Extensive participation in churches especially the Anglican, Methodist, Roman Catholic, and Spiritual Baptist (Shakers) Churches. The Methodist pastors were usually in the forefront of the socio-political movements, oft-times in a progressive way but sometimes, not.

Despite the widespread public participation in religious activities, it was becoming clear by the end of the 19th century that ordinary folks were already beginning to provide leadership for themselves. The submission of Reverend S.F. Branch of the Methodist Church before the Royal Commission in 1897 provides support for this contention. Reverend Branch, who had been Rector of St. Patrick and St. David for thirty years, told the Commission:

> There are some self-seeking persons who will teach the labourer to put pressure on his employer. We have an excitable, suspicious, and still ignorant labouring population, *drifting from the old clerical control, as shown in the numerous new friendly societies, all self-managed and not as heretofore directed by ministers of religion, and in the recent self-constituted religious societies.* (My Emphasis)
>
> The labourer, by his lay, friendly and religious societies, and his revolt from the healthy control of the clergy of the Church and Ministers of the Wesleyan body, shows he is tasting the pleasure of thinking and determining for himself. The employer in the near future must be prepared to reckon with men who are trying to think out the problem of life, but who are still uneducated, and may be dangerous in asserting what they consider their rights."

More than three decades later, in the 1930s, it is this type of thinking worker and peasant, in joinder with the progressive wing of an emerging local professional class, whom George Augustus Mc Intosh led to ignite the beginnings of the social democratic revolution in our country.

Large Lessons: Ideational Reflections on Socio-Economic Development

So far in our historical backdrop of relevance to our current quest to respair, and recover, we have addressed the origins of the just reparations' demand; the necessity and desirability of deepening regional integration; the centrality of representative government, social democracy, and solidarity as the cornerstones in the edifice of people's sustainable development; the resilience of our people in addressing extraordinary challenges in specific epochs of our history, inclusive of the role that migration has played in our political economy, historically. Now, I turn to large lessons about the strategic path to sustainable development and summary reflections on ideas for socio-economic advancement. These are vital in our quest to respair and constitute the ideational, strategic, and policy imperatives in the shaping of Budget 2022!

Over the whole sweep of our country's history from 1763 to the sunset years of the twentieth century, the economy of St. Vincent and the Grenadines was dominated by one principal agricultural crop at various periods: sugar production for some 100 years from 1766 to 1881; arrowroot from 1890s to the first decade of the twentieth century; cotton for a decade or so in the early twentieth century; arrowroot again, thereafter rejoined by sugar production, which was subsequently terminated; the growing competing dominance of bananas, with arrowroot, from mid-to-late 1950s up to the late 1960s; the supremacy of bananas from the 1970s to the late 1990s. Inter-mixing with these dominant crops were ground provisions, assorted fruits from trees, coconuts, coffee and cocoa, vegetables, cattle, sheep, pigs, and goats. Fishing, mainly artisanal, remained a constant in several communities in St. Vincent and in the Grenadines' islands. Light manufacturing emerged particularly in the 1960s onwards, although prior to that there was the production of sugar and rum, the ginning of cotton seed oil up to 1959, and the making of coconut oil and related products until the early 1980s.

The single crop dominance impacted the society, the economy and the politics. Sugar cane was grown largely on plantations owned by

Anglo-Saxons or their descendants; indeed, at the termination of sugar production in 1961-1962, two-thirds of the sugar cane were produced by plantations and one-third by peasant cultivators; the sole sugar factory at Mt. Bentinck from the immediate post-war years (post-1945) to 1962 was owned by the company that owned Mt. Bentinck Estates — the ownership was in the hands of the white planter-merchant elite. Arrowroot was initially a predominantly estate crop; most estates owned and operated arrowroot factories. There were a few independently owned and operated, like the one at Park Hill run by "Daddy" D'Andrade that processed the rhizomes from small cultivators. Much later, from the 1990s onwards, arrowroot cultivation was centred on small farms in North Windward (so-called "Carib Country" of yesteryears) and the rhizomes processed at a factory in Owia owned by the State-run Arrowroot Growers' Association. By the time of bananas' arrival as the dominant export commercial industry, substantial sub-division of the estates had occurred either through land reform led by the State, or sub-division of the large estates for sale to small farmers, by the planters. These plantation owners had by then come to realise that a plantation system of agriculture in St. Vincent and the Grenadines was an unproductive anachronism in the context of an evolving modern, social democracy, internally, and a brutally competitive monopoly capitalism, externally, with no sentiment or nostalgia for colonial-era preferential market access.

So, for some 230 or so years from 1764 to the 1990s, a dominant agricultural crop sustained the economy, society and politics of St. Vincent and the Grenadines. Over this period the central features of this essentially "colonial" economy were the following:

• The ownership of the means of production (land, buildings, machinery, equipment, tools — all objects of labour and means of labour) were concentrated in a few hands. Up to the 1960s the bulk of the land was owned by a tiny group, largely of European descent. The few commercial banks up to 1977 were all owned or controlled by British and Canadian multi-national finance institutions.

• Production was based largely on an unlimited supply of unskilled labour, including child labour, cheaply priced. Between 1764 and 1838, there was slave labour; thereafter, up to the anti-colonial uprising of 1935, the *cheap labour* was provided by former enslaved persons, indentured labourers, and the off-spring of both groups. The records show that agricultural wages were not increased for 100 years up to 1938. Thereafter, particularly after the rise and growth of militant trade unionism in the 1950s and 1960s, wages and working conditions improved, but the labour market was still a buyer's market at low wages. There was little or no trade unionism in relation to workers on small farms; it was just too problematic to organise and sustain.

• Production was subsidised either at home with production subsidies or with preferential subsidies and protections in the external market. Banana exports from the Windward Islands and Jamaica to the British market would not have prospered were it not for the market preferences, subsidies and protections offered by Britain. In the early years, 1950s to early 1970s, this suited the British given the post-war shortage in Britain of foreign currency (American dollars) to buy cheaper Latin American bananas; thereafter the economics of preferential trade in bananas was unappealing for them. In 1993, Britain's entry into the European Union Single Market and Economy combined with the "free trade" ideology of the World Trade Organisation meant the beginning of the end of the market preferences, and thus of the banana industry in our region. Without these preferences and market subsidies, banana exports from the Windward Islands and Jamaica were unable to compete with large, efficient producers with even cheaper labour in Latin America, Central America, and West Africa.

• Production centred on the growing of agricultural crops, exporting raw materials, engaging in little or no local value-added through finished manufactured commodities (the sugar itself was unrefined and the bulk of the molasses was exported), and the importation from Britain of machinery, tools and equipment. Indeed, one leading political personality in Britain had expressed loudly the accepted colonial consensus that not even *a nail or a horseshoe was to be produced in the West Indian colonies.*

The increasing modernisation of the society, the growth of services — especially tourism and the diversification of the economy — prompted competition for labour and capital. Labour shortages, labour unavailability, contradictorily amidst unemployment, and low labour productivity, began to plague the agricultural sector, even at a moderately competitive price, nominally. Only in the last two decades or so are we witnessing the emergence of a more modern, more scientific, and more diversified agricultural sector, including the introduction of new commodities such as medicinal cannabis, or the reintroduction of other commercial crops such as cocoa and coffee. In this regard, the current Minister of Agriculture, Saboto Caesar, has been a pioneering leader and moderniser. The actual numbers in the 2022 Estimates and Appropriation Act reflect this thrust in agriculture and fisheries.

As a consequence of the exhaustion of the economic model grounded in traditional colonial agricultural dominance as recommended by the Moyne Commission of 1938-1945, new perspectives and strategic approaches have been advanced.

Indeed, even before the exhaustion of the old economic model of the colonial type had become clearly manifest, there were competing, alternative, strategic policies and programmes on offer. Marcus Mosiah Garvey and Arthur Lewis, as we have hitherto noted, placed their alternative markers down.

In the aftermath of the Second World War and the wave of popular elections based on universal adult suffrage, and particularly after the dissemination of Arthur Lewis' publications on Economic Planning, Development with Unlimited Supplies of Labour, and Economic Growth, a raft of proposals for economic reform and fresh initiatives were advanced to accompany the popular democratic openings and constitutional decolonisation. In short time, other policy options came to the fore: economic planning; "industrialisation by invitation" to foreign investors; investments in seaports and airports; a diversification and modernisation of the agricultural sector and of the economy more broadly into services including people-centred tourism and financial services; and federation or other maturing forms of regional integration. Between the 1950s and late 1960s, to some degree or the other, all West Indian governments implemented these measures. Economic growth occurred and living standards were lifted even as unemployment increased and poverty/indigence in sections of the people became very visible and intractable.

The old planter-merchant elite, and many of their family successors still imbued with plantation residues, nevertheless sought protection from, or compromises with, the emerging democratic State in the region. In most regional countries, the private sector was undeveloped. This was certainly the case in St. Vincent and the Grenadines. Inevitably, the State stepped in not only to regulate the economy better but to become owners or part-owners of critical economic enterprises. A limited State capitalism arose that negotiated compromises with the old planter-merchant elite, emerging economic elites and foreign investors. In that nexus of relations, contradictions abounded, some resolved in progressive directions, others infused by the spirit and the deeds of the "ancien regime."

Swiftly, a critique developed of these policies and their practical results from the "New World Group" of towering intellectuals based at the University of the West Indies, mainly at St. Augustine, Trinidad, and Mona, Jamaica. Among the leading lights at St. Augustine were Lloyd Best and James Millette, and at Mona, the prominent personalities were the economists George Beckford, Norman Girvan, Havelock Brewster, and Clive Y. Thomas. They assessed and critiqued the old "plantation" model, the new "plantation" model, and the mixed "plantation" model. They focused significantly on skewed and unequal external exchange relations between the metropole and the Caribbean hinterland, poverty and inequality, the necessity and desirability in deepening regional economic integration of an organic, as distinct from a mechanistic kind, and internal governance arrangements of "the plantations" and the allied political systems of the so-called democratic State apparatus.

The "New World" scholars/activists churned out impressive scholarly works, including Lloyd Best in various publications on the "Plantation Economy", George Beckford on "Persistent Poverty", Havelock Brewster and C.Y. Thomas on the *Dynamics of West Indian Economic Integration*, and Norman Girvan on *Foreign Capital and Economic Underdevelopment in Jamaica*.

In short time, the intellectual umbrella of "New World Group" became fractured; the centre was unable to hold and things fell apart. In a profound sense, this fracturing was inevitable. To be sure, all in the New World Group were anti-colonial, possessed of truly democratic instincts, anti-imperialist, anti-racist, and held strongly to the uniqueness and legitimacy of our Caribbean civilisation and its trajectory for further development or ennoblement. But many had Garveyite sentiments; others were attracted to Marxism; some who were not Marxist-oriented still held up the Cuban model of socialism as a possible path for the Caribbean as a whole; some who were "Africanists" were drawn to the African socialism of President Julius Nyerere of Tanzania and his "ujamaa" or familyhood mode of cooperative economic activism in the communities, both rural and urban. Some of "the New World" members became active politically with different approaches to party-building, consciousness-raising, and political alliances.

Many in the New World Group critiqued Arthur Lewis' economic thinking by caricaturing it woefully, and wrongly, as an open-sesame of "industrialisation by invitation" along the lines of the Puerto Rican "bootstrap" model. Lewis was undisturbed and unpersuaded by the critiques. But "the New World" economic theories were themselves opaque for practical implementation, and focused, perhaps, too much on *exchange relations* externally and insufficiently on the *relations of production* within a dependent capitalist periphery or "hinterland" and its inextricable links with monopoly capitalism globally.

The "New World" critique of the old colonial economy, of Eric Williams' "state capitalism", and of Arthur Lewis' theory of economic growth and its caricatured praxis, influenced Michael Manley in Jamaica to rethink and repackage, in a new period, in the early 1970s, the People's National Party's philosophy and programme. He called it "democratic socialism" and marketed it as "Christianity in action". In Guyana, Forbes Burnham opted for "cooperative socialism", but with a heavy dose of statism in practice, authoritarianism, and an Afro-centric anti-imperialism designed to keep Cheddi Jagan's socialist People's Progressive Party, and its Indian political base, at bay in the ethnically-divided Guyana.

The substantive critique of the New World paradigm came from the Marxist left in Trinidad and Tobago, led, in part, by James Millette, a former "New World" member and in Jamaica by Trevor Munroe, a Marxist intellectual, who returned from Oxford as a Rhodes Scholar in 1970-1971 to teach at UWI, Mona, Jamaica; he founded a Marxist organisation, the Workers' Liberation League (WLL) that evolved into a communist party, the Workers' Party of Jamaica (WPJ).

The Marxists in the Caribbean saw "New World" political economy as progressive and nationalist but essentially utopian, idealist, non-scientific, and undialectical, which ignored or down-played the *relations of production* within a particular capitalist *mode of production* (*productive forces* plus *production relations*), which mode of production, the Marxists insisted, determines, always, primarily and ultimately, the contours of the economy, polity and society. Further, the Caribbean Marxists emphasised that it was the class struggle embedded within the mode of production that gives life, *dialectically*, to the objective contradictions within the capitalist mode of production itself; it is this class struggle they saw as the motor-force of change in the society and the lever to resolve the inherent *systemic* contradictions. The *mode of production*, Marxism teaches, generates a more or less mirror image in its legal, political and ideational super-structure in the composite *social formation*. Damningly, a few of the Marxists considered that "New World" political economy stylised the facts in search of a theory of explanation.

For their part, "the New World" rebuttal was that Marxism in the Caribbean resisted a proper interrogation of the specificities of the evolution of the Caribbean's political economy. As intellectual activists, the Marxists were chastised for rote learning from prescribed Marxist texts as though social science is formatted theology. Substantively, Marxists were critiqued for their easy dismissal of race and religion, which "the New World Group" insisted were relatively independent or autonomous causative behavioural factors in our region, irrespective of production relations. Moreover, "the New World" critique insisted that Marxist political praxis with its emphasis of Leninist modes of party organisation, the vanguard concept of "professional revolutionaries" in a tightly-managed party armed with an unquestioned doctrine, and democratic centralism, were alien to our Caribbean experience and were peculiarly Russian categories made universal by a jaundiced international communism. And, as regards Cuba, "the New World Group" insisted that it was "sui generis", of its own special kind, and not capable of replication anywhere else in the Caribbean. They averred, too, that there was something called a Soviet imperium — a reference to the Soviet Union's dominant presence in Cuba — that should be avoided. Neither the "New World" theorising nor Caribbean Marxism addressed the salient issue of patriarchy at all or in a wholly satisfactory manner; the issue of the oppression of women (one-half of the population) was to come to the fore later in Caribbean intellectual and policy discourses.

The revolutionary overthrow of the Eric Gairy regime in Grenada on March 13, 1979, by the revolutionary democratic New Jewel Movement (NJM) headed by Maurice Bishop gave an impetus to Marxist-Leninist ideas. The NJM's leadership contained revolutionary democrats like Maurice Bishop, in-training towards Marxism; Marxist-Leninists like Bernard Coard and his followers at various levels of cultural/intellectual sophistication who challenged the ability, and level of ideational maturity of many to absorb the scientific and philosophical nuances of Marxism; social democrats of a main-stream kind; and even progressive members of the national bourgeoisie who were social democratic and anti-imperialist. But the revolutionary democratic — Marxist leadership held the dominant sway in the NJM.

Grenada, as a very small, underdeveloped capitalist country with profound vulnerabilities and weaknesses in its economy and society, was an unlikely candidate for socialist construction.

For decades, but particularly in the 1960s and 1970s, Marxism advanced a comprehensive theoretical framework to take undeveloped economies and societies, like Grenada, not along a socialist path, but on the trajectory of a "non-capitalist path of development", alternatively called "a path of socialist orientation". In practical terms, it is advanced social democracy under appropriate leadership, a mixed economy, with a significant State sector, political democracy, anti-imperialism, and a solidarity with progressive, like-minded forces regionally and globally, all done in the interest of the people and their socio-economic upliftment. I contributed to an assessment of this literature, and its application, in a monograph I authored, entitled *The Non-Capitalist Path of Development: Africa and the Caribbean* (One Caribbean Publishers, London, 1981).

A number of seminal political developments across the region and globally caused a re-think of Marxian socialism, socialist orientation, and allied philosophical/practical constructs. In 1980, Michael Manley's "democratic socialism" became exhausted in Jamaica and was defeated by its own weaknesses and moreso by the machinations of imperialism in concert with reactionaries in Jamaica; Edward Seaga's Jamaica Labour Party (JLP) emerged triumphant with its neo-liberal philosophical stance atop a working people's base of politically-tribal support from the JLP and the followers of its founder-leader, Alexander Bustamante since the early 1940s onwards. In Guyana, the Forbes Burnham regime lost its way amidst widespread immiseration of the people, official corruption, authoritarian rule, fraudulent elections, and State violence against political opponents of the PPP and the Working People's Alliance (WPA); the "cooperative socialist republic" was a sham; in June 1980, the scholar and revolutionary activist leader of the WPA, Walter Rodney, was assassinated in Georgetown, Guyana, by hired thugs of the ruling regime. In Grenada, the revolution collapsed in 1983 through internal factionalism; Bishop, the overwhelmingly popular leader of the Revolution, and some of his comrades were killed by members of the People's Revolutionary Army and the NJM allied to Bernard Coard; and, under the direction of President Ronald Reagan, the American military invaded Grenada and occupied it until its surrogates in the region propped up a transitional government amidst overwhelming public support from Grenadians for the invasion. The NJM revolutionaries themselves killed their revolution; the Americans buried it.

Across the region, moderate social democratic governments were replaced by those wedded to neo-liberalism, the Washington Consensus, and American global hegemony. In St. Kitts-Nevis, the People's Action Movement of Dr. Kennedy Simmonds, replaced the St. Kitts-Nevis Labour Party, as the government; in St. Vincent and the Grenadines,

Milton Cato's St. Vincent and the Grenadines Labour Party was defeated at the polls in 1984 by James Mitchell's New Democratic Party. In Grenada, Nicholas Brathwaite, head of the transitional government (1983-1984), was to return as Prime Minister, as head of a National Democratic Congress government between 1990 and 1995, interposed between governments of a similar stripe. In St. Lucia, the victory of the St. Lucia Labour Party of 1979 was short-lived due to internal confusion; it was voted out of office in 1982 and replaced by John Compton's more conservative United Workers' Party. In Barbados, Tom Adams's Barbados Labour Party government had come to office in September 1976; he played a critical role in the American invasion of Grenada; in 1979, he had revoked the work permit of Ralph Gonsalves on account of the latter's left-wing, anti-imperialist political activism, and thus denied him continuance in his post as a University Lecturer in Barbados. In Dominica, the conservative, anti-communist Eugenia Charles' Dominica Freedom Party defeated the Dominica Labour Party in the general elections of 1980; she was to remain as Prime Minister for 15 years. In Trinidad and Tobago, A.N.R. Robinson's National Alliance for Reconstruction defeated the nationalist People's National Movement in the 1986 general elections to form the government.

Globally, the Union of Soviet Socialist Republic's (USSR), ("the Soviet Union"), collapsed in 1991; shortly thereafter, its allied centrally-planned, "socialist" regimes in Eastern Europe were, one by one, removed from office to be replaced mainly by "free market" ideologues and pro-American leaders. It is as though a unipolar world dominated by monopoly capitalism and the USA had triumphed unquestionably. At least one prominent American political scientist considered it "the end of history". But history, awash with multiple contradictions galore, has no such end, as the world was soon to find out.

Within a decade of the dawning years of the 21st century, the behemoth known as the People's Republic of China with 1.4 billion people advanced swiftly to become the world's second largest economy; India, with a similarly-sized population, blossomed like-wise; Brazil, with 200 million persons, emerged as the sixth or seventh largest economy in the world under President Lula of the "left wing" Workers' Party; South Africa, arising from the shadow of apartheid in the post-Mandela era was to lead an African renaissance in an African Union, of 1.3 billion people and abundant resources. And Russia re-emerged with a renewed strength of being the resourced-laden, largest country in the world in geographic size, with a population of some 140 million, still armed with nuclear weapons. These five countries were called BRICS: Brazil, Russia, India, China, and South Africa; and they worked, as circumstances and interests permitted, as a bloc, very often not in sync with the USA, Canada, and the European Union which themselves manifested searching contradictions and competing interests between and within each other.

"Emerging economies" from different corners of the world made their distinctive mark: in Latin America (Mexico, Argentina, Chile, Colombia, and the Bolivarian Republic of Venezuela under President Hugo Chavez); in the Middle East (Saudi Arabia and the anti-imperialist Islamic Republic of Iran led different wings of political Islam in a region of growing strength based on oil production); resurgent Turkey, a "secular" Muslim country, arose under Recep Erdogan's leadership with a history of Empire, of over 300,000 square miles and over 80 million people located astride Europe and Asia with a growing economy of nearly US $850 billion — the 20th in size globally — and with the second largest army in the North Atlantic Treaty Organisation (NATO) after the USA; in Asia, Japan sustained itself as the third largest economy in the world, in an area where South Korea emerged as the tenth largest economy in the world (GDP of US $1.8 trillion in 2021); Pakistan (over 340,000 square miles with a population of some 230 million — the 5th largest in the world — and an economy of US $29 billion), armed with nuclear weapons but with significant poverty and possessed of militant Islam in some sections of the population; nearby Bangladesh of 150 million persons, relatively cramped within a land area of 57,320 square miles and gripped by immense developmental challenges; and Indonesia, an archipelagic State of growing importance with the largest Muslim population of almost 300 million.

Within two decades of the 21st century the number of member-states of the European Union (EU), led by a dominant, unified Germany, grew from one dozen to 28; then Britain voted to exit the EU. Most of the new member-states are countries from the erstwhile political orbit of the former Soviet Union.

As the 21st century unfolded, flash points globally evidenced the world's multi-polarity and the end of the illusion of a Pax Americana in a unipolar world. There were the invasions of Iraq and Afghanistan by NATO forces led by the USA, and then their disorderly withdrawals in defeat after much expenditure in blood and treasure; the ongoing conflicts in Syria and Yemen; the NATO invasion of Libya, the overthrow of the Gadhafi regime, and Libya's descent into a failed State and a raging civil war; the never-ending Palestinian-Israeli conflicts; the USA's stand-off with Iran and the imposition of sanctions on the Iranian regime; the ongoing and dangerous cat-and-mouse games reflecting the chasm between the USA and North Korea over nuclear weapons; the military interventions, skirmishes, and reciprocal threats on Russia's western front especially involving Georgia and Ukraine; the virtual encirclement of Russia with NATO's troops and weapons on some of Russia's neighbours to its west and south; and America's ideological opposition to any "socialist" government in its supposed "back yard/ front yard" in the western hemisphere, as for example its unwarranted intervention in the internal affairs of, and relentless hostility to, revolutionary Cuba, Bolivarian Venezuela, and anti-imperialist Nicaragua, and its uneasy relations, despite a free trade agreement, with nationalist Mexico, the world's twelfth largest economy of 125 million people.

And on February 24, 2022, Russia embarked on military aggression against Ukraine, causing extensive physical damage, significant loss of life, huge migration, and putting the world in a terrible tailspin in political and economic terms. In the immediate aftermath of Russia's military operation in Ukraine, President Joseph Biden of the USA advanced the call for a "New World Order". But the critical queries went unanswered: What's New? Which World? And Who Gives the Orders?

All the particular flashpoints, intra-imperialist economic and political competition, the Russian and Chinese resistance to North American-Western European hegemony, the simmering of mainland China-Taiwan dispute of real moment, the internal contradictions of monopoly capitalism itself, the growth/development of international law and institutions inclusive of those under the United Nations system, the enlargement of political space for "emerging economies" and small states, the strengthening of "independent" regional blocs, and more, have conspired to provide, among other things, some political and economic space for countries like St. Vincent and the Grenadines, even in the "western orbit", to act in its own interests, relatively unencumbered, but nevertheless constrained by imperialism's hegemony in our hemisphere.

Our own experience between 2008 and 2017 in constructing the Argyle International Airport (AIA) is a dramatic and outstanding example of St. Vincent and the Grenadines utilising its sovereignty and independence creatively, with strong unwavering, leadership, in the interest of our people. An international airport is a "sine qua non" for tourism and high-priced, low-volume exports; it is basic infrastructure for sustainable development, and the construction of a modern, competitive, post-colonial economy. Given the mountainous topography of St. Vincent and the huge cost of such a venture (approximately EC $750 million to build) — the largest capital project ever in St. Vincent and the Grenadines — it was necessary and desirable to mobilise resources, in cash and kind, from all over the world. Inasmuch as our traditional friends (USA, Canada, European Union), and the usual multi-lateral lending agencies (Caribbean Development Bank, the World Bank and the European Investment Bank), baulked at the magnitude of the project, my government had to mobilise the requisite resources from alternative sources. St. Vincent and the Grenadines had limited financial resources but it possessed some skilled manpower, some land (the government sold State lands elsewhere to help with the payment for the privately-owned lands at Argyle), and the requisite bold, creative leadership.

So, we put together a compact of the willing: Cuba, Venezuela, the ALBA Bank, Petro Caribe, Republic of China (Taiwan), Mexico, Georgia, Iran, Austria, Libya (under Gadhafi), Turkey by way of monies to the CARICOM Development Fund, Trinidad and Tobago (under Patrick Manning), and Vincentians at home and abroad. As the actual airport construction neared completion, and imperialism concluded that it was a purely commercial, non-military facility, we were able to mobilise the State-export guarantee entities in the USA, the United Kingdom and Canada to secure the funding, by way of loans, dozens of millions of dollars, to purchase equipment and machinery for the airport's operation. Putting, and keeping together, this compact of the willing demanded extraordinary energy, creativity, diplomatic/political skills, and focused, quality leadership in communion with a supportive people despite the obstructionist machinations of the opposition NDP and its fellow-travellers.

At times the opposition NDP acted as fifth-columnists doing imperialism's dirty work on the ground with the vilest sorts of propaganda, centred, among other things, on the wholly false allegations that my government was a pawn in the hands of socialist Cuba, Bolivarian Venezuela, and militantly anti-imperialist Libya and Iran.

Over and over, during the near-decade long construction of the Argyle International Airport, as Prime Minister I was peppered unrelentingly by hostile questions from various officials of the American government about the role of Cuba, the Bolivarian Republic of Venezuela, Libya and Iran in the airport's construction. More than once it was suggested to me by some of these officials that the airport was essentially a military airport — an old propaganda canard from the Reagan administration's playbook about the international airport constructed in Grenada by the Revolution under Maurice Bishop's leadership. Ofttimes I felt insulted by this ignorant questioning; more often, though, I pitied their stupidity and the egregious folly of empire.

Imperialism's interrogations and their absurd queries were not restricted to low-level officials parading themselves with a make-believe self-importance. On two occasions, on my return from official visits to Libya and Iran, American delegations (officials from the State Department and the American Embassy in Barbados) came to St. Vincent and the Grenadines to cross-examine me on the role of Libya, Iran, Cuba and Venezuela on the airport construction and allied political issues. Each time I spoke truthfully in a respectful, principled and dignified manner to their queries, comments, declarations, and veiled threats; I controlled my contempt for them and their invisible masters; I hid my anger with all the skill and manners taught to us by our Caribbean civilisation, through our forbears, representing the genius of our people who have had to survive and thrive amidst adversity.

These American officials paid no attention to the assistance given to St. Vincent and the Grenadines in its construction of the international airport from Austria, Mexico, Taiwan, Mikhail Saakashvili's Georgia, or Trinidad and Tobago. The metaphoric bees in their bonnets were Cuba, Bolivarian Venezuela, Iran, and Ghaddafi's Libya. Once, after my official visit to Turkey I was quizzed briefly about the role of Erdogan's Turkey; this small group from the American Embassy in Barbados apparently had not received the memo that Turkey was a fully-paid up member of the North Atlantic Treaty Organisation (NATO) on Russia's southern border.

I confess, though, that on one occasion I let slip my wicked Caribbean humour: a small, official American delegation had visited me at the Prime Minister's Official Residence on our "Independence Day"; the tiresome questions were yet again being posed; immediately outside the Residence, on the lawn, there are two old, non-functional early 19th century cannons pointing seawards; I mockingly pleaded with the delegation to the report to the successors of Donald Rumsfeld and Dick Chaney (former Defence Secretary and Vice President of the USA) that I possessed "weapons of mass destruction" — a damning reference to America's folly in Iraq.

Today, the grateful people of St. Vincent and the Grenadines ensure that large photographs of Fidel Castro, Hugo Chavez, and Patrick Manning respectively of Cuba, Venezuela and Trinidad and Tobago hang prominently at the Argyle International Airport in recognition of their countries' selflessness and huge contributions to this existential project. A plaque thanking the Republic of China (Taiwan) is also displayed.

Many naysayers, resident in the opposition NDP in St. Vincent and the Grenadines, the modern-day Sanballats and Tobias of the Ammonites, and the men of Ashdod, mocked our government and its leadership on the Argyle International Airport; their mockery then turned to anger and conspiracy as the international airport project unfolded; they used every ruse, including written urgings to the Republic of China (Taiwan) not to provide monies, to derail the start-up, progress, completion, and operation of the airport; the opposition New Democratic Party (NDP) and its allies orchestrated a campaign — including an essentially anti-airport candlelight march in October 2005 on the eve of an official visit to St. Vincent and the Grenadines of Taiwan's President Chen Shui-bian — of lies, misinformation, and downright treacherous conduct to stop the airport's construction and operation. They all failed in similarly spectacular fashion as did the original Sanballat, Tobias, the Ammonites, and men of Ashdod during the fifth century before Christ when they sought, vainly, to prevent the Prophet-Builder Nehemiah and the Hebrew people from rebuilding the city walls around Jerusalem, which had been broken for 112 years.

Indeed, these anti-national forces that sought with such vehemence, in concert with the more revanchist elements of imperialism, to stop the international airport's construction and operation even caused some normally sensible persons, but who are weak in mind and spirit, to doubt the necessity, desirability, and efficacy of the airport. Some of it was absolutely bizarre. The history of all this is well-known.

But the construction of the international airport was a great cause; and great causes have never been won or accomplished by doubtful men and women. This "impossible" dream of generations of Vincentians took three years of preliminary preparation (2005 to 2008). The actual earthworks began symbolically on August 13, 2008 — the birthday of Fidel Castro and Vincent Beache (the first Political Leader of the ULP) — with Prime Minister Ralph Gonsalves operating, ceremonially, a bull-dozer. For starters, we had to level four hills and mountains; fill four valleys; span a river; dismantle and cause to be relocated elsewhere

135 middle-and-upper-middle-income houses; the dismantling and re-building of a church and the relocation of a cemetery; the dismantling of a hotel and an apartment building; reclaiming land seaward and the construction of extensive sea defences; the careful removal and conserv-ing of stones on which were engraved indigenous Callinago/Garifuna petroglyphs; and the excavation of an indigenous people's village, burial ground, and artefacts by trained and amateur archaeologists.

From August 13, 2008, until February 14, 2017, when the airport was formally opened in grand celebratory style, earthworks activity, construction, equipping, regulating, and organizing the functioning of the airport were in-train. It was a national effort of mammoth propor-tions, without any support from the opposition NDP (save and except, episodically, from one opposition parliamentarian pretty late in the day), but in concert with our regional and international friends and allies, in solidarity.

One week or so before the formal opening of the Argyle Interna-tional Airport, the Leader of the Opposition NDP, Dr. Godwin Friday, wrote to the Director General of the Eastern Caribbean Civil Aviation Authority to revoke or refuse approval for the airport's operation on ill-informed and spurious grounds. The Director General of ECCAA ignored Friday's folly. The Argyle International Airport duly opened on February 14, 2017.

I remind everyone that during the period of the construction of the Argyle International Airport, the global economic depression of 2008-2011, and its continuing reverberations affected St. Vincent and the Grenadines adversely, immensely; did annual storms and adverse weather events especially in 2010, 2011, 2012, 2013, 2015, 2016 and 2017 causing loss and damage in excess of EC $750 million.

Today, from Argyle International Airport, international carriers take passengers to and from Miami (American Airlines), New York (Caribbean Airlines), Toronto (Air Canada Rouge), and London (Virgin Atlantic). Several local and regional air carriers fly in and out of Argyle as do private jets, especially those with passengers destined for tourism resorts in the Grenadines (Bequia, Mustique, Canouan, Union Island, Petit St. Vincent, Palm Island, and Mayreau).

The construction and operation of the Argyle International Airport is a metaphor for the possibilities of our country: it is a prime evidential exhibit of what can be done by a united people, with quality focused leadership in communion with the people, armed with a relevant developmental approach, and in solidarity with our regional family and international friends, despite resistance from some powerful forces externally.

In drawing from these experiences, and more, and applying them to respairing in 2022, and beyond, consequent upon the pandemic, the volcanic eruptions, Hurricane Elsa, and multiple other challenges, the lessons of solidarity (internally and externally), creativity, a compelling developmental narrative, organisation, people's resilience and determination, good governance and sound State administration, and strong, quality leadership, are vital in our quest for sustainable development, inclusive of a paradigm shift to a post-colonial economy.

Chapter Two

The Quest to Build a Modern, Competitive, Many-Sided, Post-Colonial Economy

The Paradigm Shift to the Post-Colonial Economy

The review of the historical backdrop of St. Vincent and the Grenadines, and its regional and international inter-connectedness, inclusive of ideational, philosophical, and theoretical stratagems at play, prompts a viable alternative and strategic economic quest of relevance. The strategic requirement is to build a modern, competitive, many-sided, post-colonial economy that is at once local, national, regional, and global. Each of these words or formulations is pregnant with real meaning. They point to sound theoretical underpinnings, appropriate policies, and practical programmes. This economic quest is not isolated from the social, political, governance, and ideational dimensions; indeed, they are inextricably linked and form a composite whole; they feed off, and into, each other.

It is necessary and desirable to interrogate further the requisites of the ULP government's quest of building a modern, competitive, many-sided, post-colonial economy that is at once local, national, regional and global. I have written and spoken extensively on this subject, but a summary delineation and re-statement of the relevant issues are apt in the current challenging circumstances and in the context of the facts, historical and contemporary, the theoretical or ideational that help to inform economic strategy, and the role of Budget 2022 in it.

At a glance, our country's economic history from 1763 to the sunset years of the 20th century demanded a departure from the old or out-moded colonial economy either in its pure pre-1969 condition or its amended form in the three or so decades thereafter, prior to March 29, 2001, when the ULP assumed the reins of government.

No one today, save and except perhaps the most racist-and-imperialist-minded individuals, can ever condone, approve, or be enrapped in nostalgia of the British conquest and settlement of St. Vincent and the Grenadines between 1763 and 1838, the robbing of the indigenous people of their lands, the commission of widespread native genocide, the enslavement of African bodies, the establishment of an undemocratic, fascist colonial State system, and the enthronement of a colonial economy for exploitative and extractive purposes in the interest of Britain and its political and economic ruling class.

Similarly, the immediate post-emancipation 100 years (up to 1938 or thereabouts) of unbelievable immiseration of the people in a condition of nominally "free" labour (the former slaves, indentured labourers, and their offspring) were immensely dreadful in every material particular as British colonialism tinkered with the "ancien regime" of an inhuman, colonial political and economic praxis. It took the anti-colonial uprisings across the Caribbean in the 1930s, inclusive of that in St. Vincent and the Grenadines on October 21, 1935, to shake somewhat the British colonial complacency. Even so, the colonial economy with the "plantation" system at its core internally, and encumbered exchange and trade relations externally, rumbled on with a strategic political nexus between colonialism and the white planter-merchant elite, ensuring continued extraction of wealth for them, and misery for the people. This condition remained unchanged until the struggle for universal adult suffrage was won in 1951.

Between 1951, and particularly after a quasi-ministerial system emerged in 1957 *and* 1969, the devolved governmental authority to the popularly-elected governments, under Ebenezer Joshua and Milton Cato, found political and economic spaces to advance partially a range of limited initiatives in a social democratic framework. These partial advances of a social democratic kind were deepened and broadened after internal self-government between 1969 and independence in 1979 mainly by the Labour Party government of Milton Cato until 1984, and much less so by the James Mitchell-Ebenezer Joshua "Alliance" government of 1972 to 1974.

Between July 1984 and March 2001, the NDP government under James Mitchell (July 1984 to October 2000) and Arnhim Eustace (October 27, 2000 to March 28, 2001) pursued largely a neo-liberal economic model along the lines prescribed by "the Washington Consensus", which sought to reform the colonial economy, but by embedding it firmly within the vortex of monopoly capitalism overseas and a dependent capitalism locally, devoid of any large ambition for sustainable development and the advancement of our multi-faceted Caribbean civilisation.

The critique of the amended colonial economy of the 1957-2001 period is not to suggest that little or nothing of a positive nature for the people occurred over these four or so decades. On the contrary, there was much advancement, and the quality of the people's lives improved despite continued poverty and hardship for large swathes of the population and underdevelopment generally. But to avoid a developmental dead-end, a fresh paradigm was demanded. That is where the ULP government came in with its focused quest to build a modern, post-colonial economy.

As always, in our assessments of the amended colonial economy under the governments of Joshua, Cato, and Mitchell, and the post-colonial paradigm advanced by the leadership of the ULP, we must be reminded of Karl Marx's insightful observation in *The Eighteenth Brumaire of Louis Napoleon* (English Edition, 1869):

> Men (and women) make their own history, but they do not make it as they please, they do not make it under self-elected circumstances, but under circumstances existing already, given and transmitted from the past. The tradition of all dead generations weighs like a nightmare on the brains of the living.

By March 29, 2001, when the ULP assumed the reins of government, which it has exercised continuously, unbroken thus far for 21 years, and validated in five successive election triumphs (2001, 2005, 2010, 2015, 2020), it was evident that St. Vincent and the Grenadines could not continue with the amended colonial political economy of the previous 22 years or so since independence in 1979. Still, the ULP government had to build upon the efficacious initiatives of these years, and before, from Joshua's government of 1957, and be practical and mindful of the limitations of St. Vincent and the Grenadines, its immense challenges and the balance of forces globally, including the might of monopoly capitalism and our country's location within it. At the same time, we tapped into our country's strengths and possibilities, the potential of a mature regionalism, and internationalist solidarity. It was never an option for the ULP government "to roll over and play dead" to neo-colonialism, monopoly capitalism, and imperialism. The twin alternatives oscillated, as the circumstances admitted, between accommodation and creative resistance.

Immediately, it was realised that the fresh paradigm of building a modern, competitive, post-colonial economy demanded, centrally, the following among other things: a focused assault on poverty, indigence, inequality, and under-nourishment; the enhanced protection of working people, farmers, and fisher-folk; a thorough-going Education Revolution for the modern economy and society; the empowerment and protection of women, children, men and boys at risk, and other vulnerable persons; the active, practical embrace of modern science and technology in the production apparatuses of the economy, including the delivery of the revolution in information technology and telecommunications; the construction of a jet airport in Canouan and an international airport at Argyle; the joinder of the northeast of St. Vincent with its southern areas by the construction of a bridge over the expansive Rabacca Dry River, and the building of quality motorable roadways from the Dry River northward to Fancy; the improvement and expansion of the road network throughout St. Vincent and the Grenadines; the improvement of seaports throughout St. Vincent and the Grenadines and the elaboration of a plan to build a modern seaport in Kingstown to replace the aging one at Port Kingstown and the inadequate one at Campden Park; the roll-out of a Health and Wellness Revolution and a Housing Revolution; the markedly enhanced delivery of competitively-priced electricity (inclusive of renewable energy) and water, universally; the focusing on the causes and deleterious impacts of climate change, drought and land degradation, and the institution of the appropriate adaptation and mitigation measures; the significant reforming of governance and the State administration, for the better, inclusive of root-and-branch constitutional reform; the strengthening of the quality of the judiciary, law, and order; the advocacy of mature regionalism; and the fashioning of an independent, principled, and pragmatic foreign policy in our people's interest, and for global peace, prosperity, and security for all based on multi-lateralism, international law, and the precepts as laid down in the Charter of the United Nations inclusive of those relating to the equality of states, the defence of sovereignty and independence, and the non-interference and non-intervention in the internal affairs of sovereign states.

A paradigm, narrowly-defined, is essentially a world view underlying the theories and methodology of a particularly scientific subject (including in the Social Sciences). Thomas Kuhn in *The Structure of*

Scientific Revolutions (1962) identifies a paradigm as a global organising model or theory with great explanatory power. And a paradigm shift is defined as *"an important change that happens when the usual way of thinking about or doing something is replaced by a new and different way."*

Fundamental to the ULP's advocacy and practical application of a paradigm shift from the old, out-moded, or amended, colonial economy to a modern post-colonial one involved the following *core* philosophical, ideational or theoretical elements:

- The elaboration of a people-centred vision.

- The embrace of the universal principles of *advanced* social democracy as applied to the circumstances of St. Vincent and the Grenadines particularly, and the Caribbean generally.

- The recognition that St. Vincent and the Grenadines is a magnificent component of our Caribbean civilisation, itself a unique island or seaboard civilisation of legitimacy, authenticity, and nobility, having been fashioned, or has evolved, historically, in our specific landscape and seascape; and that this civilisation possesses a core of tried and tested values that are uplifting, and thus has a trajectory for further ennoblement or development for the lifting of SVG higher.

- The economic approach or strategy rests on the combining of a tripartite economy of the private, cooperative, and State sectors in such an integrated manner that the whole becomes greater than the sum of the individual parts. This approach avoids ideologically pre-conceived "laissez faire" or "statist/commandist" postures and focusses on that which is appropriate, workable, and salient in the extant circumstances, in the nation's interest.

- The achievement of optimal good governance within a constitutional order of a competitive parliamentary democracy that eschews violence or subversive disorder and extols a peaceful settlement of conflicts or disputes through established consensual or juridical mechanisms. In this regard, we hold dear the principles and ideals so majestically outlined in the Preamble to the Constitution of St. Vincent and the Grenadines, 1979.

- The pursuance of a mature regionalism in our Caribbean and an activist foreign policy of internationalist solidarity, recognising that St. Vincent and the Grenadines by itself cannot address its numerous challenges and limitations or embrace fully its strengths and possibilities without a meaningful joinder with our regional family and the global community of nations.

The outcomes of this fresh paradigm are centred on the marked improvement of the quality of our people's lives, and their opportunities, in every material particular as specified in the accompanying policies and programmes of the government in various official publications, and in the Election Manifestos and other policy statements or writings of the ULP and its leadership. Among the central outcomes is the enhanced, and equality, of access to public goods of quality (Education, Health, Housing, Social Security, Justice, Job Creation, Physical Infrastructure and so forth).

There are critical departures from the colonial/amended colonial economy of yesteryear to the modern, competitive, many-sided, post-colonial economy. Among the central ones are the following:

The post-colonial economy is premised on development with unlimited supplies of educated and skilled labour, priced at a competitive level in the chain of the international division of labour; it is not a case of unlimited or abundant supplies of cheap, unskilled labour in a largely agricultural-based economy of the colonial-type.

The post-colonial economy is more diversified and largely service-based; and even where a particular service is dominant, like tourism, it is required to be competitive regionally and globally.

The external trading arrangements of the post-colonial economy are not cocooned in a framework of reciprocal, colonial, subsidised market preferences. These trade arrangements are regulated through the World Trade Organisation (WTO) predicated on agreed trade liberalisation principles for both goods and services with particular tightly-cordoned departures for specific commodities, and regional integration mechanisms; special and differential treatment for poor countries and small island developing states to ensure fair trade, not merely free trade. In going forward, we demand trade arrangements that include quantified and binding measures to combat fiscal, financial, and climate "dumping" by rich countries, inclusive of their weaponising of the financial systems, their harmful tax regimes and policies, and the unverifiable targets of their carbon emissions.

Advanced technologies, including modern information technologies, are vital for the production apparatuses of a modern, competitive post-colonial economy; the colonial economy did not promote advanced science and technology and their efficacious applications.

The post-colonial economy demands appropriate physical infra-structure for airports and seaports, quality and comparatively-priced utilities of water, electricity, and telecommunications, proper road transportation networks, and high-quality infrastructure and services in education, health, housing, sports and culture. These have been of limited significance in, or to, a colonial economy.

Regional economic integration, particularly in respect of a single market and economy in CARICOM, and the Economic Union of the OECS. Within CARICOM, of course, there are especial provisions (Chapter 7 in the Revised Treaty of Chaguaramas) for appropriate protections of disadvantaged economies, regions, and sectors. The colo-nial economy had the primary, near-exclusive, link to the metropolitan centre, not to other regional economies.

Modern sea and air transportation to the far-flung areas of the globe are vital to the modern, post-colonial economy as distinct from one that was largely engaged in a trade between metropole and colony (except for the recruitment of labour for enslavement or indentureship) under colonialism.

The post-colonial economy is grounded in social democracy; in the ethos of our Caribbean civilisation and its Vincentian component; a mixed economy, prudence and enterprise in fiscal matters; democrat-ic governance within the frame of a liberal-democratic constitutional order; an activist foreign policy; regional community law; and interna-tional law in respect of practically all spheres of economic, social, or political activity and thus of relations between nation-states. All these are non-existent in a colonial economy.

The colonial or amended colonial economy had the working people, small farmers, fisherfolk and women on the fringes of its concerns; pa-triarchy, and only minimalist farmers', fisherfolk's and working people's considerations held sway in such an economy; in an earlier period, racial oppression, too, was the order of the day. In a post-colonial economy, the working people, farmers and fisher folk are at the centre of its pol-icies, as are women and the end of a debilitating patriarchy; and racial or ethnic prejudices or preferences are practically non-existent in the post-colonial economy and society.

The ownership of the means of production in a post-colonial economy necessarily has a far wider base than in a colonial or amended colonial economy. Broader-based private sector ownership is buttressed by State ownership of material resources (a democratic State holding such resources in trust for the people as a whole), and cooperative ownership, especially in strong credit unions.

Over the last 21 years, successive ULP administrations, unbroken, have been pursuing this strategic economic path with the central aim of lifting markedly the all-round quality of people's lives within the thrust of sustainable development.

The Rollout of the Post-Colonial Economy

The building of a modern, competitive, many-sided, post-colonial economy over the last twenty-one years is being rolled out before our very eyes with the following major requisites:

• The construction of a jet airport on Canouan and an international airport on St. Vincent for markedly enhanced movement of people and high-priced goods.

• The rollout, broadening and deepening of a thorough-going Education Revolution at all levels (Early Childhood, Primary, Secondary, Post-Secondary, Tertiary, Special, Teacher, Nursing, Technical and Vocational, and Adult and Continuing Education) to upgrade and expand the provision of education and skills (quantity and quality) for the post-colonial production apparatuses.

• The markedly enhanced physical linkage between the isolated northeast of St. Vincent (the central reserve area in which colonialism had placed the defeated Callinago and the Garifuna) by, among other things, the construction of a bridge over the expansive Rabacca Dry River.

• The reconstruction (and construction) of more roads, bridges, sea and river defences across St. Vincent and the Grenadines than any other government in our country's history in a drive to modernise and make more efficient the road network.

• The development and expansion of modern telecommunications (voice and data) infrastructure to facilitate a competitive delivery of these vital services to the modern economy and society.

• The revolutionary expansion, delivery, and universal coverage of electricity, water, and solid waste disposal through the State-owned entities: the St. Vincent Electricity Services Limited and the Central Water and Sewerage Authority.

• The unprecedented expansion of primary, secondary, tertiary, and public health care services (construction and expansion of hospitals and their services, including Smart Hospitals, a Modern Medical and Diagnostic Centre, three Polyclinics, several Clinics, Pharmaceutical and Laboratory Services, the Mental Health Rehabilitation Centre, the Lewis Punnett Home for the Elderly, the upgrade of the Milton Cato Memorial Hospital, the active plans to build an Acute Referral Hospital, the larger-scale training and deployment of health care professionals, and the embrace of very valuable medical missions from overseas.

• The unprecedented Housing Revolution including the construction of 2,000 low-and-middle income houses; hundreds of appropriately-designed houses in the Lives-to-Live Housing Programme for the Elderly and Physically-Challenged; the introduction and expansion of 100 percent mortgages (no down-payment) for central government and other pensionable State employees — this measure has created a major boost in home acquisitions for the working people and the middle class; the distribution and land-titling for the people of some 7,000 housing lots on State-owned lands; and the passage of the Possessory Titles Act to facilitate "the turning of dead property into live property."

• An unprecedented construction and expansion of sporting facilities including the Arnos Vale Sporting Complex (also used for cultural purposes), the Sir Vincent Beache Sporting Facility/Stadium at Diamond, numerous playing fields across St. Vincent and the Grenadines, inclusive of high quality ones such as at Cumberland, Hope, Park Hill, South Rivers, Chili, Stubbs, and Arnos Vale, the Tennis Complex at Villa, hard courts across the country, and the major upgrades of Victoria Park as a sporting and cultural venue.

• The unprecedented rollout of cultural programmes, activities, and facilities designed to develop further the Vincentian component of our Caribbean civilisation.

• The rollout and expansion of special employment programmes for young persons, namely the highly-acclaimed Youth Employment Service (YES) — 500 young persons annually; and the Support for Education and Training (SET) — recently up to 500 college and university graduates annually; and special public works programmes involving nearly 5,000 persons three or four times per year over ten-day periods on each occasion. These special employment and special works programmes are designed, among other things, to accommodate different categories of workers who are "in transition" in the unfolding economic transformation.

• The massive strengthening, creation, expansion, of widespread safety net supports for vulnerable persons of various kinds (children, youths, elderly, single parents, women, retirees, persons-at-risk, the poor and the indigent). These programmes are variously carried out mainly through the Ministries of Social Development, Health, Education, Housing, Finance, the Office of the Prime Minister, and other State-entities such as the National Insurance Services, and the National Lotteries Authority.

• The marked enhancement of institutional-strengthening and institutional-building of the good governance apparatus in every material particular. These touch and concern, among others, the Parliament; the Judiciary; the independent constitutional offices of the Director of Audit, Attorney General, and the Director of Public Prosecutions; the St. Vincent and the Grenadines Police Force, Coast Guard and Fire Services; the Financial Intelligence Unit; the Financial Services Authority; the Office of the Supervisor of Elections; the Passport and Immigration Office; the Central Supplies Tenders' Board; the Zero Hunger Trust Fund; the Commerce and Intellectual Property Office; the National Telecommunications Regulatory Authority; the Office of Maritime Administration; Customs and Excise Department; the Department of Inland Revenue; the National Emergency Management Office; and numerous other State enterprises.

• The deepening and strengthening of a mature regional integration through CARICOM, the OECS and their allied institutions in a range of functional cooperation initiatives; the Association of Caribbean States; the Community of States of Latin America and the Caribbean (CELAC); and the Bolivarian Alternative for Our Americas (ALBA).

• The pursuance of an activist, independent, and pragmatic foreign policy within the frame of regionalist and internationalist solidarity, regional community and international law. St. Vincent and the Grenadines has, under my government, been utilising its foreign policy to address efficaciously the immense challenges arising from the complicated external environment in the interest of our people and consistent with our principles, ideals, and commitments. In the United Nations' systems, for example, St. Vincent and the Grenadines has been the smallest country ever to hold the Presidency of the Economic and Social Council (ECOSOC) and to sit for a two-year period (January 1, 2020 to December 31, 2021) as a non-permanent member on the Security Council, the highest decision-making body at the United Nations. These achievements, among others, have permitted St. Vincent and the Grenadines to be a force for good for our people, our region, and our world. We are friends of all; we strive for a better world.

• The building of a mixed economy in which the private, cooperative, and State sectors act in an integrated manner to ensure that the whole is more than a summation of the individual parts, in the people's interest. This exercise involves an array of supportive measures and incentives for the private and cooperative sectors. It demands, too, good governance in every material particular, including the pursuance of a fiscal policy that strikes an effective balance between prudence and enterprise as the circumstances admit.

• The creation, net, of some 8,000 jobs, inclusive of quality jobs, in the period 2001 to 2019, that is, the pre-pandemic and pre-volcanic eruptions period. Similarly, the reduction of poverty from 37 percent to 30 percent of the population; the reduction of indigence from 26 percent to 3 percent; and the reduction of under-nourishment from 22 percent to under 5 percent. The pandemic and the volcanic eruptions have caused setbacks, and some reversals, in these vital indicators.

• The unprecedented multimillion dollar investments annually in renewable energy, disaster preparedness, and resilience-building in the face of climate change, as well as strenuous global advocacy for ambitious mitigation efforts to combat the worst effects of climate change.

• The increase of GDP from under EC $1 billion in 2000 to $2.3 billion in 2019 or an average per capita GDP of under EC$ 9,000 in 2000 to over $20,000 in 2019.

Sustainable Development and Economic Growth

These strategic policies, and their practical manifestations, are being built upon currently in the fashioning of a sustainable post-colonial economy, polity, and society. Two bundles of issues, immediately relevant here for policy consideration and application, are the United Nations Sustainable Development Goals (SDGs) of 2015, which we have adopted in our government as fundamental to our developmental efforts up to 2030 and beyond; and the central, enduring question of economic growth in that policy mix. These two sets of issues connect with, and build upon, the *National Economic and Social Development Plan, 2012 to 2025* of the government of St. Vincent and the Grenadines.

The history, details, analysis, financing, and more, of the 17 Sustainable Development Goals are available in various United Nations (UN) publications and other non-UN commentaries, journals, and books. This is well-traversed territory, inclusive of the actions to be taken, and the 169 targets set, in relation to each of the goals. The measurement of the goals, and targets, is effected by 232 indicators. It is necessary, though, to identify these driving goals, in their broad rubrics, summarily: (1) No Poverty; (2) Zero Hunger; (3) Good Health and Well-Being; (4) Quality Education; (5) Clean Water and Sanitation; (7) Affordable and Clean Energy; (8) Decent Work and Economic Growth; (9) Industry, Innovation and Infrastructure; (10) Reduced Inequality; (11) Sustainable Cities and Communities; (12) Responsible Consumption and Production; (13) Climate Action; (14) Life Below Water; (15) Life on Land; (16) Peace, Justice, and Strong Institutions; (17) Global Partnerships for the SDGs.

All these broad goals are interdependent; and St. Vincent and the Grenadines seeks to make them actionable through specific measurable targets, indicators, and programmes, with appropriate time-lines. They were specifically embedded in the Unity Labour Party's Election Manifestos of 2015 and 2020; they are at the core of the ULP government's socio-economic development plans for St. Vincent and the Grenadines. They are inextricably linked to our quest to build a modern, competitive, many-sided post-colonial economy.

The second relevant issue for detailed consideration is that of real economic growth in the evolving modern, post-colonial economy in St. Vincent and the Grenadines. Of course, economic growth is not an end in itself, but it provides the basis for the achievement of goals for individuals and the society as a whole. Most economists accept that economic growth is a necessary, though not sufficient, condition for broader sustainable development. In any event, the measures of economic growth by GDP metrics are problematic generally, in a conceptual sense, and in their application; additionally, in countries like St. Vincent and the Grenadines there are challenges associated with data collection, and sometimes of analysis, consequentially.

The ULP government does not insist that it has a universal formula for small-island developing states to follow in the pursuance of economic growth; it is unlikely that such a general formula exists. Each country's specific circumstances, historical evolution, and especial characteristics constitute the constellation of factual matrices out of which a viable growth strategy emerges and is pursued. In vulnerable and resource-constrained, small multi-island developing countries like St. Vincent and the Grenadines, economic growth does not occur unilinearly; inevitably there are setbacks and advances generated by both exogenous shocks or practical, material solidarity from external sources, and internal happenings of a positive or negative kind.

The economic growth strategy appropriate to the condition of a country necessarily contains short-term fixes and targeted, strategic interventions; but a sustainable economic growth strategy demands a focused, longer-term effort, commitment, and active buy-in by the people as a whole, in communion with quality, visionary leadership. To be sure, the exigencies of the actual circumstances may prompt policy-makers to take episodic zigs and zags, but they must never have a terminal point in a dead end; the composite outcomes of the strategy must always be the focus. It is true that, geometrically, the shortest distance between two points is a straight line, but economic growth cannot be so pursued; still, though, the posited, strategic outcomes are the destination, not the cul-de-sac. The achievement of the outcomes of the growth strategy demands, among other things, a patience and a calm.

I recall a penetrating and insightful Report published in 1969 on the economy of St. Vincent and the Grenadines delivered by economists and other social scientists arising from a mission led by leading economists and others from the University of the West Indies, mainly from "the New World" school. The first theoretical observation of consequence made by the Report was that the small and unique nature of the economy of St. Vincent and the Grenadines was such that none of the economic theories or models from development economics, applicable to most underdeveloped/developing economies, was applicable to St. Vincent and the Grenadines. Theoretical formulae are to be utilised, at best, as approximate proxies for understanding and prognosis of this peculiar economy, and for policy and programmatic recommendations. The Report characterized the economy of St. Vincent and the Grenadines as being in "subsistence equilibrium", which equilibrium was put swiftly in a condition of disequilibrium, upwards or downwards, depending on the presence or absence of a hike or a dip in grants, remittances from overseas, or the movement of the export price of this or that subsidized agricultural commodity at the level of production or market preferences externally. This was the fate of a colonial economy that was being amended by an emerging nationalist political class, but without a self-sustaining trajectory at that time.

In that Report, the micro-size of the economy of St. Vincent and the Grenadines was tagged as a limitation, but it was acknowledged, too, that small size is also pregnant with possibilities. It is a subject upon which scholars have been ruminating including the distinguished Caribbean political economists, William Demas, in his book *The Economics of Development in Small Countries with Special Reference to the Caribbean* (1965), *and* Lloyd Best in several of his academic and polemical writings. Indeed, in 1973, Ernest F. Schumacher, a German-born British economist, was to turn the world of economics upside down in his best-seller *Small is Beautiful: A Study of Economics As If People Mattered.* Schumacher emphasised that small, appropriate technologies, policies, and political systems were superior to the established mantra of "bigger is better"; for him, education, training and technology were critical. Of course, the relative ease of air and sea transportation and the revolution in biotechnology, information technology and telecommunications, in contemporary times, have enlarged the possibilities of "smallness".

Still, there are some general propositions on economic growth that can safely be adopted by us in St. Vincent and the Grenadines as having validity as heuristic categories and as applicable policies. One relates to the inextricable links between economic growth and public investment on infrastructure, education, and health. The highly persuasive, though not authoritatively binding, *The Growth Report: Strategies for Sustained Growth and Inclusive Development* by the Commission on Growth and Development (2008, World Bank) comprising 21 experts, including Dwight Venner, then Governor of the Eastern Caribbean Central Bank, and Chaired by Michael Spence, Nobel Laureate in Economics, Professor Emeritus, Stanford University, addressed this linkage between economic growth and public investment, thus:

> No country has sustained rapid growth without also keeping up impressive rates of public investment — infrastructure, education, and health. Far from crowding out private investment, this spending crowds it in. It paves the way for new industries to emerge and raises the return to any private venture that benefits from healthy, educated workers, passable roads, and reliable electricity.

Instructive, too, is the sage advice of *The Growth Report* on the policy underpinnings of sustained economic growth:

> The policy underpinnings of sustained, high growth create an environment of high levels of investment, job creation, competition, mobility of resources, social protections, equity and inclusiveness. Our view is that an understanding of the dynamics and a focused attention on the policy foundations will significantly increase the chances of accelerating growth. Conversely, persistent inattention to them will eventually harm it. There are many different recipes for a pasta. The precise ingredients and timing are different for each. But if you leave out the salt or boil it too long, the results are distinctly inferior.

The Growth Report further sensibly advised that:

> The ingredients for growth cover a wide range from public investment and exchange rates to land sales and redistribution, and the energy and will of the private sector. A list of ingredients is not enough to make a dish because no single recipe exists.

> Timing and circumstances will determine how the ingredients should be combined, in what quantities, in what sequence.

In the aftermath of the financial meltdown on Wall Street in September 2008, and its consequential metamorphosis as the worse global economic depression for nearly 100 years, and continuing, the Monetary Council of the Eastern Caribbean Central Bank, of which I was a long-serving member during the time of the Central Bank's Governorship of Dwight Venner, adopted an *Eight-Point Growth and Stabilisation Plan* that centred on the critical elements of economic growth, equity, plus stabilisation of the fiscal, banking and financial systems that had come under severe stress on account of the knock-on effects of the global economic depression.

The ECCB Eight Point Plan reflected, by and large, "the good ideas" of *The Growth Report* though with a specific emphasis and application in the context of the small island developing states of the Eastern Caribbean in the disruptive period of 2008-2010, and continuing.

Six "good ideas" are being emphasised in our context:

• *Accumulation*: Public Investment to accelerate infrastructure and skills. In this regard, high levels of investment are advised for infrastructure (airports, seaports, coastal and river defences, roads and bridges, energy and electricity, telecommunications and technology generally, government buildings, health and education facilities, sporting and cultural complexes, housing and community facilities). Central to all this are dramatic advances required in the development of human capital, skills, and health.

- *Innovation,* inclusive of the imitation of best practices, particularly in technology transfers and applied, appropriate technologies.

- *Efficient and Efficacious Allocation of Resources* of capital and labour. This issue relates directly to enhanced competitiveness and structural change in the following areas, among others: job creation, and open labour markets in the context of building national capacity and skills; the many-sided, diversified economic sectors within the post-colonial economy; the emphasis on the export of goods and services; development and proper regulation of competitive capital markets, capital flows, financial and banking institutions.

- *Stabilisation* to achieve macro-economic stability especially in the following respects: fiscal consolidation by way of prudence and enterprise; low-to-moderate inflation; financial sector regulation and stability; and savings for investments. Of relevance here is not only manageable public sector indebtedness but also the extent of private sector debt that may cause systemic challenges.

- *Inclusiveness:* The emphasis here is on equity and equality of opportunity, the marked reduction of poverty, and the achievement of the 17 Sustainable Development Goals.

- *Good Governance:* A cross-cutting issue of utmost significance that touches and concerns leadership in the public and private sectors; the role of the State as facilitator, regulator, and entrepreneurial partner; the promotion of civil society's engagement; mature regionalism and an efficacious bundle of policies for foreign affairs and foreign trade; climate change and disaster preparedness/management; national pride, sports, culture, and the values of our Caribbean civilisation.

All of these six bundles of "good ideas" are reflected in Budget 2022, in addition to the specific recovery issues relating to the pandemic, the volcanic eruptions, and Hurricane Elsa.

"Bad ideas" are absent from Budget 2022. In the cauldron of competitive, electoral politics one has to be on the lookout to avoid certain policies that may be superficially attractive or commanding ill-informed support from certain sections of the public. We must thus reject those ideas that are bad, wrong and subversive of the people's welfare and interests, given their large costs with little or no credible or realisable benefits comparable to the costs; or the pursuance of certain activities by the State that may be better delivered by non-State actors.

It is a bad idea to affirm, ideologically, as neo-liberalism does, that invariably the State is the problem for development and that it ought to have little or no role in the ownership, management, or regulation of the economy. Similarly, we do not accept the proposition by the American economist, Milton Friedman, made explicit in the very title of his well-known essay in 1970 "The Social Responsibility of Business is to Increase Its Profits"; indeed, a business that is entirely concerned with making money for its owners and disregards its environmental, social, or broader economic considerations is likely to be anti-developmental and subversive of the very business itself. Even rapacious capitalist enterprises are now recognizing that it is short-sighted for businesses to ignore, minimise or downplay environmental, social, and governance (ESG) impacts; more and more big businesses report on their ESGs.

"Terribly bad ideas" to avoid, include the following:

• Subsidising energy except for very limited subsidies of short duration or targeted at highly vulnerable sections of the population or in respect of a service used by the overwhelming majority of the poor and working people, like for example, the controlled, and time-bound subsidy granted by the ULP government to minibus operators when the price of fuel sky-rocketed to unprecedented heights consequent upon the extraordinary jump in international fuel prices in June-July 2008; or the recent price reduction of fuel by way of a temporary reduction of the excise duty, consequent upon the adverse knock-on price rises in fuel occasioned by the Russia-Ukraine war, *and* in the anguished aftermath of the COVID pandemic, the volcanic eruptions, Hurricane Elsa, and other adverse climatic happenings.

• Relying on the "civil service" as an "employer of last resort" to soak up unemployed persons. This is distinct from targeted-specific employment (or training arrangements) such as ramped-up, periodic road-cleaning, the Youth Empowerment Service (YES), or the Support for Employment and Training (SET).

• Reducing fiscal deficits because of short-term macro-economic compulsion by slashing spending on infrastructure investment or other public spending that yields large social returns in the longer run. Austerity in our circumstances is a wrong and dangerous idea.

- Providing open-ended protection of specific sectors, industries, firms, and jobs from competition, save and except for transitional or other strategic purposes in a small economy.

- Imposing price controls in an effort to stem inflation; this is much better handled through competition between businesses and through other macro-economic policies such as more efficient, or reduced, taxes on goods and services or effective non-price regulatory systems. In our small, open economy, the extent of price increases for goods and services comes overwhelmingly through imports; imported inflation is invariably a feature of our economy; conversely, low-to-moderate inflation is largely a consequence of price moderation/decline externally, particularly for commodities like fuel, machinery and imported food.

- Banning exports for long periods of time for protectionist purposes.

- Measuring educational progress mainly on the basis of the construction of school infrastructure or even high enrollment or generalised average pass marks on all subjects, instead of focussing on the extent of learning and quality education, quality teaching, quality school leadership, quality parenting, focused student effort, and critical subject areas such as English, Maths, Sciences, History, Literature, Foreign Languages, Technological Applications, inclusive of Information Technology, Technical and Vocational skills.

- Underpaying or over-paying public sector employees, and promoting such employees largely or purely on the basis of seniority, political partisanship, or friend-friend relations, and not on performance.

- Laissez-faire approaches to regulation, or limited regulation, of banks and other financial institutions that inevitably undermine banking and financial stability.

- Tinkering or experimenting with exchange rates in a way that undermines production, productivity, and economic stability, even if it provides temporary enhanced export competitiveness.

- Selling citizenship and passports. This is a very bad idea in principle and practice. The selling of passports/citizenship encourages official corruption; engenders wasteful consumption of high cost imported goods and services; distorts domestic production and productivity; promotes an individualistic, easy-come and easy-go, approach to money; and undermines social solidarity and a sense of community. Selling passports/citizenship boomerangs against the economy, the fiscal, the social, and good governance; any presumed nominal benefit is a mirage. The selling of passports/citizenship is not sustainable. Recently the Congress of the United States of America, the European Parliament and European Commission have signalled that they are determined to bring this practice to an end. Beyond these practical considerations, the selling of passports/citizenship transforms citizenship and its adornment, the passport, into mere commodities for sale. It devalues citizenship, which is the highest office of any nation; selling it as a commodity is unthinkable for my government.

• Under-funding regional institutions that are vital for law and order, security, health, education, lives, livelihoods, and good governance.

• Disregarding precepts and practices of good governance, constitutionalism, transparency, and accountability.

• Ignoring or disregarding the vital requisite of multi-lateralism; and displaying a lack of commitment to international law, the equality of states, our sovereignty and independence, and non-interference/non-intervention in our country's internal affairs.

• Discouraging or attacking non-governmental organisations of civil society, including trade unions and business organisations.

Clearly, this list of *bad ideas* is not an exhaustive one. These, and other bad ideas, have no place in economic decision-making or the formulation of policies generally, and these do not appear in Budget 2022, or in the ULP government's policy matrices.

There is, of course, additionally, an extensive discussion required on the efficacy of economic growth itself. Some economists argue that economic growth is at an end, at least in developed countries, and that it is not such a bad thing for the environment and the population as a whole since there are other values of far greater importance to the people in modern societies, particularly affluent ones. Additionally, it is contended by these very economists, and others, that nations and international financial institutions have become veritable slaves to the usual measurement of the economy's well-being through that of a Gross Domestic Product (GDP) assessment, which is at best an exercise in guesswork, oft-times terrible guesswork, particularly in developing countries; the GDP measure also leaves out so many things connected to the quality of life, joy, and happiness in a modernising society, that to hinge the assessment of success or failure on this faulty measure of omission and commission is to accept an absurd, fallacious proposition.

Clearly, though, all things being equal, economic growth is obviously preferable for the well-being of a country, an individual, or family than economic stagnation or regression.

An excellent discussion of the academic/theoretical controversy on the larger issues on economic growth can be found in a splendid book entitled *Good Economics for Hard Times* (2019) authored by Professor Abhijit V. Banerjee of the Massachusetts Institute of Technology (MIT) and Professor Esther Duflo, also of MIT; they were the recipients of the 2019 Nobel Peace Prize in Economics. The review of the arguments on this issue is fascinating as reflected in the writings of Robert Gordon (*The Rise and Fall of American Growth*, 2016); Joel Mokyr (Gordon and Mokyr debate "Boom vs Doom: Debating the Future of the US Economy" — *Chicago Council of Global Affairs*, October 31, 2016); Robert M. Solow ("A Contribution to the Theory of Economic Growth", *Quarterly Journal of Economics* 70, number 1, 1956); Robert Lucas Jr. ("On the Mechanics of Economic Development" *Journal of Monetary Economics*, 20, Number 1, 1988); Paul Romer ("Increasing Returns and Long-Run Growth", *Journal of Political Economy*, 94, Number 1, 1986); Thomas Piketty (*Capital in the Twenty-First Century*, 2013); and others.

Among the central queries in this debate or controversy on economic growth are: What role, and the extent of it, does technology, culture, capital, labour, institutions, production methods, the organisation of labour at the enterprise level, citizen security, government policy, or exogenous factors play? Is there a natural growth path, and when there are interruptions, when does it return, and for how long? What constitutes "balanced growth"? Is "unbalanced growth" desirable in the short run or most of the time?

And what of the "mystery" of "total factor productivity" (TFP), that is to say, the rest of the observed productivity improvement that cannot be explained by things economists can measure? The Nobel-Prize-winning economist Robert Solow amusingly referred to TFP as "the measure of our ignorance", on account of the fact that growth in TFP is what is left after economists have accounted for everything they can measure.

Banerjee and Duflo adds some clarity, yet still opaqueness, to the issue of TFP thus:

> It (TFP) captures the fact that workers with the same education level working with the same machines and inputs (what economists refer to as *capital*) produce more output today for each hour they work than they did last year. This makes sense. We constantly look for ways to use our existing resources more effectively... but total factor productivity also increases when we discover new ways to reduce waste or shrink the time either raw materials or workers are forced to stay idle. Innovations in production methods like chain production or lean manufacturing do that, as does, say, the creation of a good rental market for tractors.

At the end of an instructive review of the literature on economy growth (theory, practice, history), Banerjee and Duflo concludes:

> The bottom line is that despite the best efforts of generations of economists, the deep mechanisms of persistent economic growth remain elusive. No one knows if growth will pick up again in rich countries, or what to do to make it more likely. The good news is that we do have things to do in the meantime; there is a lot that both poor and rich countries could do to get rid of the most egregious sources of waste in their economies. While these things may not propel countries to permanently faster growth, they could dramatically improve the welfare of their citizens. Moreover, while we do not know when the growth locomotive will start, if and when it does, the poor will be more likely to hop onto that train if they are in decent health, can read and write, and can think beyond their immediate circumstances. It may not be an accident that many of the winners of globalization were ex-communist countries that had invested heavily in the human capital of their populations in the communist years (China, Vietnam) or countries threatened with communism that had pursued similar policies for that reason (Taiwan, South Korea). The best bet, therefore, for a country like India is to attempt to do things that can make the quality of life better for its citizens with the resources it already has: improving education, health, and the functioning of the courts and the banks, and building better infrastructure (better roads and more livable cities, for example)."

The best bet for St. Vincent and the Grenadines, by far, is to pursue the particular path my government has elaborated, with the particular considerations and "sui generis" applications in our peculiar political economy. The ideas laid out in this book, and the Budget 2022 as a practical exemplar of our ongoing work, constitute a viable framework and achievable programmatic details for sustainable development of St. Vincent and the Grenadines, and our people's more advanced well-being. Indeed, it is the only credible plan on offer for now, and the immediate and prospective future!

It is evident from both the presentation of the factual matrices of the budget in the next chapter, and from the Budget Address of the Minister of Finance, that the review of the many-sided historical and contemporary issues of relevance, including the ideational and theoretical discourses on the modern-post-colonial economy and economic growth, are themselves reflected in the policies and actual numbers laid out in Budget 2022.

Chapter Three

The Budget 2022

Overall Budget, Recurrent Budget, and Public Debt

On December 2, 2002, as Prime Minister and Minister of Finance of St. Vincent and the Grenadines, I introduced my address on the Budget for the fiscal year 2003 in the following terms:

> The framing of any national budget is a profoundly political and democratic exercise. To be sure, it rests upon economic and fiscal foundations but it is about people, bound together in a multiplicity of ties as a national community. So, while it is both necessary and desirable to map the domestic, regional and international economic contexts and to detail the fiscal condition of the Central Government for an efficacious grounding of the national budget itself, the heart of the budgetary process is about real flesh-and-blood persons, including their leaders, in national communion with one another.
>
> After all, behind the dry statistics and economic categories are real people like you and me, the butcher, the baker, the farmer, the worker and the proverbial candlestick maker. For example, the economic categories, "salaries and wages", are about workers; behind the economic concept of "profits" are entrepreneurs; the economic notion of "rent" is about landlords and tenants; and behind the category "taxes" is a democratic State manned at the highest policy-making levels by parliamentarians freely elected in periodic, competitive elections.
>
> For too long, the essence of a national budget and the process of budget-making have been shrouded in a mystique which has blunted genuine popular involvement and which, in turn, has caused ordinary citizens and residents to see the budget and its making as alien to them, not belonging to them. In that context, a budget came across as an imposition by the State and manipulative

politicians. In the past, people had little say in it; they thus felt no ownership of it; and, to the extent that they saw the numbers, for all they could care, they could have been written in upside-down Chinese. It was all so meaningless to them unless any of the impositions was a hurt or benefit to them immediately and directly. In any event, it was quickly forgotten.

In the past, only some politicians and public servants seemed to take the budget seriously. It is true that on the opening day of the Budget many esteemed, invited citizens and guests came to the Parliament. It is also true that in the days when there was only one radio station, many people particularly party political supporters, listened to the budget debate as a sort of substitute for an ancient gladiatorial contest between combatants. But the majority of our people felt uninvolved.

Public finances are indeed at the centre of the democratic process. Historians record that legislative assemblies emerged in Europe and the Americas in the era of modern democracy, in part, out of a quest to limit the power of the hereditary sovereign to impose taxes and determine the spending of revenues collected. There is hardly a more profound matter of practical governance which ought to agitate right-thinking persons, than the twin-issue of tax collection and the expenditure of revenues raised.

All these considerations conjoined to prompt the Unity Labour Party Government to embark on the most extensive and intensive process of consultation ever on the budget with the organised stakeholders and the public, at large. Last year, in the aftermath of the criminal events of September 11, the Government initiated and conducted a series of consultations with relevant stakeholders in its fashioning of a programme of fiscal stabilisation and a strategic path of economic recovery and renewal. This year, the Government has made an unprecedented quantum leap in democratic participation in the process of budget-making.

The evidence shows that the Government engaged itself in well-prepared, lengthy and meaningful consultations with the Chamber of Industry and Commerce, the commercial sector, the manufacturers, the tourism sector, the fisher folk, the trade unions in both the private and public sectors, the farmers, the NGO community generally, the bankers, the insurance providers, the credit unions, those involved in off-shore finance and telecommunications, contractors, and architects and managers in vital public enterprises."

These perspectives of the annual budget and budget-making continue to inform our ULP government.

As the fiscal year January to December 2021 ended, what was the fiscal condition of central government of St. Vincent and the Grenadines as a frame for Budget 2022?

A summary of the fiscal operations of the central government provides instructive lessons for guidance in the crafting of Budget 2022.
The raw data for 2021 were as follows in *Eastern Caribbean dollars*:

Total Revenue and Grants collected: $762.64 million, a 6.6 percent
increase over 2020 ($715.68 million) and a 12 percent increase over the
collections of 2019 ($680.02 million), the last immediate pre-COVID
year. Indeed, there was an 8 percent variance above the budgeted figure
of $706.29 million. Of the total collections for 2021,

Current Revenue amounted to $679.53 million or 12.1 percent over
the comparable number for 2020 ($606.27 million) and 12.9 percent
over the 2019 figure ($601.72 million). Current Revenue in 2021 was 5
percent above the budgeted figure of $647.39 million for 2021.

Capital Revenues and Grants for 2021 of $83.11 million was a 24
percent decline of the comparable number for 2020 but a 41 percent increase over the budgeted number for 2021. The "Grants" component of
this category in 2021 was 2.4 percent less than the comparable number
for 2020 and some 20 percent less than 2019.

Total Expenditure for 2021 amounted to $876.124 million or 2.7
percent over the comparable figure for 2020 of $852.99 million, 15.3
percent above that of 2019 ($760.0 million). However, total expenditure
in 2021 was 13.7 percent below the budgeted figure of $1.015 billion.

Of this Total Expenditure, Current Expenditure for 2021 was
$682.5 million or 6.3 percent above the comparable number for 2020
and 13.7 percent above, too, the immediate pre-COVID year of 2019.
Current Expenditure in 2021 was only 2.2 percent less than the sum
budgeted ($698.13 million).

Capital Expenditure out-turn (not the preliminary accounting of
$193.65 million) for 2021 was an impressive $231.6 million, above the
comparable number for 2020 of $211.178 million, and much more than
the 2019 figure of $159.56 million. Capital spending in 2021, howev-
er, was less than the revised budgeted figure of $443.8 million, which
included the approved budget ($317.4 million), and the additional capital
allocations in the Supplementary Estimates to take account especially of
the capital expenditure for the effects of the volcanic eruptions.

Current Balance for 2021 recorded a small deficit, preliminarily, of
$2.95 million compared to a current account deficit of $35.55 million in

2020, as against a small current account surplus of $1.3 million in 2019. The current account deficit in 2021 was 94 percent less than the budgeted current account deficit of $50.74 million in 2021.

The *Primary Balance* (net of the Contingencies Fund) for 2021, preliminarily, recorded a deficit of $51.4 million, 29.4 percent less than the deficit on the Primary Balance of $72.8 million in 2020 but greater than the deficit on the Primary Balance in 2019 of $10.12 million.

The *Overall Balance* in 2021 was a deficit of $100.74 million, preliminarily, compared to a deficit in 2020 of $124.46 million; the overall deficit in 2019 was $66.03 million; the overall deficit in 2021 was 66 percent less than the approved budget's overall deficit, largely because of less actual capital spending than the budgeted sum. The deficit was financed by borrowings.

The year 2021 began with great anxiety after nearly one year of the pandemic. Revenue collections for January 2021 was down a whopping $15 million below those of January 2020. Had this decline represented a trend rather than an episodic occurrence, it would have been well-nigh impossible for the central government to meet its monthly commitments, including over $31 million monthly for salaries, wages, allowances, NIS contributions for its current employees and pensions/retirement benefits for the former employees, in retirement. Every month thereafter in 2021 recorded improved revenues over the comparable months in 2020. From which sources did the increased current revenues come?

The most significant increases in current revenues in 2021 came from the categories "Alien Land Holding Licences" and the corresponding "Stamp Duty on the Sale/Transfer of Real Property". In 2021, Alien Land Holding Licences increased by 218 percent, from $11.8 million in 2020 to $37.54 million; and Stamp Duties on Sale/Transfer of real property rose from by 134.4 percent from $25.2 million in 2020 to $59.023 million in 2021.

By far, the bulk of these hefty "windfalls" came from real property transactions on the exclusive international resort island of Mustique. Mustique has 100 homes of wealthy persons, all expatriates who together constitute the Mustique Company which, in concert with the government, ensures the development of this very-high end tourism destination. At the time the COVID pandemic, Mustique has been a very safe haven; so, the usually high-priced property market experienced, and still experiences, marked enhancement in property values. This exclusive property market, in the circumstances, gave rise to above normal property transactions in volume and value; thus increased revenues due to Alien Land Holding Licences and Stamp Duties. Together these amount to nearly 17 percent of the value of property sold or otherwise transferred.

Current revenues from "Taxes on Income and Profits" remained stable in 2021 at $143.5 million or 0.1 percent over 2020, and a little higher than the $140.3 million in 2019.

"Taxes on Goods and Services" fell by 3.8 percent to $178.74 in 2021 compared to 2020. The single largest item in this category, the domestic Value-Added Tax (VAT) recorded a slight decline of 0.8 percent in 2021 compared to 2020. Given the volcanic eruptions, the dislocation of a continued pandemic, and Hurricane Elsa, this performance was not as bad as anticipated.

"Taxes on International trade" increased by 4.3 percent to $160.34 million over the comparable figure for 2020 of $153.79 million; in 2021, "the import VAT" recorded an increase of 5.9 percent over the 2020 out-turn on this tax.

"Sale of Goods and Services" recorded the sum of $71.64 million in 2021 or a 16.6 percent increase over the comparable number in 2020. The most significant item in this tax category is the Customs Service Charge which had a 25 percent increase over 2020.

The relative stability of the current revenues and the "windfall" in Alien Land Holding Licences and Stamp Duties on Sales/Transfers of Real Property were remarkable at a time of continued COVID, the volcanic eruptions, the evacuation of one-fifth of the population (20,000 persons) mainly from the red and orange zones, Hurricane Elsa, and the historical and contemporary challenges in the political economy.

Three other fiscal supports came to our country's aid, two as a consequence of important policy decisions, and the other related to regional and global solidarity. Over four years ago, the government established a Contingencies Fund to be financed by a one percentage point increase of the VAT and a US $3 disaster levy on a hotel room per night; this levy, however, was suspended in May 2020 for the duration of the pandemic. By the time of the pandemic, the Fund was capitalised at EC $40 million; the one percentage point on the VAT contributes about $12 million annually to the Fund. As at December 31, 2021, the Fund stood at $30 million. Further, in 2020, in an election year, my government decided to place an available soft loan of US $20 million (EC $54 million) from the World Bank/International Development Association (IDA) in the Catastrophic Deferred Draw Down Option (CAT-DDO) to be triggered for release, upon request, consequent upon a national disaster or a declared public health emergency. Our government accessed these resources in 2021 at the time of the volcanic eruptions. We could have spent it all in an election year, 2020, but we prudently decided to put it aside for the proverbial rainy day, rather than engage in the usual metaphoric "plucking of the chicken" for electoral purposes. The ULP won the elections despite resisting this spending temptation.

The regional and global solidarity with St. Vincent and the Grenadines at the time of the volcanic eruptions was commendable and heart-warming. We thank profoundly our regional family, and our friends and allies internationally, including regional and global financial institutions such as the Caribbean Development Bank, the World Bank, and the IMF. Most helpful, too, were the United Nations and its various agencies.

Overall, our government has been managing its fiscal condition sensibly with prudence and enterprise within a formal Fiscal Responsibility Framework, approved by Parliament. Our people's resilience, the modest uptick in the country's economic performance in the second half of 2021, and the projected capital programmes of the public and private sectors for 2022, conspired to provide optimism, despite the downside risks, as we approached Budget 2022.

The Budget address for the fiscal year 2022 was delivered on January 10, 2022, by the Minister of Finance, Camillo Gonsalves, against the backdrop of the approval by Parliament of the Estimates of Revenue and Expenditure for the year 2022 on December 13, 2021.

The Minister of Finance stressed that Budget 2022 embraced four immediate goals: *To keep Vincentians safe* from COVID and thus *to return to pre-pandemic normalcy,* from a health standpoint, as soon as practicable; *to respond* to the multi-faceted social, economic, and infrastructure toll of the volcanic eruptions; *to pursue fresh initiatives* in accelerating our economic recovery; and *to transform* further our country by creatively tackling fundamental challenges, in particular climate vulnerability, inequality, unemployment, poverty, and infrastructural deficits.

In short, the 2022 Budget is in quest of respairing, of providing fresh hope for a recovery, and more, after a near-two-year period of despondency, challenging uncertainty, and even despair. Respairing is the companion of faith and love; together they go beyond recovery, repair, rehabilitation, or even building back better and stronger. Respairing is existential; it goes to our essence as citizens, residents, visitors, friends and allies in solidarity with one another to do or be the best we can, sustainably in every material particular.

In 2020, the pandemic wrought great hardship in the society and economy and caused a contraction of the economy of some 3.5 percent. By late July 2021, consequent upon the volcanic eruptions of April 2021 and Hurricane Elsa of early July 2021, the April-June 2021 economic projection for 2021 was for a further contraction of 6.1 percent; but by year end 2021, due to a recovery of sorts in the second half of the year, it is preliminarily estimated that 2021 resulted in economic growth of 0.7 percent; these numbers are still being interrogated by the relevant professionals at home and abroad. The International Monetary Fund has projected GDP growth for St. Vincent and the Grenadines in 2022 at around 3 percent, and for 2023 it is likely to be in excess of that number. The downside risks to these projections are the continuation of the raging pandemic; the occurrence of any significant natural disaster; any knock-on adverse effects of any sluggish growth in the major world economies; the economic consequences for us of the Russia-Ukraine war and any other severe rupturing of global peace and security; and any less-than-optimal roll-out of our capital programme in the State, private, and cooperative sectors.

In the extant circumstances, what were the raw budgetary numbers crafted for 2022 to meet, satisfactorily, the goals of the Budget?

The Estimates of Revenue and Expenditure for the 2022 fiscal year amount to EC $1.329 billion or an increase of 9.6 percent over the *approved* budget for 2021 of $1.365 billion; the *revised* Estimates of 2021 included the Supplementary Estimates of 2021 in the sum of $117.9 million to address the volcanic eruptions and some additional COVID-related expenditure.

The total estimated expenditure for 2022 of $1.33 billion comprises $931.88 million for recurrent expenditure (inclusive of Amortization and Sinking Fund Contribution of $204.86 million), and capital expenditure of $397.46 million. The core recurrent Estimates for 2022, without Amortization and the Sinking Fund Contribution, amount to

$727.01 million. There is a projected current account deficit of $49.5 million, a manageable sum in the current circumstances.

The recurrent expenditure in the 2022 Estimates represents a 4.1 percent increase over the *approved* budget of 2021, but slightly less than the *revised* Estimates of $728.68 million in 2021. Amortization in 2022 is up 4.4 percent over the approved and revised Estimates; and the Sinking Fund Contribution remains flat.

The financing for the 2022 budget is expected to come from $677.51 million in current revenue and $651.8 million in capital receipts.

On the recurrent expenditure side of the Estimates, several new initiatives are reflected to address the exigent circumstances. These include:

• Subsuming the Banana Services Unit in the Ministry of Agriculture to different programmes in that Ministry, namely, the Research and Development Unit and the Agricultural Extension and Advisory Services Unit to better deliver the relevant services to farmers in the quest to enhance agricultural production, food security and exports, overall;

• The establishment of a Coastal and River Protection Unit under Economic Planning to address more efficaciously the infrastructural ravages on rivers and coastlines as a consequence of climate change;

• The creation of 108 new posts largely in the Ministry of Health (61 posts), and National Security (38 posts), but also across various ministries, to better advance and deliver the relevant services consequent mainly upon the pandemic and the volcanic eruptions.

Under the rubric of recurrent expenditure for 2022, the following are estimated to increase over the *approved* Estimates of 2021: compensation for employees, an increase of $8.2 million or 2.4 percent; other transfers (including Social Assistance, Training, Grants and Contributions to local, regional, and international organisations) are slated to rise by $7.3 million or 5.7 percent; and the provision for Goods and Services are budgeted to rise by $13.9 million or 15.4 percent.

The estimated sums for Other Transfers for 2022 are less than those for the *revised* Estimates of 2021 by $14.2 million reflecting the increases in the Supplementary Estimates occasioned by the consequences of the volcanic eruptions; and the provisions in 2022 for Compensation for Employees and Goods and Services are expected to rise by $2.2 million and $6.0 million, respectively, over the *revised* Estimates of 2021.

In summary terms, the recurrent expenditure budget for 2022, by economic categories, is as follows: Compensation to Employees $354.0 million; Pensions $60.3 million; Other Transfers $134.7 million; Goods and Services $103.9 million; and Debt Service $279.0 million (Interest Payments of $74.1 million, Amortization of $182.9 million, Sinking Fund Contribution of $22.0 million).

The largest single slice of the recurrent budget for 2022 goes to "Compensation of Employees" of $354.0 million which is broken down as follows: Salaries $287.9 million; Allowances $25.1 million; Wages $26.6 million; Employer's National Insurance Services Contribution for Employees $14.5 million. And then, one has to add Pensions of $60.3 million for retired employees, making a grand total of $414.3 million for the central government employees, current and retired, or 57 percent of the core recurrent budget of $727.01 million (that is, without Amortization and the Sinking Fund Contribution).

Those public sector trade union leaders who demand an even greater share of the budget for central government employees are acting without any sense of social solidarity with the rest of the population, particularly in these especially challenging times; these union leaders are unashamedly in pursuit of the enthronement of a veritable "aristocracy of labour" comprising exclusively central government employees with a security of tenure.

No one can reasonably begrudge the central government employees their emoluments, allowances, retirement provisions, and other substantial benefits (training, paid study leave, annual increments of nearly 2 percent for nearly one-half of employees, no-deposit home mortgages, and security of tenure), or any quest to enhance them reasonably. But it must be acknowledged, seriously and sincerely, that the central government resources cannot be applied for the near-exclusive benefit of its employees. In any event, the Minister of Finance announced in his Budget Speech for 2022 that sometime in the second half of this year, discussions will be held with the public sector unions to arrive at a package of salary/wage enhancements for the years 2023, 2024, and 2025.

As the head of a Labour government which champions the cause, always, of the working people, including the central government's employees, it is not at all unreasonable to request enhanced social solidarity from government employees (with a security of tenure) and a practical recognition of their obligations, even as their rights and self-interests are being championed. Fortunately, the overwhelming majority of the central government employees do not share the partisan, political bombast of a politically-partisan, anti-government kind exhibited by some sections of the leadership of the public sector unions. I have discussed this matter extensively in my 2019 book entitled *The Political Economy of the Labour Movement in St. Vincent and the Grenadines.*

The 2022 budget for "wages and salaries" is 2.0 percent higher than the amount estimated for the wages and salaries bill in 2021; there are new posts in 2022 Estimates; this fact contributes, in part, to the increase in that category of expenditure.

The thorny issue of the unsustainability of the current pension arrangements for pensionable employees in the central government, ought to be acknowledged, and appropriate reform measures instituted as necessary and desirable. In 2022, it is estimated that $74.8 million will be spent on retirement benefits for government employees (Pensions of $60.3 million; and the Government's counterpart contribution of $14.5 million, as employer, to the National Insurance Services (NIS) which provide additional pension payments and other employee-related benefits). St. Vincent and the Grenadines is one of the few countries in the Caribbean and the world with two pension arrangements of this kind: a fully-funded pension by the government and a NIS pension partly funded by the government's contribution as employer. One central effect of this arrangement is that as the NIS system matures, the maximum would be reached around 2030 in which both the solely-funded pension by government and the NIS pension would amount to 127 percent of the employee's salary at the point of retirement. This matter, with all its attendant political risks, has to be resolved reasonably. There are various options on the table for possible resolution; this is a public policy issue of some urgency.

The details of the "Other Transfers", that is the category other than "Transfers – Pensions", in the 2022 recurrent budget, amounts to $134.6 million (Grants and Contributions $97.1 million, Training $15.9 million, and Social Assistance $21.6 million). This category of recurrent spending covers payments of public assistance to the poor and vulnerable, scholarships and other financial support for tertiary education, and grants and contributions to State entities, local non-governmental agencies, regional and international organisations. The grants to State agencies amount to $67.2 million; to local NGOs, $2.02 million; and regional and international organisations, $23.2 million, the bulk of which goes to regional organisations.

The main State entities that receive grants are the following: SVG Tourism Authority ($16.0 million); SVG Community College ($14.25 million); Buildings, Roads, and General Services Authority – BRAGSA ($14.0 million); Argyle International Airport Incorporated ($6.2 million); Financial Services Authority ($2.8 million); Invest SVG ($1.5 million); Financial Intelligence Unit ($1.1 million); Bureau of Standards ($1.3 million); Local Government bodies ($4.6 million); Central Water and Sewerage Authority ($1.4 million); National Parks Authority ($2.3 million); National Broadcasting Corporation ($0.6 million); National Sports Council ($0.7 million); SVG Postal Corporation ($0.8 million); Centre for Enterprise Development ($0.6 million); Housing and Land Development Corporation ($0.4 million); Tobago Cays Marine Park ($0.8 million); and Carnival Development Corporation ($0.5 million).

Of the numerous non-governmental bodies which receive grants and contributions from the government, the Assisted Secondary Schools get the single largest sum, $1.33 million.

The delivery of good governance in St. Vincent and the Grenadines is inextricably entwined with its membership of numerous regional and international organisations that provide significant specific services, and general benefit, to our country. The main contributions to regional organisations are as follows: Eastern Caribbean Supreme Court ($2.2 million); the University of the West Indies ($6.5 million); the OECS ($4.3 million); CARICOM Secretariat ($1.5 million); the Regional Security System ($2.0 million); Eastern Caribbean Civil Aviation Authority ($0.9 million); the Seismic Research Centre ($0.4 million); the Caribbean Disaster Emergency Management Agency ($0.3 million); the Caribbean Institute for Meteorology and Hydrology ($0.3 million); the Caribbean Public Health Agency ($0.1 million); and the CARICOM Implementation Agency for Crime and Security ($0.3 million). Each of these entities is vital to the good governance of St. Vincent and the Grenadines; for these eleven regional bodies, we budget $18.6 million in 2022.

Excluding the funding for the University of the West Indies, which may fluctuate during the year depending on the number of Vincentian students in enrollment, the other ten regional entities are now funded, through "automaticity of financing" as distinct from a purely "voluntary" approach. A relevant law, passed by Parliament last year, imposes upon the Director General of Finance and Planning and the Accountant General to pay over "automatically" the budgeted funds on a periodic basis to the scheduled regional bodies during the fiscal year. A one percentage point of the Customs Service Charge is currently earmarked to provide for this "automaticity of funding". As usual, the imposition of the one percentage point increase in the Customs Service Charge for this purpose was met with incandescent rage by the opposition NDP; their opposition was both demagogic and hypocritical, lacking any real appreciation of the especial governance tasks at hand regarding the judiciary, the regional integration thrust of CARICOM and the OECS, public health, seismic monitoring of the volcano, tackling climate change and drought, civil aviation, and security.

The funding for St. Vincent and the Grenadines' membership of international organisations includes resources for the United Nations and its agencies, the Commonwealth, the Organisation of American States, the Association of Caribbean States, the Community of States of Latin America and the Caribbean, the Organisation of African, Caribbean and Pacific States, and international bodies touching and concerning activities such as, for example, postal services, sports and anti-doping, telecommunications, police and security, education, health, the seabed, international law, labour, atomic energy and nuclear weapons, trade, climate change, civil aviation, tourism, food, and agriculture.

The financial contribution to each of these global organisations is not individually significant, but in the aggregate, they amount to a sizeable sum but far less than for the regional organisations. Indeed, all the funding of St. Vincent and the Grenadines to regional and international organisations for 2022 amount to $23.2 million; for the regional organisations together the aggregate sum is in excess of $20 million; thus, for the international organisations the financial outlay is relatively much smaller but the benefits derived for us are great.

It is to be noted that the annual capital subscriptions to the regional and international financial organisations (the Caribbean Development Bank, the World Bank and the International Monetary Fund) are budgeted separately. For example, for this year, the allocation to the World Bank amounts to $2.5 million and constitutes part of the capital budget of the Ministry of Finance and Economic Planning.

The disbursed outstanding public debt of St. Vincent and the Grenadines (central government debt and the debt of public enterprises) has increased over the past two years both *absolutely* as a consequence of necessary borrowings to finance additional expenditure occasioned by the extreme challenges of public health and major natural disasters, and as a proportion of GDP due, too, as a result of the contraction of the macro-economy. As at December 13, 2019, the disbursed public debt stood at 73.5 percent of a total GDP of EC $2.273 billion; by September 30, 2021, the debt was 98.1 percent of a diminished GDP of $2.125 billion. The actual public debt at September 30, 2021, was $2.1 billion or 13.1 percent more than the total disbursed outstanding public debt for the comparative period in 2020. In early May 2022, Venezuela accorded St. Vincent and the Grenadines full debt relief amount to (100 percent) of the balance of the Petro Caribe debt amounting to in excess of EC $110 million, a huge demonstration of regional/international solidarity!

Of the $2.1 billion public debt as at September 30, 2021, the total domestic debt was $525.4 million or 1.6 percent or $8.7 million *less* than for the comparable period in 2020. However, the external debt as at September 30, 2021, had *increased* to $1.6 billion or 19.2 percent or $251 million more than for the comparable period in 2020.

The main changes in the domestic debt in the 2020 to 2021 period were as follows: the balance on overdrafts owed by the public sector *increased* by $0.8 million or 1.6 percent; the local loans portfolio *fell* by 1.4 percent or $1.5 million, as a result of amortization on a number of loans during the period, including a loan of the State-owned Agricultural Input Warehouse which was repaid; and total "government bonds and notes" issued and outstanding over the period *decreased* marginally by $0.1 million.

In respect of the external public debt, the main drivers of the *increase* in 2021 of $251.3 million or 19.2 percent over 2020 are the following: supplemental financing of loans from the World Bank/International Development Association (IDA), namely, the Second Reform and Resilience Development Policy Credit (EC $135 million), and the second Fiscal Reform and Resilience Development Policy Credit (Catastrophe Disaster Deferred Drawdown Option – CAT-DDO) of EC $54.0 million; the Caribbean Regional Digital Transformation Programme ($3.9 million); the OECS MSME Guarantee Facility Project ($2.7 million); the Regional Disaster Vulnerability Service Delivery Project ($5.9 million). All of these are soft loans on very concessionary terms by the World Bank. It is to be noted that at December 31, 2019, the disbursed outstanding debt (DOD) owed to the World Bank/IDA was $190.9

million; by September 30, 2021, the DOD owed to the World Bank/ IDA had increased to $540.6 million, almost $350 million more — all on very favourable concessional terms.

Over the same 2020-2021 period, *net repayments* were recorded on a number of external loans. The more significant ones are: $1.3 million repaid on a number of loans from the European Investment Bank; $6.8 million repaid on loans from the Republic of China (Taiwan); $1.9 million repaid on loans owed to the ALBA bank; $1.6 million repaid on loans from the CARICOM Development Fund; and $11.6 million repaid to bondholders of government instruments.

A disaggregation of the *domestic debt* as at September 30, 2021, reveals Sinking Fund Securities of $61.4 million; Amortized Bonds of $188.5 million; Treasury Bills of $10.8 million; Bank Overdrafts of the Accountant General and State entities of $52.056 million; Domestic loans of $115.1 million; and other domestic debts (insurance deposits and accounts payable) of $4.8 million. The interest rate on these domestic debts (except the payables) ranges from 1 percent to 8 percent (overdraft).

A disaggregation of the *external debt* as at September 30, 2021, shows indebtedness to the following: Caribbean Development Bank $343.4 million of which $327.77 is directly owed by the Central Government and $15.7 million in guarantees for loans not financed by the government's budget; Republic of China on Taiwan ($89.13 million); World Bank/IDA ($540.6 million); International Monetary Fund ($80.2 million); ALBA Bank/government of Venezuela ($139.0 million); Other Loans ($177.0 million of which the principal ones are $109.56 million owed to Petro Caribe, $12.4 million to Damen Shipyard, $18.9 million to North Star Trade Finance, $7.4 million to OPEC Fund for International Development); $128.81 in Bonds (Sinking Fund Securities of $28.16 million, $100.65 million in Amortised Bonds); and Treasury Bills of $53.15 million. The bulk of the external debt, by far, is on concessional terms.

In the short-to-medium term, the public debt will undoubtedly increase with disbursements over the next three or so years from significant loans in respect of the modern port project (US $172 million); the two State-hotels (Marriott at Mt. Wynne and Holiday Inn Express at Diamond — together US $80 million); the Modern Parliament Building and the Modern Court Complex (US $20 million); the Volcano Eruption Emergency Project (US $42 million); the strengthening of Health

Resilience, inclusive of the Acute Referral Hospital (US $98 million); and Fishing Vessels and Little Tokyo (US $9 million). All of the loans are concessionary (low interest rates over lengthy amortisation periods) from lenders such as the Caribbean Development Bank, the World Bank, ALBA Bank, the OPEC Fund for International Development (OFID), and the Republic of China. They will fuel economic growth and social development; the port, the hotels, and the fishing vessels are expressly generators of income themselves to finance the loans.

It is important to note the following about the public debt of St. Vincent and the Grenadines: it is overwhelmingly concessionary; there is very little commercial borrowing in our debt portfolio; the debt is generated to increase growth, create jobs, transform education and health, build up further the physical infrastructure, bolster climate resilience, provide strengthened social safety nets and equity, or to advance good governance. And St. Vincent and the Grenadines pays its debts; we have never defaulted. Over the medium term, beyond three or so years, the debt-to-GDP ratio will stabilise, then commence its fall, and will decline thereafter as the borrowings on the big projects taper and the GDP increases. It is to be noted that borrowings connected to strengthening climate resilience as a consequence of man-made climate change are huge and growing, although St. Vincent and the Grenadines contributes little or nothing to adverse climate change; yet, we bear a heavy burden on the front-line of climate change.

Capital Spending/Development Budget

The estimated capital expenditure of EC $397.5 million for 2022 represents a 25.2 percent or $80.1 million increase over the *approved* capital budget for 2021, but less than the *revised* capital budget for 2021 of $435.7 million. In 2020 and 2021, actual capital spending by the central government was in excess of $200 million in each of these years ($211.2 million in 2020; $231.6 million in 2021) — significant sums.

Capital spending by the central government is buttressed by capital expenditure of the major State entities such as St. Vincent Electricity Services Limited, Central Water and Sewerage Authority, National Properties Limited, Agricultural Input Warehouse Limited, the National Lotteries Authority, and the National Insurance Services, and by the private sector. The State sector, outside of the central government, plans to execute capital expenditure in excess of $70 million in 2022. The private sector (local and foreign) especially through hotel and tourism development, manufacturing, telecommunications, agriculture including medicinal cannabis, fisheries, and housing construction are targeting to invest some $400 million in capital projects in 2022.

Given the probable capital expenditure, public and private, in the region of $650 million in 2022, the question arises about the capacity of both the public and private sector to execute the extent of these capital works. This capacity relates to the availability of a sufficiency of skilled labour, raw materials especially for infrastructure development, equipment, and managerial systems. In 2022 to 2025, all these levels of capacity are likely to be tested to the fullest.

In the capital budget of the central government for 2022, five Ministries, in the aggregate account for 90 percent or $357.1 million: Ministry of Transport and Works ($94.8 million); Ministry of Urban Development, Energy, and Airports ($76.3 million); Ministry of Finance and Economic Planning ($138.3 million); Ministry of Education ($26.7 million); and Ministry of Agriculture, Fisheries and Rural Transformation ($21 million).

An analysis of the budget by main heads of functional classification reveals that 70 percent or $277.9 million of the capital budget is accounted for by three of nine functional heads. These are:

Economic Affairs: This category receives 44.6 percent of $177.3 million of the capital budget in order to facilitate the stimulation of economic growth in the main productive sectors of the economy.

Environmental Protection: This category has been provided with $71.3 million or 17.9 percent of the capital budget aimed at strengthening the country's resilience to natural disasters.

Education: This functional classification head of spending has been allocated $29.4 million or 7.4 percent of the capital budget. The aim here is to enhance further the quality of education and technical/vocational training for our people.

Under the Category Economic Affairs, the following sixteen (16) major projects are allocated the respective sums in millions (m) of dollars for 2022:

Modern Port Project	$42.5 m
Construction of Secondary and Feeder Roads	$11.0 m
Diamond Hotel Project — Holiday Inn Express	$22.4 m

Mt. Wynne Hotel Project — Marriott	$21.0 m
Agricultural Modernisation and Development	$2.5 m
Agricultural Production Support	$1.0 m
Energy Efficiency and Solar PV Plant	$6.0 m
Arrowroot Industry Revitalisation	$4.0 m
Capitalisation of Medical Cannabis Authority	$2.0 m
Volcano Eruption Emergency Project (VEEP)	$24.4 m
La Soufriere Eruption Disaster Relief II	$2.3 m
Public Access Village Enhancement (PAVE)	$2.5 m
Promoting Youth Microenterprise (PRYME)	$1.4 m
Enhancement of Tuna Fishing Industry	$1.3 m
Road Rehabilitation and Repair Programme II	$3.1 m
Caribbean Digital Transformation Programme	$10.8 m
Retrofitting of Building for Inland Revenue and Financial Services Authority	$3.5 m.

Under the Category Environmental Protection six major projects are among those funded as follows:

Natural Disaster Management Rehabilitation (Roads: Mainly Rivers and Coastal Defences)	$21.8 m
Regional Disaster Vulnerability Reduction	$6.7 m
Sandy Bay Defence Resilience Project	$3.5 m
Purchase of Aggregate	$1.0 m
Dengue Eradication Campaign	$1.3 m
Volcano Recovery and Reconstruction	$9.9 m

Under the Category Education, seven major capital projects, among others, are being funded:

School Improvement programme (9 schools)	$12.7 m
Technical and Vocational Education and Training	$5.5 m
Upgrade of School Premises	$1.2 m
Redevelopment of Mary Hutchinson Primary School	$1.0 m
Book Loan Scheme (Phase II)	$1.0 m
Computer Replacement for Secondary Schools	$0.7 m
OECS Programme for Educational Advancement	$0.9 m

Additionally, there are important projects under three other major categories: Health, Community and Housing; and General Public Services. Twelve significant projects, among others, highlighted here and funded in 2022 are:

Upgrade of Health Facilities II	$1.0 m
Purchase of Equipment at Milton Cato Memorial Hospital	$1.0 m
Human Development Service Delivery Project	$6.9 m
Housing Reconstruction/Rehabilitation Projects	$6.0 m
Clare Valley Housing Reconstruction Project	$0.7 m
Land Purchase II	$5.0 m
Modern Parliament	$10.5 m
Modern Court Complex	$5.0 m
Community Improvement Project	$2.0 m
OECS Regional Tourism Competitiveness Project	$4.8 m
Diamond Sporting Facility	$4.2 m
Diamond Multi-Purpose Centre	$1.6 m

I am including as an Appendix the 195 capital projects (each $300,000 or more) listed in the 2022 Estimates, by Ministry, for ease of reference, to show the extent of the capital development programme.

Current Revenue and Capital Receipts

The current revenue for 2022 is estimated at $667.51 million which is 4.7 percent or $30.1 million more than the amount budgeted in the *approved* Estimates for 2021; the approved estimates of revenue for 2021 were $6.2 million more than the *revised* Estimates for 2021.

The current revenue for 2022 comprises tax revenue of $582.55 million and non-tax revenue of $94.98 million. Tax revenue is estimated in 2022 to rise by 5.3 percent over the approved estimates for 2021; non-tax revenue is expected to increase by 1.7 percent over the 2021 approved estimates.

The increase in the forecast for tax revenue for 2022 is due to expected increases in at least three main revenue drivers:

Taxes on Incomes and Profits are expected to rise by 0.8 percent or $1.2 million;

Taxes on Goods and Services are assessed to be increasing by 2.2 percent or $4.2 million; and

Taxes on International Trade and Transactions are forecast to increase by 4.1 percent or $6.7 million.

There are no increases in tax rates or levies in 2022!

On the non-tax revenue side, the bulk of the receipts is expected to come mainly from "Sales of Goods and Services" which is projected to generate $75.7 million or $0.7 million more than the amount collected in 2021. Other miscellaneous non-tax sources are expected to raise some $2.1 million.

Of the $582.5 million of tax revenue estimated for 2022, the five principal sources, in summary are:

Taxes on Incomes and Profits	$156.2 m
Taxes on Property (including Stamp Duties and Alien Land-Holding Licences)	$ 61.3 m
Taxes on Goods and Services	$192.1 m
Taxes on International Trade and Transactions	$169.3 m
Other Taxes	$ 3.6 m

The non-tax revenue category includes five bundles:

Property incom	$8.86 m
Sales of Goods and Services	$75.7 m
Fines, Penalties and Forfeits	$1.66 m
Transfers (not elsewhere classified)	$3.2 m
Other Revenue (not elsewhere classified)	$5.5 m

It is useful to drill down on certain details of current revenue and the locales of collection.

The Registry and the High Court is estimated to collect $39.5 million in 2022, the principal item being $35.7 million as stamp duties charged on the sales or other transfers of real property.

At the Office of the Prime Minister, $22.8 million is estimated to be collected, of which $20.6 million is expected to come from Alien Land-Holding Licences on the purchase by, or transfer to, an "alien" (a non-citizen) of real property.

The Ministry of Finance, Economic Planning, and Information Technology is estimated to collect the bulk of recurrent revenue in 2022, amounting to $596.3 million. The principal revenue sources in this Ministry are:

Policy, Planning, and Administration Department and Accounting Division of $25.1 million, the main drivers being:

Property Income of $3.2 million as dividends from the government's shareholding in St. Vincent Electricity Services, WINERA, Bank of St. Vincent and the Grenadines, and Eastern Caribbean Flour Mills.

Property Income of $5.1 million, mainly consisting of $5 million from the Mustique Company as per that company's agreement with the government.

Sales of Goods and Services of $3.29 million of which $3.1 comes from International Financial Services.

Taxes on Goods and Services of $12.5 million, all of which is for interest levy.

Customs and Excise Department which is projected to collect $267.6 million through the following mainly:

Taxes on Goods and Services of $44.2 million of which the main items are: Excise Duty of $42.2 million; Yacht Licences of $0.504 million; and Cruise and Charter Tax of $1.4 million;

Taxes on International Trade and Transactions of $167.8 million, driven mainly by import duty ($60 million), vehicle surtax ($7.4 million), and VAT ($100.03 million).

Sales of Goods and Services of $50.4 million of which the main revenue items are: Customs Service Charge ($48.1 million), personal fees ($1.1 million), television licences ($0.7 million), and Customs Handling Fees ($0.5 million).

Other Revenue of $4.3 million.

Inland Revenue Department which is slated to collect $291.9 million of which the following are the major revenue items:

Taxes on Incomes, Profits, and Capital Gains of $156.2 million consisting of Income Tax – Individuals ($95.3 million), Income Tax – Corporate ($47.0 million), and Income Tax – Non Resident ($13.6 million).

Taxes on Property of $4.99 million comprising of Property Tax ($4.77 million), and Estate and Succession Duties ($0.117 million).

Taxes on Goods and Services of $124.8 million of which the main items are: VAT ($91.7 million), Excise Duty ($8.7 million), Insurance Premium Tax ($6.7 million), and Motor Vehicle Licence ($15.7 million).

Sales of Goods and Services of $5.4 million, mainly drawn from Drivers' Licences and Fees ($3.99 million) and Registration of Vehicles ($1.4 million).

Telecommunications, Science, and Technology to provide an estimated revenue of $5.4 million in Taxes on Goods and Services, all of which is scheduled to come from Telecoms and Broadcasting Licences.

The Ministry of National Security is expected to bring in revenue of $9.92 million in 2022 from the following main sources: Maritime Administration – Taxes on Goods and Services in merchant shipping licences of $4.1 million; Police Administration with revenue collections of $3.2 million for Sale of Goods and Services of which the principal items are the Inspection and Examination of Vehicles ($2.8 million) and Traffic Tickets of $0.3 million; Airports with revenues of $0.669 million; Passport and Immigration Department with revenues of $1.9 million coming entirely from the Sale of Goods and Services, mainly passport replacements ($1.41 million), and emergency travel documents ($0.205 million).

The Ministry of Agriculture, Rural Transformation, Forestry, and Fisheries is expected to bring in revenues of $2.3 million for 2022 mainly under Taxes on Goods and Services of $1.0 million for Medical Cannabis Authority Licences; Taxes on International Trade of $1.0 million in export tax; and Sale of Goods and Services ($0.248 million).

The Ministry of Transport, Works, Lands, and Physical Planning is slated to bring in the relatively small sum of $0.399 million in current revenues.

The Ministry of Health and the Environment is projected to bring in only $5.5 million in revenues from Hospital Services in the form of Sales of Goods and Services. The main items of revenue under this head of current revenue are: Hospital fees ($0.693 million); Radiology Fees ($0.613 million), Hospital Laboratory Fees ($3.2 million), Out-Patient Fees ($0.452 million), Clinical Rotation Fees for Medical Students ($0.424 million).

Given the recurrent expenditure of Health of $88.3 million of which Hospital Services are $31.8 million, the sum budgeted for revenues from the Ministry of Health is quite small, and thus very protective of the population, especially the poor.

Capital Receipts

The capital budget is financed in the year 2022 through Domestic Receipts of $105.2 million (capital revenue of $1.0 million and Local Loans of $104.2 million); the Domestic Receipts amount to 16.1 percent of the capital receipts; and External Receipts of $546.7 million or 83.9 percent of the capital receipts, comprising of Grants ($69.7 million), Loans ($211.6 million), and Other Receipts ($265.4 million).

The specific funding sources for the Capital Budget in 2022 are as follows:

Grants ($69.7 m)

Caribbean Development Bank (CDB)	$2.112 m
European Union (EU)	$14.945 m
United Nations Development Programme	$1.186 m
Global Environment Fund (GEF)	$1.597 m
United Nations Environment Programme	$1.143 m
Republic of China (Taiwan)	$12.945 m
Pan-American Health Organisation/ World Health Organisation	$1.1 m
United Kingdom CIF (Caribbean Investment Fund)	$20.0 m
United Arab Emirates – Masdar	$2.561 m
United Nations International Children's Emergency Fund	$0.148 m
CARICOM Development Fund (CDF)	$3.875 m
India	$2.0 m
Japan	$1.0 m
Inter-American Development Bank (IDB)	$0.538 m
Global Partnership for Education (GPE)	$0.900 m
Italy	$0.700 m
Morocco	$0.102 m
Other	$2.8 m

External Loans ($211.574 million)

European Investment Bank (EIB)	$5.973 m
Government of Kuwait	$4.82 m
Caribbean Development Bank (CDB)	$84.666 m
International Development Association (IDA)	$64.31 m

Republic of China (Taiwan)	$35.66 m
CARICOM Development Fund (CDF)	$11.45 m
OPEC Fund for International Development (OFID)	$4.10 m

Domestic Funds ($118.160 million)

Local Loans	$104.160 m
Revenue	$12.0 m.

In the operation of the recurrent expenditure budget there are invariably savings amounting to roughly 5 percent thereof; almost always, too, current revenue tends to out-perform the usually cautious current revenue estimates. Clearly, though, the budget is constrained by the share of it that goes to salaries, wages, allowances, pensions, and payments on the public debt. This is the structural challenge of a vulnerable, small island developing State encumbered by limited material resources, a legacy of underdevelopment, and the continuing threat of climate change, in the quest to build a modern post-colonial economy in pursuance of sustainable development. This development quest is awash with limitations, weaknesses, and contradictions amidst immense strengths and possibilities.

Chapter Four

Good Governance, Parliamentary Democracy, Small Island Exceptionalism, and Budget Debate 2022

In this chapter I shall address four bundles of relevant issues to our nation's recovery, rebuilding, and sustainable development. These issues touch and concern Good Governance and Institutional Building, Parliamentary Democracy and an Alive Constitutionalism, Small Island Exceptionalism, and the very Debate itself on Budget 2022.

Good Governance and Institutional Building

Over the past 21 years, there have been significant advances in good governance, institutional strengthening, and institutional building. Every single critical governance institution has had its structure and functioning enhanced; and an extensive bundle of fresh institutions has been created to address specific responsibilities. In each case the institutional alterations and enhanced functioning have been focused on much-improved delivery of a range of services to the public, and in accord with the relevant laws and regulations, grounded in the principles of fairness, accountability, transparency, and effectiveness.

The constitutional offices of the Attorney General, the Director of Public Prosecutions (DPP), the Director of Audit, the Supervisor of Elections, among others, have been strengthened immeasurably. Let us provide first a brief review of these four constitutional offices; we will then proceed to address several critical government departments, statutory bodies, and other public enterprises.

Office of the Attorney General

The *Office of the Attorney General* provides authoritative legal advice to the government. Such advice ought to be independent and non-partisan, politically. In a small country such as St. Vincent and the Grenadines, it has proven to be wise not to appoint an activist politician to that Office; it is far preferable, as the ULP government has done, to cause the appointment of a public service, non-partisan Attorney General. Further, it is unwise, as governments other than those of the ULP have done, to conjoin the Office of Attorney General with one or more Ministerial portfolios.

Since independence in 1979 up to March 29, 2001, the appointment of partisan political personages to the Office of Attorney General with attached ministerial portfolios has repeatedly caused or occasioned these Attorneys General to be embroiled in partisan controversies with negative consequences for them and their governments. Under the Milton Cato Administration 1979 to 1984 the Attorneys General Arthur Williams and Grafton Isaacs were quite controversial, though each had chalked up considerable achievements; both Williams and Isaacs were shifted from the post of Attorney General. Under the James Mitchell administrations (1984 to 2000) controversy and resignations followed a succession of "political" Attorneys General: Emery Robertson, Parnel Campbell, Carlyle Dougan, and Carl Joseph — all of whom were persons of merit and worth, and in the case of Campbell, extraordinarily so.

Further, under Mitchell's NDP government the Offices of the Attorney General and Director of Public Prosecutions were, for a time, compromised by having the same person acting in both roles!

Under my leadership, I have preferred the "public service" Attorney General, first in the person of Judith Jones-Morgan who was actually a public servant prior to her appointment as Attorney General — she served some 17 years as Attorney General and demitted her Office at her retirement age; and secondly, the current Attorney General, Jaundy Martin, a former public servant. These appointments have worked well, and independently of partisan politics. The informed public appreciates this way of proceeding in the interest of good governance.

Office of the Director of Public Prosecutions

Up to 2001, under the NDP government, *the Office of the DPP* was not highly regarded despite its central role in initiating, continuing, or discontinuing criminal prosecutions. As noted above, on one occasion the person who acted as DPP was Attorney General, and sat in the Cabinet; and on another occasion, the Solicitor General acted as DPP.

Further, in 2001, the Office of the DPP had three professionals (DPP and two other lawyers) and four non-professional staff, with an annual budget of EC $0.331 million; in 2022, there are 12 professionals (DPP, nine other lawyers, and two administrative professionals) and ten non-professional staff; in 2022, the annual recurrent budget for this Office is $2.022 million. (In 2022 dollars, the 2001 allocation would be approximately $0.450 million). The annual salary of the DPP in 2001 was $66,224; in 2022, the comparable salary is $116,064, much higher than 2001 even after a 40 percent discount for inflation. The allowances in 2022 are correspondingly higher than 2001. The physical facilities that accommodate the DPP's Office today are excellent and are far superior than in 2001. There is, too, a National Prosecution Service, with the DPP at its centre, functioning under a well-articulated *Prosecution Code*. The two latter initiatives were the handiwork of an excellent reforming DPP, Colin Williams, now a High Court Judge in the Eastern Caribbean Supreme Court.

Office of the Director of Audit

The *Office of the Director of Audit* in 2001 had a staff of 32 with an annual budget of $1.78 million. In 2001, it had one Deputy Director; today, it has two. In 2001, the Office lacked the full extent of specific divisions; today, in addition of the Office of the Director, which contains the Director and a Deputy, there are five specific units: the Administrative Support Unit; the Pensions and Salaries Unit; the Financial Audit Unit; the Compliance Audit Unit; and the Performance Unit.

In 2001, the physical premises of this Office were an embarrassment. There were insufficient space, desks and chairs for the staff; there was little equipment and the two computers were non-functioning; rats and bats abounded; and the place was thoroughly unhealthy. Today, the Office of the Director of Audit is located in spacious accommodation, has adequate furniture and equipment and a healthy work environment.

The Audit staff are all much better paid than in 2001, even taking account of inflation; allowances are more, as are abundant training opportunities.

Up to 2001, the constitutional independence of the Office of the Director of Audit was severely compromised in that the Director of Audit was required to seek permission from the Prime Minister to travel overseas to audit our country's diplomatic missions and tourism offices overseas. I put a stop to all that. Accordingly, in the Estimates of Expenditure from 2002 onwards the Office of the Director of Audit has a specific line item titled "International Travel and Subsistence". Upon her retirement one Director of Audit wrote to me with thanks for my non-interference in the work of the Office of the Director of Audit; for funding, accommodation, and equipping it well; and for ensuring the maintenance of the Office's constitutional independence.

In the discussion on Budget 2022, the Director of Audit expressed satisfaction with the allocations in the Estimates. Moreover, no requests for funding, additional to those allocated, were made to me or to the Ministry of Finance.

The Office of the Director of Audit was further strengthened post-2001 with the passage of a modern Audit Act of 2005 that repealed the former Finance and Audit Act that was in place since 1964. The upgraded statute consolidates the Director of Audit's constitutional duties and extends her statutory role considerably.

The Reports of the Director of Audit are vital in the work of the Public Accounts Committee (PAC), chaired by the Leader of the Opposition. Unfortunately, the NDP in opposition has failed and/or refused to put the PAC to work. Their spurious reasons for abdicating their responsibility in this regard are entirely untenable; they are false and bogus.

Office of the Supervisor of Elections

The *Office of the Supervisor of Elections* is of supreme importance in our competitive democracy. Free and fair elections are the cornerstone of the process to elect representatives, in our representative democracy, to the House of Assembly.

It was the St. Vincent and the Grenadines Labour Party government under Milton Cato that modernised the Representation of the People Act in 1982, strengthened the constitutional independence of the Office of the Supervisor of Elections, provided for continuous registration and a picture-identification card for each voter. Since then, free and fair elections, substantially in accordance with the law and regulations, have been conducted in St. Vincent and the Grenadines. Constitutional reforms, including the establishment of a more secure and a stronger Independent Elections Commission, were opposed by the NDP. However, in each of the general elections subsequent to 2001, that is to say, 2005, 2010, 2015, and 2020, the opposition NDP, the loser in each of these elections, has falsely contended that the elections were stolen by the ULP. On each occasion the independent foreign observers variously from CARICOM, the Commonwealth, and the Organisation of American States (except that the OAS was not an observer in 2020), and the National Monitoring and Consultative Mechanism (NMCM) headed by the SVG Christian Council, pronounced that each of these elections was free and fair and represented the will of the people.

In the aftermath of the 2015 elections, which occasioned the NDP's fourth successive election defeat at the hands of the ULP, the NDP took to the streets in protest and instituted election petitions in two of the constituencies the ULP won in the vain hope of overturning the ULP's 8 to 7 majority of elected representatives.

For five years, 2015-2020, the NDP and its anti-ULP and anti-Ralph fellow-travellers, protested repeatedly on the streets about stolen elections and demanded "fresh elections". Practically every day a NDP front organisation, calling itself "Front Line", protested noisily outside the Office of the Supervisor of Elections; the holder of that Office was a woman of utmost personal integrity, Ms. Sylvia Findlay-Scrubb, a former school principal, a high-quality administrator and a pillar of the Anglican Community.

Practically every day, oft-times with members of the NDP leadership present, the protesters verbally-abused, insulted, assaulted and threatened Ms. Findlay-Scrubb. On no occasion did the NDP leadership denounce these illegal tactics; indeed, they encouraged and condoned this lawlessness against an innocent, law-abiding, professional woman.

Meanwhile, the election petitions wound their way through the High Court and up to the Court of Appeal and back on this or that preliminary point of law and practice. In April 2019, the case was finally heard by Justice Stanley John of Trinidad and Tobago, an experienced and highly-regarded Caribbean jurist. After days of sifting the evidence through numerous witnesses, examination and cross-examination, evidential review of documents, and submissions by learned Senior Counsel on all sides, Justice John dismissed the election petitions and reaffirmed the two ULP representatives as having been duly elected in the North Windward and Central Leeward constituencies respectively.

On the day of the High Court's decision, the Leader of the NDP Opposition, Dr. Lorraine Friday, a trained lawyer, took to the streets with a small group of supporters shouting "No Justice, No Peace". Apparently, "justice" is done only if they had won the petitions; and the absence of "peace" is undoubtedly "war". The NDP pledged to appeal the case, but other than filing the Notice of Appeal and associated initial formal documentation, they did absolutely nothing to pursue the appeal. They never, apparently, compiled the Record of Appeal; if they did, they did not file it, nor did they serve it or anything else other than the initial Notice of Appeal on the respondents in the appeal. Yet, they insisted publicly that the Court of Appeal was not hearing the appeal on a timely basis. It was dishonesty, pure and simple.

In time, the Notice of Appeal became academic upon the dissolution of the House of Assembly by the Governor General and the holding of fresh general elections on November 5, 2020, after the usual five-year term. The ULP increased their parliamentary majority among representatives. In 2015, the ULP had a majority of one; now they commanded a majority of three even though the NDP gained a sliver of a majority on the popular votes, mainly because of their huge majorities in the two Grenadines' constituencies, their historic strongholds.

In 2001, in the Recurrent Estimates (the last of the NDP government's Estimates) there were 10 staff members at the Office of the Supervisor of Elections, including the Supervisor and Deputy Supervisor, and a budget of $1.0 million, during an election year; the 2001 elections were held on March 28th. The physical facilities of this Office were poor and decrepit. In 2020, in the year of general elections of November 5th of that year, the expenditure on the elections was $4.2 million. In 2022, in a non-election year, the recurrent budget is for a permanent staff at this Office of 17, with an allocation of $1.5 million. For over ten years now, this Office has modern, spacious accommodation with advanced information technology for a highly trained staff.

The law and practice of general elections in St. Vincent and the Grenadines are such that it is impossible for an election to be conducted that is not free and fair. Of course, the NDP continues to demand "fresh elections", the basis of which is known only to them. The CARICOM

Observer Mission and the NMCM observers concluded authoritatively that the elections of 2020 were free and fair and reflected the will of the people. Trumpism (the praxis of former President Donald Trump of the USA) seems to have infected the NDP badly. They are doing a great disservice to our democracy and our free people!

Passports and Immigration Department

The critical *Passports and Immigration Department* has witnessed a complete transformation in its structure, functioning, and output since 2001.

Up to 2001, the passport was relatively easy to forge, and it was frequently done. A vital source document for the passport's issuance, the birth certificate, was sometimes forged and oft-times misrepresented as belonging to another. People's names were changed relatively easy. Many such changes were done with the intention to deceive the authorities in St. Vincent and the Grenadines and countries to which the persons were migrating, including those in the Caribbean, United States of America, Canada, and the United Kingdom.

The official issuance of the passport in 2001 was done by Police Officers, many of whom were untrained in border security; the head of the Passports and Immigration Department was also a Police Officer. The department itself was under the general administration of the Police Force. The law and regulations governing passports and immigration were outdated and required modernisation and strengthening from a security standpoint. Passports were issued overseas at diplomatic missions in a sloppy fashion; and the Director of Audit reported, repeatedly, that blank passports sent to the overseas missions for issuance went missing, and monies related thereto were unaccounted.

The physical facilities, equipment, quality and quantity of personnel were insufficient for the tasks at hand; and generally-speaking the delivery of services was inadequate and oft-times tardy. International law, including the regulatory framework of the International Civil Aviation Organisation, was given scant attention.

Immediately, the ULP government recognised upon being elected to office that this undesirable state of affairs could not continue. After all, the two most important books in the people's households were, and are, the Holy Bible and the passport; clearly, the passport required greater security, higher quality, and far better processes for its issuance.

Further, the rise of terrorism, globally, especially after the terrorist attack in the USA on September 11, 2001, demanded greater strides swiftly to reform the passport and immigration services for the better.

Over the past 21 years, the following, among other things, have been done in this regard:

The passport and immigration services were civilianised, taken from under the wings of the Police Force, and placed under a separate department. Some of the police officers were retained and retrained and passport/immigration officers of a high quality were recruited for this specific business within the broader rubric of "border security".

The law and regulations were changed, especially in relation to the services rendered by the Department but also in respect of the Advanced Passenger Information Systems (APIS) to better secure our borders.

The British authorities were invited to review our processes and make appropriate recommendations. The upshot of all this was a set of reforms, including the important matter of secure and safe source documents. In this latter respect, a modern Birth Certificate with security features was rolled out with assistance from the Organisation of American States.

Some $20 million were spent on the passport infrastructure and border security to deliver first a machine-readable passport, then an E-passport of the highest international quality through the procurement of the professional services of "Canadian Bank Note", a Canadian company of very high repute in this field.

The purchase, modernisation and equipping of a multi-million dollar building for the Passport and Immigration Department, which it shares with the Electoral Office (Office of the Supervisor of Elections).

In 2001, the Passport and Immigration Services were delivered without a budget separate from that of the Police Force; it was subsumed within that entity. In 2022, these services are a separate and distinct civilianised Department with a staff of 83 and an annual recurrent budget of $5.8 million. In the 2001 Estimates the Immigration and Passport Services did not merit even one line in the "Key Results" of the Office of the Prime Minister under which the Police and the Immigration and Passport Service were located ministerially and administratively. In the 2022 Estimates, there was reportage on six "Strategic

Priorities" (formerly "Key Results") of the Department from 2021, a listing of ten "Strategic Priorities" for 2022, a performance measurement of five "Outcome Indicators" from 2021, and a further listing of eight "Output Indicators" for 2022 with comparisons for 2021 and projections for 2022 and 2023. One of the "Strategic Priorities" for 2022 is the reform and modernisation of the Immigration (Restriction) Act, the core of which was legislated in 1937.

Accountability and security systems were minimal in 2001; they are emphasized in 2022 in the delivery of the services of this Department.

National Emergency Management Office

The *National Emergency Management Office (NEMO)* was formally established in 2006 by the National Emergency Management Act to address efficaciously the preparation for, and the management of, natural disasters, including health pandemics. NEMO has a permanent staff of nineteen and an annual recurrent budget for 2022 of $2.6 million. NEMO has a management network headed by the National Emergency Council, a broad-based inter-ministerial body with the participation of relevant State agencies, the private sector, and civil society entities, chaired by the Prime Minister. Under the Council is a National Executive Committee, chaired by the Director of NEMO, consisting of 15 high-level professional State officials, the Red Cross and the Rainbow Radio League; ten functional sub-committees; and over forty district disaster management committees across St. Vincent and the Grenadines.

Up to 2001, the disaster preparedness office doubled as a local government office. In the 2001 Estimates, which were passed on December 6, 2000, the last by the previous NDP government, the rubric was headed "Local Government/Disaster Preparedness". This unit, located within the Ministry of Housing, Local Government, Community Development, Sports and Youth Affairs, had a staff of two, comprising a Local Government Officer/National Disaster Coordinator and a Senior Clerk, with an annual budget of under $100,000 of which $60,972 were for salaries for the two staff members. The head of the Unit had an annual salary of $38,076 at a grade, nine grades below that of the most highly-paid public servant (Director General of Finance and Planning – DGFP). That Unit carried out its functions in 2001 in accord with a piece of inadequate legislation of 1947. Today, the annual salary of the Director of NEMO is $93,024; her grade is only four grades below that of the DGFP. The top nine employees of NEMO are *above* the comparable grade level of that of the Disaster Preparedness Coordinator of 2001. All of them are trained professionals.

Significantly, from April 2001, within a month or so of the ULP government taking office, the Prime Minister assumed ministerial responsibility for national emergencies, disaster preparedness and management, and that responsibility has remained his since then. Indeed, swiftly after the ULP assumed office it put in place, administratively, a precursor to what became the statutory NEMO, by a similar name that transitioned into NEMO. Disaster preparedness and management were so low on the NDP government's totem pole of governance that for nearly three years it did absolutely nothing on a World-Bank financed project to set up a NEMO-type entity, to build the requisite headquarters, to construct a seawall at Layou to save that town and the main road to North Leeward from the ravages of the sea, and to carry out other miscellaneous activities such as training, community involvement, and requisite legislative alterations. The soft loan from the World Bank amounted to EC$16 million, but none of it was ever drawn-down by the NDP government; its tardiness cost the tax payers an extra $5 million more from local government sources when the ULP government promptly and actively engaged the World Bank on the issue.

Under the ULP, NEMO has become a household name across St. Vincent and the Grenadines. It has prepared and managed well numerous natural disasters over the years, particularly a series of them from 2010, almost annually. NEMO has been, and is being, severely tested with COVID-19, the volcanic eruptions of April 2021 and their consequences, Hurricane Elsa of July 2021, and the droughts of 2021; but it has done and is doing magnificent work. Since March 2020, the Health Services Sub-Committee of NEMO, chaired by the Chief Medical Officer, has been exemplary in addressing the pandemic. NEMO has been a major accomplishment of the ULP government.

Financial Intelligence Unit and Financial Services Authority

The Financial Intelligence Unit (FIU) and the Financial Services Authority (FSA) are creations of the ULP government. Under and by virtue of the Financial Intelligence Unit Act of 2001 (Chapter 17 of the Laws of St. Vincent and the Grenadines) that came into effect on December 28, 2001, the FIU was created; the FIU began its operation in February 2002. The FIU Act provides for the establishment of the FIU as the national, centralised unit in St. Vincent and the Grenadines to collect, analyse and disseminate suspicious transaction information to the competent authorities in and out of the jurisdiction of St. Vincent and the Grenadines. In a few short years, the FIU was admitted to the elite "Egmont Group" of similar units globally; it swiftly became, arguably, the most professional financial intelligence agency in the Eastern Caribbean to which the regional FIUs have been sending their personnel for training and attachments. The FIU works very closely with its regional and international partners, including from North America, the United Kingdom, and the European Union.

The FIU Act was passed, and the FIU was created in the wake of a mountain of credible allegations of money laundering and the criminal misuse of the proceeds of crime in the latter years of the twentieth century under the NDP government. Indeed, the British government in 1999 had refused the NDP government debt-relief under the Commonwealth Debt Initiative on four stated grounds namely: the offshore finance sector was insufficiently regulated; the country was riddled with "official corruption"; the existence of widespread money-laundering and the illegal use of the proceeds of crime were not being tackled effectively or at all; and the government had no credible poverty reduction programme in a country with high levels of poverty and indigence.

When the ULP government was elected there were several "blacklists" already imposed, or imminently pending, on St. Vincent and the Grenadines including one by the global Financial Action Task Force (FATF) due to the poorly regulated offshore finance sector, money-laundering, and the misuse of the proceeds of crime. Indeed, in December 2000, the principal corresponding bank in the USA, Bank of America, for the then wholly State-owned National Commercial Bank (NCB), severed abruptly corresponding banking relations with the NCB, threatening in effect to reduce the NCB from the status of a commercial bank to a poorly-run savings bank. The NCB was itself in a thorough mess and was on the brink of insolvency. It was a small, under-capitalised bank with liquidity challenges and non-performing loans amounting to some 20 percent of all loans; internally, the bank's controls were weak, and for the years 1998 and 1999, the auditors gave a "qualified opinion" on the audited statements of accounts.

On September 11, 2001, the terrorist attack on the Twin Towers in New York City brought very sharply into focus the issue of "terrorist financing". Across the world this matter assumed prominence in financial transactions. Various countries pronounced on it, and so too, did the United Nations' Security Council. In St. Vincent and the Grenadines, our Parliament passed a modern Proceeds of Crime and Anti-Money

Laundering Bill, which was in draft and under public consultation before September 2001. Immediately thereafter, the Financial Intelligence
Unit Bill was also passed; subsequently, the Proceeds of Crime Act was
further strengthened.

Meanwhile, the process of reviewing, repealing, and amending the
entire menu of offshore finance legislation and practice was underway;
the Confidentiality Act, essentially an act to protect secrecy in offshore
finance transactions, was repealed. The Offshore Finance Authority was
revamped and its regulatory powers strengthened, first as the International Financial Services Authority, and later as a fully-fledged *Financial Services Authority* (FSA). The FSA was rolled out to regulate all
non-domestic banking financial businesses/transactions in St. Vincent
and the Grenadines, including international banking and other offshore
entities, credit unions, all insurance companies, building societies, money
services, and large Friendly Societies. The legislation in each of these
areas of finance and international (offshore) banks was modernised and
provided for far better regulation in accord with international standards.
The domestic banking laws, the regulatory oversight of them by the
Eastern Caribbean Central Bank (ECCB), Securities Legislation, and
supportive institutions were reformed and fortified.

There are no "black lists" anymore against St. Vincent and the
Grenadines on any matter touching and concerning banking, finance,
proceeds of crime, or money-laundering. For all intents and purposes, St. Vincent and the Grenadines is a "clean" jurisdiction with sound
regulatory systems and excellent external cooperation. All of this is
good news for the economy and good governance, however inconvenient
and expensive it may sometimes be regarding legitimate, non-suspicious
transactions.

In the 2022 Budget, the sum of $3.9 million has been allocated for
these two institutions in respect of financial regulation: $1.1 million for
the FIU; and $2.8 million for the FSA. Additionally, the Estimates pro-
vide annual contributions to the allied Caribbean Financial Action Task
Force, the OECD Forum on Tax Transparency, and the Base Erosion
and Profit Sharing (BEPS).

Office of the Supervisor of Insolvency

The Office of the Supervisor of Insolvency was created under the
Insolvency Act of 2007, a modern piece of legislation addressing bankruptcy and insolvency along the lines of the Canadian model, adapted to

our circumstances. The Insolvency Act repealed the woefully inadequate and out-dated Bankruptcy Act of 1928 based on the pre-1927 legislation in force in England, including the Deeds of Arrangement Acts of 1914. The Office of the Supervisor of Insolvency, within the framework of the modern insolvency laws, greatly strengthens the business climate and the ease of doing business. In Budget 2022, the Office has been allocated the sum of $84,939.00.

Commerce and Intellectual Property Office

This Office was established by the Commerce and Intellectual Property Office Act of 2002 (Chapter 310 of the Laws of St. Vincent and the Grenadines). Among the functions of this Office is to register and protect intellectual property, namely, literary and artistic work; performances of performing artistes, phonograms and broadcasts; inventions in all fields of human endeavor; scientific discoveries; industrial designs; trademarks, service marks, and commercial names and designations; protection against unfair competition; and all other rights resulting from intellectual activity in the industrial, scientific, literary or artistic fields. CIPO thus functions in practical terms for the registration and regulation of copyrights, patents, and trademarks. It also has, centrally, the responsibility as the registry for companies, business names, charitable and commercial associations.

CIPO is a well-staffed, modernised registry in comfortable surroundings. It is all part and parcel of the ULP government's quest to modernise and make more efficient the delivery of government services in a modern, competitive, more diversified post-colonial economy. Intellectual property rights are particularly important in the many-sided production and sale of goods and services.

CIPO has a Registrar, Deputy Registrar, and nine other staff members. Its operational budget in the 2022 Estimates is $0.8 million. It is slated to bring in close to $1.5 million in revenues in 2022. In other words, it more than pays for itself, while contributing immensely to the orderliness and productivity of the modern economy. Its services are reasonably and competitively priced.

The National Lotteries Authority

The National Lotteries was established in early July 1984 by the Labour Party government under Milton Cato a few weeks before it was voted out of office and replaced in late July 1984 by James Mitchell's

NDP. Before the ULP assumed governmental office in March 29, 2001, the National Lotteries functioned for 17 years without a well-defined legislative structure and with very little ministerial oversight. In its financial year 2000, it grossed revenues of just under $10 million.

I had long seen the potential of National Lotteries to contribute immensely to sports, culture, educational and health support, but it was structured in a minimalist way with an insufficient ambition. Indeed, when I was Leader of the Opposition and Chairman of the Public Accounts Committee (PAC) in Parliament for the period October 1999 to March 2001, I summoned the National Lotteries to the PAC to answer queries about its operation. Within one week of being elected Prime Minister, I invited the Manager of the National Lotteries, Mr. Mc Gregor Sealey, who had been the Manager at its founding and has continuously been its Manager, to discuss with me ideas for the National Lotteries' further development. As a consequence of this conversation, a series of transformative innovations were made.

First, the National Lotteries was placed on a sound legislative footing. In early 2002, Parliament passed the National Lotteries Authority Act, establishing formally the National Lotteries Authority (NLA). The Act provides additionally for the constitution, powers, duties, management and staff of the NLA; provision is made, too, for its funds and resources, its borrowing powers, reserve fund, application of funds, annual business plan, its accounts, its auditing, and the reportage of its audited financial statements to the House of Assembly. The Bill for an Act to establish the NLA was actually drafted by Mr. Sealey's daughter, Petrona Sealy, (who at the time was a Legal Draftsperson with the Attorney General's Chambers), with reviews of it by me personally. We worked together on weekends to produce the draft Bill. The Act's operation commenced on March 28, 2002.

Between then and now the NLA has chalked up impressive achievements. To begin with, its gross revenues have jumped from under EC $10 million annually to $85 million for its 2021 financial year, despite the pandemic and the volcanic eruptions; its gross revenues for 2021 increased by some $5 million over the 2020 figures; it is on target to achieve gross revenues of over $90 million in 2022. Some eighty percent of the NLA's revenues go towards prize monies; the remaining twenty percent, or so, pay for administration, sports, culture, and other purposes.

The NLA during the ULP years in government purchased and developed its substantial headquarters in capital city, Kingstown; that property also contains two squash courts. The NLA also owns valuable property in lower Kingstown, which currently houses the annex of the Kingstown Anglican Primary School. The NLA owns a television station, VC3, through which it broadcasts live its Lottery draws; VC3 promotes local sports and culture in its programming. Currently, the NLA is rolling out plans for a tourism development property (cabanas, a restaurant, a small casino) at the former Emerald Valley Hotel and Casino; it has negotiated the purchase of the existing property from the State-owned National Properties Limited; it is in partnership with Canadian Bank Note on the management of the casino. Canadian Bank Note Company is a very reputable Canadian company that provides the technology required for the operation of the lotteries themselves. The NLA is the most successful national lotteries entity in the Organisation of Eastern Caribbean States (OECS) despite the fact that it does not, as a matter of policy, run popular, but quite addictive, video lottery games.

The NLA has been assigned the responsibility to develop and manage Victoria Park, the premier mass, cultural facility in St. Vincent and the Grenadines. It has done a splendid job in developing and maintaining this facility. The NLA has built and/or redeveloped significantly major sporting facilities, including the following: playing fields at London (Sandy Bay), Park Hill, South Rivers, Chili, North Union, Evesham, Calliaqua, Hope, Cumberland, and Green Hill; Hard Courts at Lowmans Leeward, Choppins, and Union Island; and dozens of other sporting and cultural facilities have been repaired or expanded.

The NLA under Chairman, Murray Bullock and Manager, Mc Gregor Sealey have been doing an excellent job over the last 21 years.

Carnival Development Corporation

The Carnival Development Corporation Act establishing the Carnival Development Corporation (CDC) came into operation on December 31, 2002. Prior to the legislative establishment of the CDC as a State-run statutory body, incorporating all relevant stakeholders into it, with a permanent staff, it functioned as a loose, episodic administrative body called the Carnival Development Committee. The Legal Draftsperson, Petrona Sealey, René Baptiste (a lawyer and the then Minister of Culture), and I worked on weekends on the draft Bill to establish the CDC. For decades, hitherto, there was a popular demand to put the CDC on a legislative footing as a statutory corporation, but nothing was ever done; in less than two years in office, the ULP government did it!

The CDC organises and manages the premier mass cultural event, Carnival ("Vincy Mas"), annually. René Baptiste's leadership made Vincy Mas bigger and better in every way, particularly with calypso, pan music and "mas". Vincy Mas is popularly-driven; it is a festival of creativity; it earns money for the individual artists and artistes; and it is a boon to the economy. Moreover, the "ten days of mas and fun in the Vincy sun" culminating in a two-day street festival is a fantastic release of the metaphoric pressure valve of life, living, and production for the society. Over the past two years (2020 and 2021) the pandemic prevented the holding of Vincy Mas.

In Budget 2022, the CDC receives a subvention from the government of $500,000 to run the permanent office of CDC annually. Further, for the festival itself, the CDC usually receives $1 million from the NLA plus much in-kind assistance. Sponsorship and gate receipts provide the bulk of the "other receipts" for the CDC.

Agency for Public Information/ National Broadcasting Corporation

The Agency for Public Information (API) is the renamed and refashioned agency that succeeded, in April 2001, the Government Information Service (GIS), to provide information on government policies and programmes, and other relevant "public" information on the events or happenings in the wider society.

The API works closely with the State-owned radio station, *National Broadcasting Corporation* (NBC), VC3 (the NLA television station), and other public information entities or persons in various ministries and other public enterprises across the State administration. The NBC was established under the National Broadcasting Corporation Act of 1986 to enable the State-owned radio station to be properly run as a statutory corporation rather than as a department or unit of government. In Budget 2022, it receives an annual subvention from government of EC $0.5 million. At the time of the establishment of the NBC, it was the only radio station licensed to operate in St. Vincent and the Grenadines. Today, there are a dozen or so privately-owned and operated radio stations.

The API is located within the Ministry of Information, which is currently under the Office of the Prime Minister. In the Estimates for 2022, the API is allocated $2.046 million; it has a full-time staff of 33, mainly professionals in the field of communications, under the leadership of a Director and a Deputy Director.

This year 2022, a provision is made under the Office of the Prime Minister for a Director/CEO of the Amalgamated Information Services. It is the public policy of the government to amalgamate the API, the National Broadcasting Corporation that runs the State-owned radio station, VC3, and some other ministries' information networks, to provide greater synergies and effectiveness as a precursor to a more unified and restructured delivery of public information services to fit the changing communications' landscape nationally, regionally and globally.

It is accepted by the ULP government, and by all modern governments, that communication is a vital function to be performed in an open, democratic, political system. Various functions in the political system are provided by specific structures: interest articulation is done by pressure groups and non-governmental entities; interest aggregation is performed by political parties; rule-making is legislated by Parliament or subsidiary bodies empowered by Parliament; rule-execution is carried out by the Cabinet and the State administration; rule-adjudication is performed by the independent judiciary. The output of all of this has to be communicated to the public from whom feedback (positive or negative), demands, and supports, enter as inputs to the political system as a whole. This latter function of communication, in part by a coordinated State agency, is vital. Of course, in a free, democratic society there is freedom of the press/media exercised by an array of private or cooperative entities. A coordinated State agency for public information, in this framework, is thus vital for good governance.

St. Vincent and the Grenadines Community College

The SVG Community College (SVGCC) was incorporated by statute, the St. Vincent and the Grenadines Community College Act of 2005. It integrated into one body four hitherto separate entities: the SVG Community College (an "A" Level College pursuing almost exclusively programmes for Cambridge General Certificate of Education at Advanced Level); the SVG Teachers' College; the SVG Technical College; and the SVG School of Nursing. In the integration process, four divisions of the SVGCC were established: the Division of Arts, General Studies, and Sciences (the former "A" Level College); the Division of Teacher Education; the Division of Technical and Vocational Education; and the Division of Nursing Education.

The SVGCC Act does the following: establishes the integrated Community College; sets out the objectives, powers, and functions of the College; establishes and provides for a Board of Governors, Executive and Finance Committee of the Board, the Academic Council; makes provision for the College's administration, the Director and Deputy Director of the College, Registrar, Bursar, Deans and Vice-Deans for the various Divisions of the College; addresses the issue of the staff of the College, their appointment, matters of discipline and dismissal of staff, retirement, secondment of public officers, emoluments, and pensions; provides details of financial arrangements, accounts, business plans, audit, reportage to the House of Assembly; sets up a students' loan fund; and miscellaneous provisions relating to students, a Students' Council, alumni association, and regulatory framework.

The SVGCC offers a range of courses at a post-secondary and tertiary education level leading to various qualifications: Caribbean Advanced Proficiency Examinations (CAPE) qualifications of the Caribbean Examination Council (CXC); Associate Degrees; Certificates; Diplomas including post-graduate university diplomas; Bachelors' Degrees; and Masters' Degrees. The SVGCC pursues one set of programmes leading to qualifications internally granted but which are registered or approved by the independent National Accreditation Board, and/or recognised by various tertiary institutions, including the University of the West Indies. The College also conducts educational and training programmes through a process of articulating these programmes leading to qualifications offered by other accredited universities and tertiary-level institutions overseas.

Locally, the SVGCC and the Open Campus of the University of the West Indies are the backbone of the offerings of post-secondary and tertiary education/training programmes. These are two critical institutions in providing the skilled and educated manpower immediately, or for better preparation for the production apparatuses of the modern, competitive, many-sided, post-colonial economy.

In 2001, when the ULP arrived in governmental office, the four entities that now make up the integrated SVGCC had a total enrollment of some 600 students. Currently, there are some four times that number of full-time students (2,489) and in excess of 120 part-time students. In 2001, the budgeted contribution to the four entities that now make up the integrated SVGCC was $4.4 million; in 2022, the budgetary allocation for the SVGCC in $14.25 million. Today, the SVGCC receives additional revenues from other sources.

The physical plant of the various divisions of the College has undergone massive improvement and expansion. At the main campus at Villa, which houses the College administration, the Division of Arts, General Studies and Sciences and the Division of Teacher Education, the expansion has been phenomenal. The small building of 2001 is dwarfed by the expansion: a library and learning resource centre; over 80,000 square feet of additional floor space for lecture theatres, class-rooms, language labs, science laboratories, computer labs, students' faculties and eating facilities, meeting areas, and staff room; sports facilities were also further enhanced.

The Education Revolution has been well underway for some 20 years and is being deepened and broadened. Still, much more remains to be done particularly in respect of the enormous educational challenges at the time of COVID-19.

Buildings, Roads, and General Services Authority (BRAGSA)

The Roads, Buildings and General Services Authority Act establishing BRAGSA was passed in Parliament in 2008, but its date of commencement was July 1, 2009. BRAGSA essentially replaced the former buildings and road repairing divisions within the central government operations in the Ministry of Transport and Works.

Since the ULP came into office on March 29, 2001, it was being felt, increasingly, that the relevant divisions in the Ministry of Works were not functioning as speedily and efficiently in respect of the repairs of buildings, roads, and the general delivery of small-scale infrastructure works and services as was demanded by the general public and policy-makers. The structures and systems in the Ministry itself were too bureaucratic, slow and cumbersome. The idea was, and still is, that the Ministry of Transport and Works would reorganise itself to address the large infrastructure projects, and provide overall technical advice and supervision, but BRAGSA would be the activist entity on the ground with a large measure of statutory autonomy but still under the aegis of the Ministry.

Accordingly, the Ministry of Transport and Works was reorganised as follows: Policy, Planning and Administration headed by the Minister and Permanent Secretary, with supportive staff; the Engineering and Project Management Services (Office of the Chief Engineer and Project Management Services) in the 2022 Estimates under this administrative programme are 51 staff members comprising a number of relevant professionals, headed by the Chief Engineer.

BRAGSA, on the other hand, was structured by statute broadly to encompass the following: establishment and incorporation of the Authority; powers and functions of the authority; its relationship to the State and other bodies; directions, requests and approvals by the Minister; Board of Management; appointment of staff; transfer of officers and preservation of pensions; financial provisions and accountability; borrowing power and guarantee of loans; annual business plan and its work plan; accounts and audit; reportage to the House of Assembly; and a number of miscellaneous provisions necessary for its functioning.

As a result, BRAGSA repairs roads, bridges, public buildings; it does road-cleaning; and it constructs or oversees the construction of manageable projects financed by the government. BRAGSA also undertakes, under contract, works for other State enterprises. BRAGSA in the 2022 Estimates receives an annual subvention of $14 million to run its operation in accord with its work plan. Beyond the work plan to which the subvention relates, substantial additional resources are provided to BRAGSA from other sources: for example, the four-times-per-year "road cleaning" programme is financed separately as are established programmes such as repairs to schools, clinics, police stations, hospitals, other government buildings, all funded through the respective line Ministries in the national budget.

During, and subsequent to, the volcanic eruptions of April 2021, BRAGSA did yeoman service in the clean-up programme, financed from other sources. BRAGSA is well-staffed by the requisite professional and technical personnel for the work under its authority. It also sub-contracts out work to ensure speedy and effective completion of tasks. BRAGSA has proven to be an excellent innovation in the good governance arsenal.

National Parks, Rivers and Beaches Authority

This authority was established by the National Parks and Protected Areas Act of 2002. This Act makes provisions for national parks and the establishment of an authority for national parks; it provides for the preservation, protection, management and development of natural, physical and ecological resources, and the historical and cultural heritage of St. Vincent and the Grenadines. This statutory body is structured in the usual manner to reflect the basic principles of good governance, made operational in relation to the Authority's central purposes. This Authority has been assigned to the Ministry of Tourism, Civil Aviation, Sustainable Development, and Culture. For the 2022

Estimates, it has been allocated a subvention of $2.3 million to operate recurrently. Capital resources in relation to particular relevant projects have also been allocated. This Authority does excellent work towards the goal of sustainable development. It works closely with other associated agencies of government, including the Tobago Cays Marine Park Board.

Eight Post-2001 Economic-Type Public Enterprises

Argyle International Airport (AIA) Incorporated; National Properties; SVG Tourism Authority; Invest SVG; National Centre for Technology and Innovation; SVG Bureau of Standards; SVG Postal Corporation; and Agricultural Input Warehouse Limited

The *Argyle International Airport Incorporated* is a wholly-owned State company, established to manage the Argyle International Airport (AIA), which was opened on February 14, 2017. This airport is vital for the economy of St. Vincent and the Grenadines, its diversification, investments in hotels, and the development of tourism. In the 2022 recurrent budget, the AIA has been allocated $6 million; and $5 million on the capital side for rehabilitation of the runway and the terminal building.

The annual reports and accounts of AIA Incorporated are filed, under the companies' law, at CIPO. The public has access to these reports and accounts.

I shall return to the AIA Incorporated in more detail later in the next chapter of this book.

The *SVG Tourism Authority* (SVGTA) was established by statute in 2007 and became operational in April 2008. The SVGTA was formed to manage, direct, regulate, market tourism (inclusive of interfacing with the airlines) in St. Vincent and the Grenadines. Tourism is the largest economic sector currently in St. Vincent and the Grenadines. In the recurrent budget for 2022, $16 million has been allocated to the SVGTA to do its work as laid out in the SVG Tourism Authority Act. The Act provides, among other things, for its annual reports and audited statements of accounts to be presented to Parliament.

The *National Properties Company Limited* is the State-owned property company established by the ULP government. It holds substantial real estate assets. Sales of State-owned lands that were transferred to National Properties, were instrumental in assisting the financing of the construction of the Argyle International Airport. It is the lead entity, currently, in pursuance of the public policy to develop the decommissioned E.T. Joshua airport site. Its annual reports and accounts are filed at CIPO.

Invest SVG is a State-owned company established by the ULP government to drive investment promotion in St. Vincent and the Grenadines. Our country has one of the highest rates of foreign direct investment to GDP in CARICOM. The 2022 Recurrent Estimates have provided $1.5 million for the day-to-day operations of Invest SVG. It is a well-staffed entity and professionally-run. It has a critical role to play in economic development and the quest to build a modern, competitive, many-sided post-colonial economy.

The *National Centre for Technology and Innovation* located within the Ministry of Finance, Economic Planning, and Information Technology is the spur for technology and innovation in the economy.

The Standards Bureau and the Postal Services (Post Office) pre-dated the ULP government, but they have been transformed into autonomous statutory entities respectively as the *SVG Bureau of Standards* and the *SVG Postal Corporation*. The former, the Bureau of Standards, sets and applies standards across a range of economic activities, especially in the manufacturing sector. It is located under the aegis of the Ministry of Agriculture, Forestry, Fisheries, Rural Transformation and Industry. In the recurrent budget for 2022, it has a subvention of $1.3 million. It is a well-staffed, well-equipped, and professional outfit.

The *SVG Postal Corporation* has had to be established to save the delivery of postal services in an age of information technology. The SVG Postal Corporation has diversified its activities to earn more revenue. Still, in the recurrent budget of 2022, it has received a subvention of $0.8 million for its operation. It belongs to both the Caribbean Postal Union and the Universal Postal Union, the subscriptions of which are paid by the central government.

The Agricultural Input Warehouse

The Agricultural Input Warehouse (AIW) Limited is a wholly-owned State corporation registered under the Companies Act of St. Vincent and the Grenadines in May, 2003. Prior to its incorporation it existed as a department or unit of the government; it was originally set up by the former NDP government, but its operations were limited and restricted.

The AIW is the principal importer of agricultural inputs (fertiliser, basic agricultural tools, and other inputs). Under the ULP government it was accorded the monopoly to import sugar into St. Vincent and the Grenadines. The AIW operates to ensure, among other things, that a sufficiency of agricultural inputs at the lowest prices is available on an ongoing basis fECGCor the farmers of St. Vincent and the Grenadines. The AIW makes certain, too that the profits from the importation and wholesaling of sugar, subsidise the cost of the agricultural inputs sold to farmers.

The cheapest fertiliser of all kinds sold in the Eastern Caribbean (outside of Trinidad and Tobago) is at the AIW. Indeed, some farmers from more than one country of the Organisation of Eastern Caribbean States (OECS) get local farmers in St. Vincent and the Grenadines to buy fertiliser for them from AIW, and ship to them. The fertiliser sold at AIW is heavily subsidised.

Since the AIW's incorporation it has secured ownership of its own headquarters in capital city, Kingstown. It has also been handed the management of the State-owned Kingstown Fish Market. The AIW makes a small profit annually. It is a well-run, professional entity.

Maritime Administration:

Given the massive significance of the seascape, the oceans, and shipping to our multi-island nation, the ULP government established, for the first time ever in St. Vincent and the Grenadines, a structured system of Maritime Administration. It is located in the Ministry of National Security, headed by the Prime Minister. The central function of the administrative programme known as Maritime Administration is to provide general supervision, and to regulate matters, relating to maritime affairs.

In the 2022 Recurrent Estimates, $0.6 million is allocated for the annual operating costs of Maritime Administration. This division is headed by a Director and has on its staff of nine, a Surveyor of Ships, a Registrar of Ships and Seafarers, a Senior Inspector of Ships, and associated support staff.

The division of Maritime Administration oversees the application of a bundle of maritime legislation, some pre-2001, but also important reforms that were introduced post-2001. The following legislative measures in the field of maritime law, passed in the post-2001 period, include: Carriage of Goods by Sea Act (2002) repealing the former Act and incorporating the United Nations Convention on the Carriage of Goods by Sea 1978; the Convention on Oil Pollution Damage Act (2002) that repealed the former Act and implemented the 1992 International Convention on Civil Liability for Oil Pollution Damage and the 1992 International Convention on the Establishment of an International Fund for Oil Pollution Damage; the Dumping at Sea Act (2004), a modern piece of environmental legislation; the Management of Ship-Generated Solid Waste Act (2002) providing for the powers and jurisdiction in relation to pollution of the seas from ships and to give effect to the International Convention on the Prevention of Pollution from Ships together with its Protocol of 1978; the Maritime Security Act (2002) giving effect to the Convention for the Suppression of Unlawful Acts against the Safety of Maritime Navigation, 1988, and the Protocols for the Suppression of Unlawful Acts Against the Safety of Fixed Platforms located on the Continental Shelf, 1988, which supplements that Convention; and the Shipping Act (2004), which repeals and replaces the former, out-dated Merchant Shipping Act.

The Shipping Act of 2004 provides for: The registration of ships; the national character and flags of ships; the regulation of proprietary interests in ships and terms of engagement of masters and seafarers; the provision of the prevention of collisions at sea, the safety of navigation and life at sea, the safety of submersibles, the regulation of load lines, the carriage of bulk and dangerous cargoes, unsafe ships, wreck, and salvage; the control of persons on ships, the liability of shipowners and others, and inquiries and investigations into maritime casualties; and to consolidate the law relating to shipping and matters incidental thereto.

The Shipping Act of 2004 is a comprehensive statute consisting of 408 sections. It is supported by substantive regulations, including the Ship and Port Facility Security Regulations of 2004, and the Merchant Shipping (Standards of Training, Certification and Watchkeeping for Seafarers) (No. 2) Regulations of 2005.

When the ULP arrived in office on March 29, 2001, it met several black lists against St. Vincent and the Grenadines, including two immediately impending ones connected to matters maritime, namely: (a) The failure or refusal of the NDP government to incorporate certain international conventions into our law especially the International Convention on Standards of Training, Certification and Watchkeeping, 1978, as amended in 1995 (STCW Convention); and (b) the on-going breach by St. Vincent and the Grenadines of the International Convention for the Conservation of Atlantic Tuna. The late Sir James Mitchell, former Prime Minister of St. Vincent and the Grenadines, drew this latter matter to my attention when he visited me at the Office of the Prime Minister on April 3, 2001, a few days after the 2001 elections that brought the ULP to office. I addressed both of them successfully.

In the case of the first-named, impending black list, my government swiftly amended the pre-existing Shipping Act to satisfy the requisites of halting the black list and then proceeded to put in place a comprehensive, modern Shipping Act. In this effort, my government secured legal assistance from our country's Maritime Commission in Geneva, Switzerland. Our Attorney-General, Judith Jones-Morgan, did magnificent work on this and other maritime legislation; as did the late Sir Vincent Beache who was at the time our Minister of National Security, responsible for shipping. The Shipping Act of 2004 established for the first time the Directorate of Maritime Administration and the Office of Maritime Commission and the Commissioner for Maritime Affairs. The Maritime Administration works very closely with the SVG Police Force, the Coast Guard, the SVG Port Authority, and our regional and international partners on matters maritime.

Annually, Maritime Administration, including our Maritime Commission in Geneva, brings in over $4 million in revenue.

This bundle of laws and administrative networks are critical to the development of a viable Blue Economy. Budget 2022 is replete with initiatives for the Blue Economy.

Strengthening Ten Existing Public Enterprises

VINLEC, CWSA, NIS, BOSVG, HLDC, Arrowroot Industry Association; National Sports Council, Government Printery, SVGPA, and NCF

Each of these State-owned entities has been strengthened immensely under successive ULP administrations, namely: The St. Vincent Electricity Company (VINLEC), the almost exclusive provider of electricity; the Central Water and Sewerage Authority (CWSA), the almost exclusive provider of water and solid waste collection and disposal services; the Housing and Land Development Corporation (HLDC), which was moribund for 17 years up to 2001, has become over the last 21 years the principal implementing agency of the ULP government's Housing Revolution; the Arrowroot Industry Association (AIA), the manager and regulator of our arrowroot industry, overall. The National Sports Council (NSC), the Government Printery, the SVG Port Authority (SVGPA), and the National Cultural Foundation (NCF), National Insurance Services (NIS), and the Bank of St. Vincent and the Grenadines (BOSVG) (majority State-owned), as each name suggests, each covers vital areas of the economic and social life of St. Vincent and the Grenadines.

Each of these has advanced by leaps and bounds. Each is of importance to our modern economy, society, and good governance. VINLEC, CWSA, SVGPA, NIS and BOSVG are, by far, the most significant and largest of this group of enterprises; they are also quite profitable; they are very well-run. They will be discussed more fully later in the next chapter of this book.

Student Loan Company (SLC)

This State-owned company was formed in 2012 to lend money to economically-disadvantaged students who are pursuing tertiary education at home and abroad, mainly in the Caribbean region. Its predecessor, the State-resourced Economically-Disadvantaged Student Loan Committee, was established in 2002. Over the past near-20 years both the Committee and the Company have, in the aggregate, lent in excess of EC $100 million to over 2,000 students who have accessed tertiary level education in areas of approved priorities. The resources for both entities have come from the central government funds and loans from the National Insurance Services (NIS), guaranteed by the government. The SLC has had real property assets — the Learning Resource Centres — transferred to it by the government; these assets are valued at approximately $22 million.

The loans to economically-disadvantaged students have transparent criteria. The borrowers do not require any guarantor; the government is the guarantor. The loans attract interest during the borrowers' student years; the payment of the principal sum commences one year after the student-borrower graduates from university or college. The delinquency rate on the loans is about roughly 20 percent. The SLC operates on the basis of a revolving fund and is capitalised by the government from time-to-time.

Officials from the State administration and the NIS constitute the members of the board of the SLC. The board selects the membership of the screening committee for the loans that are channelled through one or other commercial bank or credit union for which a guarantee is given under the signature of the Minister of Finance. The officials from the Ministries of Education, Finance, the Chief Personnel Office, and the NIS are the drivers of the SLC.

The SLC, inclusive of its predecessor Committee, has been hailed by a former Vice Chancellor of the University of the West Indies as a "best practice". Without these loans, students from economically-disadvantaged families with matriculation qualifications for university/ college but whose grades are insufficiently competitive to be awarded national scholarships, national exhibitions, special awards, other scholarships, bursaries and tuition grants, are unlikely to be able to pursue tertiary education. Of course, many students who receive loans are also eligible for discretionary grants or financial support of one kind or the other.

Undoubtedly, loans for the SLC are one mechanism, among many others, to push St. Vincent and the Grenadines towards the reachable target of one college/university graduate on an average, per household by 2030. Education, training, science and technology are vital in their applications to the building of a modern, competitive, many-sided, post-colonial economy. Such an economy is built, centrally, with unlimited supplies of educated and skilled labour.

In the Capital Estimates for 2022, the SLC is slated to receive $0.5 million for its further capitalisation.

Farmers' Support Company (FSC)

This State-owned company was established in 2014 to provide soft-loans to the farmers and fisherfolk up to a maximum of EC$ 20,000, per loan, at an interest rate of 2 percent. There is a bundle of criteria to access this "revolving fund" in the FSC. Since 2014, the FSC has lent some $15 million to over 3,000 farmers and fisherfolk, but mainly farmers. In the capital budget for 2022, there is an allocation of $1.5 million to capitalise further the FSC. The delinquency rate hovers around 40 percent on the loans. Storms, landslides, droughts, and the volcanic eruptions have undermined farmers' efforts to repay their borrowings.

The FSC is one of a raft of measures initiated by the government to assist farmers and fisherfolk. Competitive production, diversification, and equity are guiding principles and goals of the FSC.

Medicinal Cannabis Authority (MCA)

This State-owned authority was set up in 2018 to drive the establishment of a medicinal cannabis industry, mainly for export but also for local consumption. The ULP government has reformed the laws on cannabis in accord with the relevant international conventions and the local circumstances. The MCA is a highly professional outfit, grounded in science, export orientation, and traditional cultivators' participation. The medicinal cannabis industry in St. Vincent and the Grenadines has attracted, thus far, investment of over EC $25 million, mainly from foreign entities, to *acquire* relevant licences; a number of traditional cultivators' licences have been issued, too, to individuals and local co-operatives. Significantly, more investment has been made by companies in growing medicinal cannabis, setting up laboratories, and processing facilities. There is a state-of-the-art research and regulatory laboratory owned jointly by a foreign investor and MCA. Over 200 persons are currently employed in the medicinal cannabis industry in St. Vincent and the Grenadines.

Recently, the Caribbean IMPACT Justice Project, a 13-country justice-sector reform project funded by the Government of Canada and implemented by the University of the West Indies, evaluated the state of cannabis legislation across the Caribbean and stated thus:

> SVG is the only country in the region that has implemented medicinal cannabis legislation that is fully compliant with the rules and obligations of the International Drug Treaties, and the legislation has been approved by the International Narcotics Control Board (INCB). It will therefore be the first country to be able to conduct legal commercial international exports of medicinal cannabis." (Caribbean Impact Justice, vol. 8, Nos 1-3, January 2021-October 2021, p. 11).

In early January 2022, a German importer received a licence to import into that country 150 pounds of medicinal cannabis, and the government of St. Vincent and the Grenadines issued correspondingly an export licence. By mid-January 2022, the export of the medicinal cannabis left Argyle International Airport for Germany; it was the first such export. It is expected to be the first of many. Meanwhile, medicinal products from cannabis are being produced in St. Vincent and the Grenadines. And locally, trained medical practitioners are dispensing medicinal cannabis for a range of legally-scheduled ailments or medical conditions. In May 2022, an enterprising entrepreneur engaged in hotel, restaurant, and tourism business generally, opened the first medicinal cannabis café to the public, established under the reformed medicinal cannabis laws of St. Vincent and the Grenadines.

In the 2022 capital budget, the sum of $2 million has been allocated to the MCA for its further capitalisation.

Zero Hunger Trust Fund

The Zero Hunger Trust Fund (ZHTF) was established by an Act of Parliament in 2016. Its central mandate is to assist in the achievement of Sustainable Development Goal 2 (SDG2) "to end hunger, achieve food security, and improve nutrition and promote agriculture."

Despite successful efforts by the ULP government to reduce poverty generally since 2001, and to roll back indigence significantly from 26 percent of the population in 1997 to under 3 percent in 2009, there were, and are, intractable pockets of indigence, hunger, and undernourishment. As a consequence, the ULP government decided to set up a specific agency, with innovative ideas, to work in tandem with other policies and entities to put certain initiatives in place to end hunger, hopefully by 2030.

The ZHTF is managed by a highly qualified Board, appointed by the Cabinet through the Minister of Finance and Economic Development, and operates out of that Ministry. It focusses especially on families especially the children, women, the youths, and the elderly with a mixture of programmes that run the gamut of social safety net supports, practical hands-on training in traditional and modern technologies, and some production supports. It has built and equipped kitchens and classrooms in primary schools in areas where the Census data show poverty or indigence to be more elevated than elsewhere.

The ZHTF is funded by a 2 percent levy on international telephone calls made on cellphones, and by donations from within and without St. Vincent and the Grenadines. The major external donor for several years has been "Dubai Cares", an entity located in Dubai in the United Arab Emirates.

I was actively involved in the drafting of the Bill for an Act to establish the ZHTF along with the Attorney General's Chambers and Laura Anthony-Browne, the immediate past Director of Economic Planning. Immediately after the ZHTF's formation, Ms. Anthony-Browne opened the ZHTF's account at the Bank of St. Vincent and the Grenadines with $10 of her own money. The first deposit was a cheque from me personally, my entire Prime Minister's salary for that month; in the process I pledged to deposit a further one month's salary for each year of the succeeding four years into the ZHTF account. I kept my pledge. In this way, this Fund was born!

Since its formation, ZHTF has positively affected the lives of hundreds of families and has been effective in making progress towards SDG2.

ZHTF is very well-managed and wedded to the principle of transparency, accountability, and effectiveness. It reports to Parliament through the relevant Minister.

Unfortunately, in the parliamentary debate on the Bill for an Act to establish the ZHTF, the opposition NDP opposed it on the grounds that it was unnecessary because there were enough anti-poverty and anti-hunger measures and entities and that the funding mechanism will impose further taxation on people! The work of the ZHTF has shown the NDP's first contention to be unfounded; as regards the second, most people do not notice the 2 percent levy on international calls on cellphones, and if they do, they support it fully.

At the same time, the Minister of Agriculture, Saboto Caesar, piloted through Parliament a motion on "The Parliamentary Front Against Hunger", requested by the Food and Agricultural Organisation (FAO). On this occasion the opposition was in support. Interestingly, though, the NDP has never taken up the legislative offer to nominate a person to be appointed to the Board of the ZHTF.

Contingencies Fund

The Constitution of St. Vincent and the Grenadines (Section 72) makes provision for the establishment of a Contingencies Fund. Between 1979 and 2018, no government since independence had set up such a Fund. In 2018, the ULP government did so. It is funded by a one percentage point of the domestic Value Added Tax (VAT), and a Disaster Levy of US $3 per room per night in a hotel; in May 2020, the Disaster Levy was suspended for the duration of the COVID pandemic. Statue law and appropriate regulations provide the legal framework for the operation of the Contingencies Fund. The Fund has been critical in helping to provide monies for the relief and restoration from the pandemic and the volcanic eruptions. As of January 10, 2022, the Contingencies Fund had EC $30 million in it. On the basis of the one percentage point of the domestic VAT the fund increases annually by some $12 million. Good governance is at work again despite the opposition to it by the NDP.

Petro Caribe (SVG) Limited

The Petro Caribe initiative commenced in St. Vincent and the Grenadines in 2005. This initiative was the brainchild of two Caribbean and Latin American political titans, President Hugo Chavez of the Bolivarian Republic of Venezuela and President Fidel Castro of Cuba, both now deceased. The unilateral, illegal sanctions of the U.S. government, first under President Obama and subsequently in more draconian terms under Donald Trump, against Venezuela effectively brought this excellent initiative to a halt due to the practical constraints imposed on shipping and cross-border payments' systems, whether or not the payments were made in American dollars or other foreign currency. The weaponising of the international banking system by the American government was a huge blow to Petro Caribe.

In May 2022, in a meeting with President Nicolas Maduro of the Bolivarian Republic of Venezuela, I was informed that plans are afoot to re-start the Petro Caribe initiative through fresh modalities that are unlikely to run afoul, in practical terms, of the illegal sanctions of the U.S. government.

The Petro Caribe initiative of Chavez was based on a simple idea, but with profound implications in terms of internationalist/regional solidarity, generosity, and impact on the recipient/beneficiary countries of the Caribbean: Venezuela provided energy products (diesel, gasoline, and cooking gas — Liquified Petroleum Gas) on very favourable terms to Caribbean countries that signed on to the initiative, St. Vincent and the Grenadines among them. Between 40 to 50 percent of the cost of energy products was paid for within 90 days of delivery; the remainder of the price was considered as a long-term loan over a 25-year period at 1 percent interest per year. From 2005 until the initiative was effectively closed down by the U.S. government, St. Vincent and the Grenadines obtained long-term financing support of in excess of EC $230 million. In 2017, Venezuela accorded St. Vincent and the Grenadines 50 percent debt relief on the Petro Caribe debt; in May 2022, it received further relief, in full, on the remainder of the debt: These monies were utilised in programmes and projects relating, among other things, to poverty reduction, productive enterprises, education and health, security, and physical infrastructure, including airport construction.

Between 2005 and 2007, VINLEC (the State-owned electricity company) functioned as the agent of the government of St. Vincent and the Grenadines on the Petro Caribe initiative simply because we imported only diesel from Venezuela, for the Lowmans Bay Power Plant. Between 2007 and 2009, the Ministry of External Trade was the relevant agency of the government; Liquified Petroleum Gas (LPG) was also then imported. From October 2009 up to the current time, the wholly-owned State corporation, Petro Caribe (SVG) Limited, has been the operational agency of the government of St. Vincent and the Grenadines in this matter; this company was actually formed in 2005.

Petro Caribe (SVG) Limited also holds 45 percent of the shares of a company, incorporated in St. Vincent and the Grenadines also in 2005, known as PDV (SVG) Limited. Petróleos de Venezuela, S.A. (PDVSA), the State-owned petroleum company of Venezuela, is the majority shareholder with 55 percent of the shares. PDV (SVG) Limited owns the Hugo Chavez Storage Facility at Lowmans (Leeward), which stores diesel, gasoline, aviation fuel, and LPG. The government of St. Vincent and the Grenadines provided the lands upon which the facility was built; the Venezuela government constructed it at its own expense — estimated at US $30 million. This facility increased the storage capacity of fuel in St. Vincent and the Grenadines from two weeks' supply to three months' supply, thus enhancing energy security on the ground.

In 2016, the Petro Caribe (Special Purpose Fund) Act was passed by Parliament. The Petro Caribe (SVG) Limited was embedded in the Act for the establishment of the Special Purpose Fund so as to facilitate better the management and expenditure of the monies from the Petro Caribe initiative; it also anticipated the debt relief that was already under discussion at the highest levels of the respective governments. The Director of Audit is authorised under the Act to audit the accounts of the Special Purpose Fund.

The reports and audited accounts of Petro Caribe (SVG) Limited are submitted as required under the company laws to CIPO. The company is well-managed under the leadership of an experienced public servant, Fay Fergusson.

From the very beginning, the long-term financing debt of the Petro Caribe initiative in St. Vincent and the Grenadines has always been entered into the debt profile of the government of St. Vincent and the Grenadines and published in the annual Estimates that are approved by Parliament; the expenditure was accounted for in the Estimates. The International Monetary Fund (IMF) routinely commended our government for this debt's inclusion in the overall public debt, contrary to the practice in some other Caribbean countries.

St. Vincent and the Grenadines looks forward to a full resumption of the Petro Caribe initiative. This small, vulnerable country has suffered collateral damage as a consequence of the illegal, unilateral sanctions by the U.S. government against Venezuela. And the USA are our friends!

Central Supplies Tenders Board/Central Procurement Board

The Central Supplies Tenders Board (CSTB) established under the Purchasers and Tenders Procedure Orders of 1967 was replaced by the Central Procurement Board (CPB), buttressed by the Central Procurement Office, pursuant to the Public Procurement Act, number 34 of 2018. The CSTB was and its successor CPB is, respectively, the independent procurement authority providing the oversight and regulatory functions over public procurement for the central government of St. Vincent and the Grenadines. The CSTB was and the CPB is the body authorising, through competitive bidding, all purchases of goods and services, and approving contractors for works carried out in excess of EC $20,000. Additionally, the CSTB was and the CPB is engaged in issuing guidelines to govern the general conduct of procurement activities undertaken by all ministries and departments of the central government.

The CTSB, under the chairmanship of the Director General of Finance and Planning, the top public servant relating to financial and economic planning matters in the government, served the country quite well. However, its legislative framework required modernisation and strengthening in accord with international best practices of institutions such as the Caribbean Development Bank (CDB), the World Bank (WB), and the European Investment Bank (EIB). Accordingly, in 2018, Parliament passed a modern Public Procurement Act that meets the highest international standards, inclusive of the requisites of bolstering the procurement authority's independence, fairness, openness, transparency, and effectiveness.

Indeed, for a decade or so prior to the passage of the Act, the ULP government took steps to shed more light on the CSTB's decisions by causing, on a quarterly and yearly basis, to publish core relevant facts of each contract awarded for the purchase of goods and services by, and the execution of public works on behalf of, the central government. Annually, too, the CTSB published a full report of its activities. These publications are required now, as a matter of law, to be done by the CPB. The publication is done through the three newspapers in St. Vincent and the Grenadines, in the official Gazette, and online. These reports detail the names of the successful competitive bidders, the nature of the contracts awarded, the dates for the commencement and terminal point of each of the contracts, and the value, in monetary terms, of each contract.

The functions of the CSTB were and of the CPB are vital to the country's good governance, the securing of value-for-money, and the building of a modern post-colonial economy.

The Public Procurement Act is a very comprehensive piece of legislation consisting of 75 sections and 5 schedules detailing every aspect of modern procurement in line with the highest international standards. The membership of the CPB comprises eight persons: The Director General of Finance and Planning as Chairman; two permanent secretaries (relating to the ministries of trade, and transport and works), the Accountant General, and three members from the private sector appointed by the Minister of Finance and Planning (done through the Cabinet).

The work of the CTSB was and of the CPB is routinely approved and commended by major regional and international lending agencies such as the CDB and WB. The ULP government has been placing great store on the maintenance and promotion of the CSTB/CPB's strict compliance with the law and regulations to ensure, among other things, the unquestioned integrity of the procurement authority's structure and functioning.

National Accreditation Board/Sector Skills Development Agency

The National Accreditation Board (NAB) was established pursuant to the Further and Higher Education (Accreditation) Act which was passed in Parliament in 2006, but which came into operation on January 29, 2008.

This Act provided for the setting up of the NAB, the vesting in that Board the power to accredit institutions and programmes of study in St. Vincent and the Grenadines and elsewhere, the detailing of the process and mechanism of accrediting such institutions and programmes of study, and the enactment of other related matters.

The NAB's remit concerns the accreditation of the institutions and programmes of study in post-secondary education, which leads to the award of sub-baccalaureate qualification, baccalaureate degree, and post-graduate degree. Thus, for example, the St. Vincent and the Grenadines Community College and the four medical schools in St. Vincent and the Grenadines come under the aegis of the NAB.

This institutional development was considered by the government to be necessary and desirable in light of the huge expansion of post-secondary and tertiary education for Vincentians in St. Vincent and the Grenadines and abroad. The NAB is vital for quality assurance in post-secondary and tertiary education. It is an important institution in the country's Education Revolution.

The Sector Skills Development Agency (SSDA) was established pursuant to the Sector Skills Development Agency Act of 2010. This agency is located juridically in the Ministry of Education. Its focus is on the preparation, implementation, and oversight of the national policy for technical and vocational education and training. The enactment of the SSDA highlights the emphasis the government places on technical and vocational education and training in the roll-out of the post-colonial economy.

National Telecommunications Regulatory Commission (NTRC)

The NTRC was legally established under the Telecommunications Act that was passed in the House of Assembly, with full bipartisan support, on October 19, 2000; the Act commenced operation on April 1, 2001. This Act gave effect to the Treaty establishing the Eastern Caribbean Telecommunications Authority (ECTEL) to provide for the regulation of telecommunications; to establish the NTRC; and to provide for related or incidental matters. In the process, the Act repealed the Radio and Communication Services Act of 1988 and the Wireless Telegraphy Act, 1949, of the United Kingdom in its application to St.

Vincent and the Grenadines. The contracting parties to the Treaty are five member-states of the Organisation of Eastern Caribbean States (OECS), namely, Dominica, Grenada, St. Kitts and Nevis, St. Lucia, and St. Vincent and the Grenadines; the Treaty was signed on May 4, 2000, and forms part of the Act as the Second Schedule.

It is instructive to quote the Preamble to the ECTEL Treaty to grasp the significance of an altered, and altering, landscape of telecommunications, and fresh policy initiatives accordingly, in our sub-region, including St. Vincent and the Grenadines:

The Governments of the Contracting States,

Desirous of creating a competitive environment for telecommunications in the Contracting States:

Conscious that the benefits of universal telecommunications services should be realised by the people of the Contracting States:

Determined to provide affordable, modern, efficient, competitive, and universally available telecommunications services to the people of the Contracting States:

Convinced that a liberalised and competitive telecommunications sector is essential for the future economic and social development of the Contracting States:

Recognising that a harmonised and co-ordinated approach by the Contracting States is required to achieve a liberalised and competitive telecommunications sector,

agreed to the provisions of the Treaty.

In each of the five OECS countries there is a NTRC that functions within the framework of the policies developed by ECTEL and in accord with ECTEL's regulatory advice. Each of the respective NTRCs then makes the regulatory decisions at the national level. ECTEL is headquartered in St. Lucia.

The requisite of creating a regional regulatory system for telecommunications in the OECS emerged from a condition in which a monopoly provider, Cable and Wireless Limited, delivered poor and limited telecommunications services at high prices. Clearly, in a modernising society and economy, this situation had become an untenable obstacle to meaningful economic diversification, especially in financial services and information technology, an optimal flow of information, administrative efficiency, improved good governance, and socio-economic development generally. A regional regulatory system in telecommunications also afforded benefits of economies of scale.

The twin issue of the liberalisation of telecommunications and a regional regulatory system arose, tentatively, at first in an OECS Economic Diversification Project funded largely by the World Bank and the Caribbean Development Bank. One dimension of it swiftly morphed in 1998 into the OECS Telecommunications Project funded by the World Bank and executed through the OECS Secretariat in St. Lucia. The quest for liberalisation in telecommunications, however, was highly dependent on ending the lengthy, exclusive licensing agreements Cable and Wireless had secured in each of the five OECS member-states, including St. Vincent and the Grenadines; there were legal and financial implications at stake. And the monopoly provider was neither willing nor eager to go gently into the proverbial night. There were difficult negotiating months immediately ahead in which the ULP government was intricately and deeply engaged.

In April 2001, the NTRC in St. Vincent and the Grenadines got off the ground when the newly-elected ULP government appointed the first Commissioner of the NTRC. On November 3, 2001, the NTRC was installed in its own rented office space. Its operation began with five permanent members of staff headed by its first, and still Director, Apollo Knights.

Over the next few months and years, thereafter, Statutory Rules and Orders were issued and published to fortify the provisions of the Telecommunications Act, touching and concerning relevant matters such as Confidentiality in Networks and Services, Terminal Equipment and Public Network, Licence Classification, Private Network Licensing, Retail Tariff, Licensing and Authorisation, Dispute Resolution, Fees, Spectrum Management, Universal Service Fund, Numbering, and Interconnection.

Under the Telecommunications Act there are detailed provisions regarding the composition and functioning of the NTRC. The NTRC consists of not less than three and not more than five Commissioners, one of whom is designated as Chairman. Section 10 of the Act specifies 17 functions of the NTRC; in the exercise of its functions, the NTRC is obliged to consult and liaise with ECTEL.

The NTRC does not receive an annual subvention from the central government, and never did so except in its first year of operation. Its funding depends largely on the fees collected for spectrum usage. The NTRC also collects fees such as for applications, numbering, licenses, and the Universal Service Fund. The Licence Fees are transferred to the central government on a quarterly basis while the other fees go towards the NTRC's annual budget. The spectrum fees collected by each NTRC goes into a common regional fund managed by ECTEL. Each year, a budget is approved by the Council of Ministers of ECTEL; an allocation of funds is thus made to each NTRC and the ECTEL Directorate. Any surplus funds are returned to the member-states. The NTRC in St. Vincent and the Grenadines has never had to enter an overdraft arrangement with its bankers.

As at December 31, 2021, the NTRC of St. Vincent and the Grenadines had assets of EC $5.2 million. It now has a staff of 15 persons.

Over its 20 years of operation, NTRC has served the people of St. Vincent and the Grenadines very well, in accordance with its legislative and policy mandates. Immediately following its establishment, it swiftly put in place its requisite systems, procedures and personnel to function as a high quality, professional entity. It has ensured, too, that the critical regulations were authoritatively issued and gazetted. It has granted appropriate licences. The NTRC in St. Vincent and the Grenadines was the first in the ECTEL region to collect spectrum fees from service providers and thus became self-sufficient by its second year of operation. It was also the first to set up its Universal Service Fund (USF) in 2008 and collected USF fees, accordingly.

The NTRC has had as a central focus "connectivity for all", and the most efficacious delivery of international communications technology (ICT) to the people of St. Vincent and the Grenadines. In the execution of its mandate, the NTRC has been collaborating with all the relevant stakeholders. Some major highlights of its initiatives have been:

Installed Wi-Fi access in all schools (first in the OECS).

Installed Wi-Fi access in all Police stations.

Installed Wi-Fi access in all Hospitals and clinics.

Installed a Global Maritime Distress Safety System (GMDSS) network to provide digital emergency communication in our seascape. (First in the OECS). Network coverage will be expanded in 2022.

Installed Wi-Fi access at all community centers and LRCs.

Installed Wi-Fi access at a number of tourism and public sites.

Executed a program to provide Broadband internet to low-income households at $10 EC per month.

Developed and fully funded an Associate Degree program in Cyber Security at the SVGCC.

Developed a program that offers full funding for our youth to undertake short term certified online courses in ICT areas.

Developed the annual MyAPP summer program to inspire our youth in the age group 13-18 years to get into ICTs and Robotics.

Developed the annual icode784 mobile app competition to inspire our secondary students and young entrepreneurs to get into software development.

Worked closely with the central government and the World Bank in getting the subsea fibre project executed allowing residents and businesses in the Grenadines to have similar broadband experiences as those on the mainland St. Vincent.

Donates approximately 150 computers to our schools on an annual basis.

Offers VHF maritime radios at 50% subsidy to our fisherfolk.

Established a program in collaboration with a local IT business in 2021 offering laptops on credit purchase to customers, inclusive of a built-in cap on the mark up and interest rate, thus making the laptops affordable for households.

The NTRC is seeking to move into its own building within the next 12 months as it has outgrown its current accommodation. The NTRC is alive to the extant and prospective challenges and possibilities in the telecommunications space and sector. It continues to work with ECTEL, the government of St. Vincent and the Grenadines, regional and global partners, including the telecommunications' providers for optimal delivery of services.

Judiciary, Police, Coast Guard, Prisons, Border Security

The Judiciary, the Police, the Coast Guard, the Prisons, and Border Security are all part and parcel of the delivery of justice, law, order, and security. The total recurrent cost of these institutions is hefty. A summary from the recurrent budget for 2022 is as follows:

Eastern Caribbean Supreme Court	$ 2.0 m
Registry and High Court	$ 5.3 m
Magistracy	$ 1.5 m
Family Court	$ 1.1 m
Office of the DPP	$ 2.02 m
Commerce and Intellectual Property Office (CIPO)	$ 0.8 m
National Security (Police, Coastguard, Prisons, Border Security, etc.)	$ 70.4 m
Legal Affairs	$ 3.6 m
Regional Security System	$ 2.0 m
CARICOM Implementation Agency for Crime and Security	$ 0.278 m
Other Regional and International Security Organisations	$ 1.341m
Total	$ 90.339 m

This sum of $90.34 million amounts to 9.7 percent of the total recurrent budget for 2022. The allocation on the capital side for these core security services is approximately $7.5 million.

The judiciary in St. Vincent and the Grenadines is independent, impartial, easily accessible, and of a high quality. There are challenges with delays and back-logs of cases, both civil and criminal. These are being addressed, on-going, by the responsible authorities. Of especial concern are persons who are on remand in prison awaiting trial for longer periods than desirable. I have formally written the Judiciary, the Police, the Office of the DPP, and the Attorney-General on this matter for amelioration and resolution; and I have repeatedly discussed this issue with all the relevant office-holders and authorities.

It is to be noted that St. Vincent and the Grenadines receives high grades from reputable international organisations and governments for its quality delivery of justice and the protection of civil, political, and economic rights. Always, however, we must improve our work constantly in this area, and be externally vigilant!

The Royal St. Vincent and the Grenadines Police Force has expanded in size, quality, physical facilities and equipment, as have the Fire Services, the Coastguard, the Prisons, and Border Security (Passport and Immigration Services). All these services in 2001 had a complement of 880 personnel; in 2022, the number has jumped by 604 to 1,484. The breakdown is as follows:

Categories	2001	2022
Police	(Inclusive of Passport and Immigration 665	(Excluding Passport and Immigration) 1,034
Fire Services	57	109
Coastguard	65	119
Prisons	93	139
Passport and Immigration	-	83
Total	880	1,484

The budgeted recurrent expenditure for these services in 2001 was $23.09 million; in 2022, the comparable sum is $60.84 million or an increase of 163.5 percent, a whopping rise even after a 40 percent discount for accumulated inflation. It is to be noted that the country's population has not increased sizeably since then: In the 2001 Census the population was 109,022; by the 2012 Census the population edged up to 109,991 or an increase of only 969 persons, absolutely! A similar rise between 2012 and 2022 would put the population at no more than an estimated 111,000.

Additionally, the private sector has, in recent years, been providing security services for private businesses through a number of security-related firms. These security firms are being regulated under the Private Investigations and Security Guards Act of 2004.

Since 2001, the ULP government has built modern Police Stations at Georgetown, Biabou, Mesopotamia, Questelles, and Canouan, and improved the other 21, in some cases extensively. Still, ongoing repairs are required and monies ($0.5 million) are allocated in the capital budget for this purpose in 2022; this is an ongoing programme, annually. The Police Force has also become better equipped, better trained, and far better structured than hitherto.

Similarly, the physical facilities of the Prisons have been improved immensely. A modern Correctional Facility was built at Belle Isle for over EC $20 million; this currently houses over 250 of the 380 prisoners in the system. A modern female prison at Belle Isle is nearing completion. The remainder of the prisoners are at the late-nineteenth century Kingstown Prison; twelve of these are females in the female wing of the Prison at Kingstown. Renovations and repairs have been done at Kingstown and $169,000 has been earmarked in Budget 2022 for a continuation of these repairs. A further $100,000 is in the 2022 Budget to complete the female prison block at Belle Isle and a trade/industrial workshop.

Prison reform has been instituted and Prison Officers are far better trained than hitherto. Still, much more work needs to be done to modernise and improve further the prison facilities, particularly at Kingstown.

The St. Vincent and the Grenadines Coastguard is far better resourced, equipped, and trained than ever. In the last three years, the Coastguard has acquired, among other assets, an Offshore Patrol Vessel (named "Captain Hugh Mulzac" at a cost of almost EC $20 million and a Medical Vessel (named "Balliceaux") at a cost of $5 million. The "Captain Hugh Mulzac" is the only such type of vessel in the countries of the Organisation of Eastern Caribbean States (OECS); it was built by Damen Shipyard of Holland and has the capacity to patrol extensively, and for prolonged periods without returning to base, in our country's exclusive economic zone (200 miles) particularly on our country's western seascape. The Medivac Vessel is vital for medical evacuations from the Grenadines and on the northeast and northwest of St. Vincent and the Grenadines. In the recent evacuations consequent upon the volcanic eruptions in April 2021, the work of the Coastguard was extensive and even heroic. The Coastguard also mans a vital radar network system around St. Vincent.

In the 2022 Capital Estimates, there is an allocation of $0.4 million to complete renovations at its Calliaqua Base. There is a further $0.30 million in the capital budget to improve the access road to the Canouan Sub-Base built under the ULP government with resources from the government of the United States of America to facilitate marine patrols in the Southern Grenadines.

Similarly, the Fire Services located within the Police Force have developed markedly over the last 21 years. The Fire Services are far better equipped and the officers are far better trained. There is an excellent base for the Fire Services at the Argyle International Airport. The Central Water and Sewerage Authority is working assiduously to extend and improve the system of fire hydrants in the capital city and other main population centres across St. Vincent and the Grenadines.

The discussion on border security was sketched in our coverage earlier on the work of the Passport and Immigration Department.

The security forces of St. Vincent and the Grenadines are linked inextricably with the Regional Security System, the CARICOM Implementation Agency on Crime and Security, INTERPOL, and numerous intelligence and security agencies internationally. St. Vincent and the Grenadines is a safe and secure country; still, we can never be complacent given the activism of national, regional, and global criminal networks.

Parliamentary Democracy and an Alive Constitutionalism

Upon its election to government in March 2001, the Unity Labour Party (ULP) resolved, in its quest to advance, strengthen, and consolidate "good governance" to do the following, among other things: (a) Uphold and defend optimally, in every material particular, the liberal democratic Constitution of St. Vincent and the Grenadines; and (b) Reform, root-and-branch this very Constitution in order to improve, dramatically, its liberal, democratic, and national character so as to ensure the best governance possible and practicable in our circumstances. Our government has succeeded on the first limb, but failed on the second, even though it tried mightily.

Central to upholding and defending the Constitution and an alive Constitutionalism, in practice, has been its uplifting of the work of Parliament and parliamentary democracy. In order to grasp the extent of our progress in this regard, a brief review of parliamentary maladies as at March 2001 is necessary and desirable.

First, under the New Democratic Party (NDP) government (July 1984–March 2001), the unicameral legislature, called the House of Assembly, consisting of a majority of elected representatives and a minority of appointed Senators, met infrequently. Indeed, in one year, 1992, when the NDP had all the seats in the House (on account of the results in the 1989 elections), it did not meet at all for four months between early August and early December; the Governor-General upon the advice of the Prime Minister James Mitchell, prorogued Parliament in early August 1992; its resumption did not occur until the date for the presentation of the annual Estimates of Revenue and Expenditure, and Appropriation Bill in December 1992.

Secondly, neither the Parliament nor the citizenry knew when the House of Assembly would next meet. At the end of every meeting, the House was never adjourned to a particular date, but to the indefinite "sine die".

Thirdly, the vital parliamentary mechanism of "Question Time", through which the Opposition may hold the Government to account at each sitting of the House with up to seven questions (three for oral answers and four for written answers) for each non-Cabinet member, was accorded scant regard by the former NDP ministers of government. The questions (prior to March 2001) were never read out, only the "question number" on the Order Paper of the House, available only to Members of the House. Thus, no "stranger" in the gallery listening was able, properly, to follow any answer, having not heard the question. Further the NDP ministers tended to answer the questions in a peremptory manner, more intent on obfuscation than elucidation. Even the Prime Minister, James Mitchell, once memorably stated in the House that the government was obliged to answer the questions, but not necessarily fully or truthfully!

Fourthly, save and except for the week during the debate on the Estimates and the Appropriation Bill, broadcasts of the proceedings of the House were not permitted either by radio or television. So, the general public was unable to follow the proceedings of the House save for the small number who were able to be accommodated in the gallery, if they were so inclined to attend. Indeed, so undemocratic and farcical was this practice under the NDP, on one occasion in 1999 the Speaker of the House, Nolwyn Mc Dowall, whom I had defeated in the general elections in 1998 in the constituency of North Central Windward, threatened to use the House's power of arrest in relation to the late radio journalist/activist Glen Jackson, for his temerity in surreptitiously taping the proceedings and then broadcasting excerpts later. Even at "budget time", in the debate on the Appropriation Bill, the Leader of the Opposition's speech would be cut short on radio and television if it exceeded the time the Prime Minister/Minister of Finance took to deliver his budget address the evening before. According to the Rules of the House, the principal Opposition spokesperson had four hours allotted within which to deliver the response to the Finance Minister's budget speech; so, if the Minister took two hours for his address that was all the time accorded on radio and television for the Opposition spokesperson!

Fifthly, the NDP government routinely broke the Constitution's requirement in respect of the presentation of the Estimates and Appropriation Bill. Indeed, every government did so since independence in 1979, a carry-over from pre-independence practice. This breach of constitutional law short-changed the public and the Parliament from receiving a thorough-going analysis of the annual budgetary exercise.

Under Section 70(2) of the Constitution of St. Vincent and the Grenadines, it is stated, thus:

"When the estimates of expenditure (other than expenditure charged upon the Consolidated Fund by this Constitution or by any law enacted by Parliament) have been approved in the House, a bill, known as an appropriation bill, shall be introduced in the House providing for the issue from the Consolidated Fund of the sums necessary to meet that expenditure and the appropriation of those sums, under separate votes for the several services required, to the purposes specified therein."

The plain meaning of this constitutional provision was for the Estimates to be presented first to the House of Assembly and passed *prior* to the introduction of an Appropriation Bill. What the NDP government did for the first 11 years of its nearly 17 years in office was to circulate the Estimates and the printed copy of the Finance Minister's budget address on the Appropriation Bill *after* the address was delivered. So, both the Estimates and the Appropriation Bill were introduced to the House at the same time.

When the ULP first entered the House after the general elections of 1994, we insisted that the constitutional provision be scrupulously followed. It is amazing that during the NDP's governance, prior to the ULP's presence in the House, the government did not even bother to hold, on more than one occasion prior to the presentation of the Estimates and the Appropriation Bill, a meeting of the Finance Committee (a Standing Committee of the Whole House) to approve these Estimates and the Bill, and to lay the minutes of that Committee's meeting in the House before the presentation of the Estimates, as required by the Standing Orders of the House. In short, the NDP government took unacceptable and unconstitutional short-cuts in the presentation and debate on the most important annual exercise of the parliamentary calendar — the raising of revenues and their expenditure! This was not a matter of the NDP applying or interpreting the rules in a manner to its political advantage, it was an egregious breach of constitutional and parliamentary order!

Sixthly, the NDP government's disregard of the House of Assembly was also evident in its woeful neglect of the Parliament Building. It was drab, not maintained, and was unbearably hot — no air conditioning. It was as though the Executive was interested in having its efforts quickly rubber-stamped, with as little debate as possible. As a work environment, it was quite uncomfortable; still, in my seven years in Opposition (February 1994 to March 2001) my colleagues and I were determined to do our duty to the people of St. Vincent and the Grenadines, however uncomfortable the physical surroundings.

Upon the ULP's election to government, we swiftly altered these maladies the NDP government had inflicted upon the Parliament.

First, we spruced up the building and air-conditioned it; we have continued to maintain it even as it is falling apart on account of its age and the historic failure, hitherto, to maintain the facility properly. Indeed, when in 2020 I introduced a Bill in the House to approve a US $20 million (EC $54 million) soft-loan from the Export-Import Bank of Taiwan to renovate the existing Parliament building and build a separate modern Parliament *and* to construct a Supreme Court Complex, both at Richmond Hill, the opposition NDP vehemently opposed the Bill. Opportunistically, and demagogically, the NDP insisted that, at the time of COVID, the money should be spent on displaced workers. The fact was that the displaced workers and others were already being accorded an extended safety net beyond the provisions allocated similarly anywhere else in the Caribbean. Moreover, the loan I had negotiated in August 2019 and signed *prior* to the pandemic was specifically for the Parliament building and the Court Complex. Thus, the loan could not have been drawn down to be applied elsewhere; repeatedly this was explained but the NDP continued with its demagogic mantra right up to, and through, the campaign for the general elections of November 5, 2020, which it lost.

The physical condition of the Parliament building has been deteriorating so quickly that in late 2021, the government gave approval to the Speaker and the Clerk of the House to relocate the Offices of Speaker and the Clerk, and the support staff, to rental accommodation elsewhere outside the city limits, even as we continued to patch up the existing building. In the meantime, a temporary Parliament building is being constructed at Calliaqua; upon its completion, the Parliament will move there and the existing building that also houses the Supreme Court downstairs, will be vacated, and completely renovated; thereafter the entire building would be used for the Law Courts; at the same time the modern Parliament will be constructed at Richmond Hill.

Under the ULP government, the House of Assembly has been meeting very frequently, and the dates of the meeting are almost always known upon adjournments. All the proceedings of the House are broadcast live on more than one radio station, on a special television channel, and on "live streaming". The Constitution has been followed scrupulously under the ULP in respect of the presentation of the Estimates and Appropriation Bill. Further, the Estimates have always, since 2001, been circulated in ample time prior to the meeting of the Standing Committee on Finance and the parliamentary debate on the Estimates. And "Question Time" in Parliament since April 2001 has been a lengthy and engaging process; we on the government side take this aspect of parliamentary life very seriously and we give full and truthful answers to questions that are themselves read out, by the questioners, for the entire country to hear.

The ULP government has ensured hefty increases in emoluments for the Speaker and the Clerk of the House in accord with their responsibilities and status. Similarly, the supportive staff have been better trained and better compensated.

In October 2002, the ULP government formally started the process towards a root-and-branch reform of the independence Constitution of 1979; it did so with the bipartisan support of the opposition NDP. Indeed, the motion I moved in the House on this subject in October 2002 was seconded by the Leader of the Opposition, Arnhim Eustace. Among other things, this motion called for the establishment of a broad-based Constitutional Reform Commission (CRC), involving representation from both parties, and membership, too, from Parliament, civil society, the Vincentian diaspora, and distinguished individuals. In February 2003, the CRC was formally established, initially with Professor Nicholas Liverpool of Dominica as the Chairman and with the late Parnel R. Campbell, a distinguished former Attorney General of St. Vincent and the Grenadines as his Deputy. An appointment of Professor Liverpool, shortly thereafter, to a high office elsewhere, prompted him to demit the Chairmanship; Campbell replaced him and carried out these duties over the next seven years, magnificently.

Out of the blue, in July 2007, the Leader of the Opposition withdrew from the constitutional review process even though three weeks earlier he and I had yet again acted cooperatively on a mater in the House of Assembly to advance further the reform process. In terminating the NDP's cooperative involvement, Eustace cited three specious and unconnected reasons: that the ULP had not removed as yet one of its election billboards of December 2005 from Sion Hill; that the Supervisor of Elections had not yet published his report on the general elections of December 2005; and that the ULP's General Secretary, and competitor of Eustace in the East Kingstown constituency, was yet to explain his alleged assertion that he knew which Syrians voted for him.

These excuses offered by Eustace were laughable. He acted opportunistically, pure and simple. We were in the final stages of the extensive public consultations in the constitutional reform process; a comprehensive draft of the reformed constitution was to be prepared for further consultation; then the matter was scheduled to go to Parliament for a vote prior to being put to a popular referendum requiring a two-thirds majority for approval. Eustace realised that the referendum had to be held before the general elections in 2010; so, he opted to oppose the reforms confident that without the Opposition's support, the requisite two-thirds majority in a popular referendum was well-nigh impossible. Thus, he anticipated that the ULP and its leader would sustain a defeat and so weaken them in the run-up to the 2010 general elections.

In the upshot of all this, Eustace was proven correct about the referendum. The people rejected the reform constitution by a majority of 55 percent to 45 percent in a referendum on November 25, 2009. But he was wrong about the general elections held on December 2010; the ULP was again returned to office for a third consecutive term. The ULP is still in office for a fifth consecutive term as a consequence of the general elections in November 2020. In 2022, it is 20 years since the constitutional reform process started; and it is over 12 years since the referendum defeat of the proposed reform constitution. The nation's governance is worse-off because of the popular rejection of the proposed reform constitution.

Sound as the 1979 Constitution is in its liberal-democratic dispensation, there are areas that demand reformation. The ULP had pressed for constitutional reform for the following central reasons: (i) To conclude the national democratic tasks of the unfolding social democratic revolution by replacing the Queen of Great Britain as our symbolic and substantive Head of State with a home-grown, non-Executive President elected by Parliament after appropriate screening through a "Council of Elders"; (ii) to strengthen the quality, independence, and Caribbean character of the judiciary by replacing the Privy Council in England as the final appellate court by our own regional Caribbean Court of Justice (CCJ); (iii) to fortify the fundamental rights and freedoms of individuals and to bolster their juridical protections; (iv) to make Parliament entirely an elected body on the basis of a mixed electoral system (first-past-the-post and proportional representation), and to remove the unelected, nominated element in the appointment of Senators; (v) to set-up an independent Elections Commission to oversee the conduct of general elections; (vi) to lessen the powers of the Prime Minister and to increase those of the Leader of the Opposition and other independent bodies such as the Public Service Commission, the Office of the Director of Audit, and the Public Accounts Committee; (vii) to improve governance by decentralisation through appropriate local government; (viii) to establish strong supportive democratic/accountability institutions such as a Human Rights Commission and an Ombudsman; (ix) to strengthen regionalism and the prospect of achieving a Caribbean political union; and (x) to generally deepen democratic participation in governance.

The highlights of the draft reformed Constitution, which was popularly rejected in the referendum at the strident urgings of the NDP, include: (i) The establishment of the office of a home-grown non-Executive President as Head of State; (ii) the joinder of the CCJ by St. Vincent and the Grenadines; (iii) the strengthening of the independence of the Magistracy; (iv) the diminution of the powers of the Prime Minister in respect of the appointments to the Public Service and Police Service Commissions; (v) the establishment of a Human Rights Commission; (vi) the establishment of the Office of an Ombudsman to address complaints by individuals about administrative abuses; (vii) the establishment of Local Government; (viii) the strengthening of individual rights and freedoms including property rights, freedom of expression and freedom of the press, the rights of women and children, trade union rights and other rights at the workplace; (ix) the making of an entirely representative unicameral, enlarged House of Assembly (27 members) with representatives elected on a first-past-the-post system and senators on the basis of a "list system" of proportional representation — a mixed electoral system; (x) the establishment of an independent Elections and Boundaries Commission to replace the Office of the Supervisor of Elections; (xi) the bolstering constitutionally of the Office of the Director of Audit, the Public Accounts Committee, and the setting up of a Teachers' Service Commission; (xii) the renaming of the divisive title "Leader of the Opposition" as "Minority Leader" with enhanced powers; (xiii) Liberalising the access to the Constitutional Court (the High Court) for persons seeking constitutional redress; (xiv) Detailing a bundle of values and objectives as non-justiciable declarations to guide the workings and interpretation of the Constitution, including the affirmation of a marriage being a union between a biological male and female at birth, and the requirement that one-third of election candidates of a party in a general election be female; (xv) removing the disqualification of a dual citizen (a Vincentian citizen who holds another citizenship) to be a member of Parliament; and (xvi) removing the requirement of a referendum for a political union between St. Vincent and the Grenadines and any of the member-states of CARICOM, and replacing it by a requirement for a two-thirds majority of the House of Assembly.

All objective observers, including two of NDP leaders (its Chairman Dr. Linton Lewis, a Senator, and Parliamentary Representative and Vice President St. Clair Leacock) considered the reformed Constitution to be superior in every respect to the 1979 Constitution. But partisan politics trumped the national interest for many people. The British firm of self-proclaimed mind-benders, Strategic Communications Laboratories (SCL), the precursor to Cambridge Analytica employed by Donald Trump's Presidential campaign in the USA, ran the NDP's rejection campaign of "NO"! SCL was financed by external interests. Imagine this: a British firm steeped in colonialism, Empire, and even racist attitudes, campaigning against a reformed Constitution to get rid of, among other things, the Queen as Head of State and the Privy Council as the final appellate court! SCL even boasted by telling the false tale that they happily worked for "free" on this campaign. Those who led the campaign against the reformed constitution and misled the people with untruths and scare-mongering tactics are unlikely to fare well at the bar of history.

In urging a "NO" Vote in the referendum, the NDP delivered demagogic, deceitful, and at times contradictory messages from their platform. Depending on who was speaking, the Queen was necessary and desirable; others said that changing her as Head of State was unimportant; one sectarian religious group, the Thusians, the leadership of whom was, at the time, in the political bosom of the NDP, alleged that the reformed Constitution did not affirm that all rights were inalienable and came from God, ignoring completely that the retention from the

1979 Preamble to the Constitution "affirmed that our Nation was found-ed on the belief in the supremacy of God and the freedom and dignity of man and woman"; this Thusian allegation metamorphosed quickly into one that Ralph, the ULP, and the draft Constitution were "ungod-ly"; falsely, the NDP alleged that the reformed Constitution would take away people's fundamental rights; incredibly, they alleged that this was a grab by Ralph for more power when the reverse was the case; NDP activists alleged, from their platform and in print, that removing the Queen would reduce the value of the Eastern Caribbean dollar (SVG's currency) and that her face on the currency would be replaced by those of Ralph and Hugo Chavez of Venezuela; and generally the NDP mocked the real constitutional changes of substance as totally insignifi-cant and irrelevant to people's lives.

But today, more and more people, including many who misled per-sons to vote "NO", regret the defeat of the proposed reformed Consti-tution. For me, personally, the rejection of the reformed Constitution has been my greatest political disappointment, by far. I do not think that for the remainder of my political life this would ever again be on the active political agenda. I feel truly sad about all this as a nationalist, an advanced social democrat, and a strong advocate of the deepest form of popular democracy, justice, freedom, and regional integration.

Small Island Exceptionalism

St. Vincent and the Grenadines is a small, multi-island developing State: Thirty-two islands and islets, nine of which are inhabited; 150 square miles of land; approximately 11,000 square nautical miles of seascape; 110,000 persons at home, nearly thrice that number overseas; Gross Domestic Product (GDP) of approximately US $850 million.

St. Vincent and the Grenadines is one of 33 independent small island states in the United Nations. Collectively they have a population of 40 million and a GDP, in the aggregate, of US $650 billion. Camillo M. Gon-salves, Minister of Finance of St. Vincent and the Grenadines, has sought to make sense of the phenomenon of small island developing states, partic-ularly those in the Caribbean, and their place in the global political econo-my. In the process, he has advanced the concept of "small island exception-alism" in his thoughtful and exquisitely written book entitled *Globalised. Climatised. Stigmatised.* (2019, Strategy Forum, Inc, SVG). These consider-ations are reflected in his 2022 budget address, and in the 2022 Estimates and Appropriation Bill in St. Vincent and the Grenadines.

Let us quote Camillo's book at some length, on "small island exceptionalism" and related issues:

> ...the Caribbean's outsized influence on sports and culture, and the litany of legendary individuals that have planted the flags of superlative Caribbean achievement in diverse pursuits across the globe, are mere manifestations of a more fundamental truth: That the islands of the Caribbean are different. The constraints of small size, the backdrop of a complex history, the confluence of cultures and races, the geopolitical imperatives and the geographic and topographical realities have conspired to produce societies and nations that exist beyond conventional frames of reference or forecasting models. By those conventions, be they economic, political or sociological, the countries of the Caribbean are not viable. They should not exist as independent nations.
>
> But here we are. Surviving, thriving even, in a geopolitical order that neither anticipated nor accounted for our existence.

Camillo goes on to introduce the notion of "small island exceptionalism" in the following terms:

> The nations of the Caribbean are sui generis. And while the precise ingredients of their uniqueness are not replicated elsewhere on the planet, they do share enough basic similarities with some small states scattered across the Atlantic, Indian and Pacific Oceans to discern a common small island exceptionalism. This exceptionalism is not in the triumphalist, "we're number one" vein of today's manifestations of jingoistic great power exceptionalism, nor is it simply the 'island mentality' or 'small island syndrome' born of isolated navel-gazing and limited horizons. Instead, small island exceptionalism spans regions and civilisations. It is shaped by the practical realities of smallness, of islandness, and of the delicate dance of alternately accommodating, resisting and adapting to tremendous exogenous pressures. Through this dance, small island states have forged a personality and developmental outlook without parallel in any other group of countries in the world.

In his book, Camillo argues that:

> This uniqueness — this small island exceptionalism — is indispensable to any analysis that considers the past, perspective or path of independent small island states. We are islands first. We fit neatly into no other paradigm. Our achievements and aspirations cannot be understood without first understanding this obvious, but often overlooked fact.

In enlarging upon this insight, Camillo Gonsalves insists that:

Political thought, economic theory and the prescriptions applied or imposed on small island states have gradually moved beyond yesteryear's 'one-size-fits-all' orthodoxy. However, there is a persistent belief that analyses and advice can simply be scaled down – almost mathematically — from other experiences and mechanically applied to the small island context.

This is folly. Just as 'one-size-fits-all' is inapplicable, so too is 'one-concept-fits-all.'

What are some of the major ways in which "the external" has afflicted the small island developing State? Camillo first identifies the broad philosophical and policy matrices that constrain the small island states, thus:

The global entrenchment of neoliberal orthodoxy as our planet's guiding philosophical underpinning, and the erection of its corresponding financial architecture on the foundations of monopoly capitalism, represent the gilded cage that confines the developmental aspirations of small islands. Like much of what ails our global village, island states played little role in constructing the cage we now inhabit.

The consequences of this philosophical and policy orientation are thus assessed by Camillo:

The contradictions and constraints of those policies and practices have caused island states to suffer the unholy trinity of being globalised, climatized and stigmatised to varying harmful degrees. This trinity of anti-island action has produced some cruel socioeconomic paradoxes, including:

The smallest contributors to climate change are the most affected.

The lowest contributors to terrorist financing or banking impropriety are the most constrained.

The smallest producers of global goods and services are most restricted by the rules of international trade.

The most indebted are among the least likely to get debt relief or concessional financing.

These paradoxes, and the systems that produced them, pose existential threats to the sustainability of island states. However, today, there is little popular appetite for quixotic quests by small island states to revolutionise or reinvent the global socioeconomic order. Pragmatic reform is the order of the day.

There is real potential for carefully selected pragmatic reforms to improve lives and alter the islands' developmental trajectory.

These bundles of issues and considerations are reflected in the practical roll-out of the on-the-ground programmes and numbers in Budget 2022, especially in the capital or development budget Estimates.

The overall approach is thus accommodation or creative resistance in concert within our interest and the extant circumstances. In the process, at a global level, we insist that "small island exceptionalism" must be accorded an especial juridical basis beyond the narrow confines of "special and differential treatment."

Still, Goal 17 of the Sustainable Development Goals (SDGs), agreed to by all states in the United Nations in September 2005, provides a framework for the requisite global partnership for sustainable development and the infusion within it of the notion of small state exceptionalism. Goal 17 of the SDGs is designed to: *"Strengthen means of implementation and revitalize the global partnership for sustainable development."*

Goal 17 of the SDGs has 19 targets to be achieved by 2030, broken down into five categories: Finance, technology, capacity building, trade, and systemic issues. Progress towards these targets is being measured by 24 indicators:

The targets of SDG17 (Goal 17 of the SDGs) are as follows:-

Mobilise resources to improve domestic revenue collection.

Implement all development assistance commitments.

Mobilise financial resources for developing countries.

Assist developing countries in attaining debt sustainability.

Invest in least-developed countries.

Knowledge sharing and cooperation for access to science, technology and innovation.

Promote sustainable technologies to developing countries.

Strengthen the science, technology and innovation capacity for least-developed countries.

Enhance SDG capacity in developing countries.

Promote a universal trading system under the World Trade Organisation (WTO).

Increase the exports of developing countries.

Remove trade barriers for least-developed countries.

Enhance global macroeconomic stability.

Enhance policy coherence for sustainable development.

Respect national leadership to implement policies for the SDGs.

Enhance the global partnership for sustainable development.

Encourage effective partnerships.

Enhance availability of reliable data.

Further develop measurements of progress.

Various international organisations utilise the relevant indicators to measure progress on these targets. These organisations include the International Monetary Fund (IMF), the World Bank, the Organisation for Economic Development and Cooperation (OECD), UN Conference on Trade and Development (UNCTAD), International Telecommunication Union (ITU), United Nations Environmental Programme (UNEP), World Trade Organisation (WTO), Department of Economic and Social Affairs – Statistics Division (DESA – UNSD), and United Nations Educational, Scientific and Cultural Organisation – Institution of Statistics (UNESCO – UIS).

High level progress reports for all the SDGs are published through the Office of the UN Secretary General, the most recent report is April 2020. The implementation process of the SDGs has been uneven, in many cases, fragile. The paucity or absence of data and the COVID pandemic have hampered the monitoring of progress on the SDGs.

One matter of concern for small island developing states is the measurement of progress and the basis of eligibility of concessional finance for development; the near sanctity accorded to "per capita Gross Domestic Product (GDP)" by international finance institutions, is not tenable. It ought to be clear to all objective persons that this index of measurement is highly-flawed especially for small island developing states that are so vulnerable to exogenous shocks, including climate change. Thus, a "multidimensional vulnerability index" (MVI) is required to be constructed within the frame of "small island exceptionalism" to supplement or replace per capita GDP criteria for concessional financing. Advocacy work continues in this regard through the Association of Small Island States (AOSIS). Actual technical work is being done through the UN Panel of Experts on the MVI. The Caribbean is well-represented at the highest levels on both the UN Panel and the AOSIS Task Force on the MVI.

Unfortunately, opportunist and demagogic political opposition elements across the Caribbean, including in St. Vincent and the Grenadines, frequently undermine domestic support for SDG17 by asserting that "global development partnerships" are about demeaning "begging". The simple fact is that the SDG17 imposes on developed countries an obligation to assist with development finance. The notion that a small island developing State like St. Vincent and the Grenadines can on its own generate enough surpluses to finance development from its current domestic economic base is entirely fanciful. These demagogic opposition elements do not admit to the historic legacies of underdevelopment, the contemporary challenges arising from the global economy, and the external pressures including the adverse impacts of climate change, and small size (inclusive of scarce natural resources), as the main drivers, structurally, of our developmental challenges. To be sure, there are domestic issues that demand resolution, but they pale into insignificance in comparison to the externally-sourced challenges and their imposed anti-developmental limitations.

In respect of SDG17, it is clear that a consolidated regionalism and an efficacious foreign policy are vital instruments in the quest for more meaningful global developmental partnerships. These policy imperatives are reflected in Budget 2022 in quest of our respairing.

The ULP government places great store on the 17 SDGs. They have been central in our party's Election Manifestos of December 2015 and November 2022. The SDGs form an integral part of all our public policies as we seek to build a modern, competitive, many-sided post-colonial economy in pursuit of sustainable development.

The Debate on Budget 2022

The Budget Debate 2022. The debate on the Appropriation Bill 2022 was scheduled for the week beginning Monday January 10, 2022. The Estimates for 2022 were passed in the House of Assembly in December 2021, but the debate on the Appropriation Bill was postponed to January 3, 2022, on account of the funeral arrangements for the former Prime Minister Sir James Mitchell. Unfortunately, a COVID infection arose in the home of the Speaker of the House; she was the caregiver of an infected person. Accordingly, the start of the debate was postponed to Monday, January 10, 2022.

As scheduled, the Minister of Finance, Camillo Gonsalves, delivered his Budget Address on the evening of Monday, January 10, 2022. A number of persons on the government side of the House of Assembly, all vaccinated, contracted the coronavirus that disrupted the debate and caused several persons to be absent from the House. In the process, a many-sided controversy developed between the government and the opposition in the House. Still, the government secured passage of the Appropriation Bill and the Public Sector Investment Loan Bill (a Bill to secure authority to borrow up to EC $125 million to assist, in part, the financing of the capital budget) on the evening of Friday, January 14, 2022. The whole story is worth telling; it illustrates foremost the purposefulness of the government in its offering of fresh hope at a very challenging time, and its commitment to the principle and practice of representative government; at the same time, it laid bare the irresponsibility, folly and obstructionism of the opposition NDP, in complete disregard of the people's interest.

Prior to Monday, January 10th, two ministers of government, Saboto Caesar (Minister of Agriculture) and Curtis King (Minister of Education) tested positive for COVID on Saturday, January 8th, on Palm Island, one of the Grenadines' islands. Two other members of Parliament were on Palm Island, the Prime Minister, and Carlos James (Minister of Tourism) both of whom tested negative for COVID on Sunday January 9th.

On the morning of Tuesday, January 11, 2022, three other members of the government side tested positive — the Minister of Finance, Camillo Gonsalves, Senator Julian Francis (Minister of Urban Development) and Senator Rochard Ballah (Parliamentary Secretary in the Office of the Prime Minister). Accordingly, on advice of the Chief Medical Officer and pursuant to a consequential ruling of the Speaker, the sitting was suspended to Wednesday, January 12th, for the Leader of the Opposition's response to the Budget Address, which took the allotted four hours. On the said Wednesday, Minister Montgomery Daniel reported sick and was absent from the House; later that day he tested positive for COVID.

During the luncheon suspension on Wednesday, January 12th, the Minister of Health, Wellness and the Environment, St. Clair "Jimmy" Prince tested positive for COVID-19. At the resumption after lunch, it was reported that Minister Frederick Stephenson was not feeling well, so he was absent; he later tested positive for COVID that very evening. The Speaker, on the advice of the Chief Medical Officer, suggested a further suspension to ensure that all members of the House present that morning be PCR-tested for COVID and that the Chamber of the House be fully sanitised. The members of the Opposition refused to be tested. All remaining six members on the government side tested negative (the Prime Minster, the Attorney General, Ministers Carlos James, Orando Brewster, Senator/Minister of State Keisal Peters, and Senator Ashelle Morgan). The House was suspended until the morning of Friday, January 14th.

In the House there are 14 members, including the Attorney General on the government side; on the opposition side only five of their eight members were available to attend (three who were unvaccinated *and* had been in contact with a member who was positive, were in quarantine for seven days — the national protocol — and thus would be absent from the debate). The Opposition made it plain publicly that it would not return to the House to continue the debate unless there was a suspension for at least seven days; according to them they were concerned about their health and safety, but in reality they did not want to be present to constitute a quorum of the House (eight members) to ensure passage of the Appropriation Bill.

During the recent period of COVID, both the government and opposition had agreed that neither side would raise the issue of a quorum — eight members — save and except at the time of voting. The Speaker had directed that at any one time, other than at voting, no more than six members on the government side and three on the opposition side would be permitted in the House.

So, at the suspension on Wednesday, January 12th, there were six members on the government side who were able to attend the meeting of the House, and five members, too, from the opposition seats. But the Opposition refused to attend any further. Thus, the debate could go on with six members but no voting on any Bill was possible, legally, without eight members being present.

On Thursday, January 13th, in the afternoon, Saboto Caesar tested negative (he had tested positive six days earlier) and was cleared to attend Parliament, as per the rules of the Health Protocols. Curtis King was not cleared. Camillo Gonsalves, Senator Julian Francis, Senator Rochard Ballah, Jimmy Prince, Frederick Stephenson, and Montgomery

Daniel were still in quarantine — all members on the government side.

Thus, early Friday morning, January 14th, under Section 29(2) of the Constitution of St. Vincent and the Grenadines, the Prime Minister advised the Governor General that Senator Ballah's appointment be revoked and in his stead René Baptiste, who had been an elected representative for the Unity Labour Party in West Kingstown between 2001 and 2010, be appointed as Senator under Section 28(2) of the Constitution. Both the revocation and the appointment were done by the Governor General by 9 a.m. on Friday, January 14th. Within twenty minutes René Baptiste was sworn into the House and took the requisite Oath of Allegiance. Just in case another member had tested positive, another former member was on stand-by to be sworn-in to replace Senator Francis who was still in quarantine.

So, on the morning of Friday, January 14th, the House resumed with eight members on the government side; the opposition was absent; they were still boycotting, even after they were wrong-footed by the astuteness on the government side. Later that evening while the Prime Minister was wrapping up the debate on the Appropriation Bill, Minister Curtis King arrived in the House, he having been cleared from quarantine that very evening by virtue of a negative test.

Accordingly, at the conclusion of the debate on the Appropriation Bill and on the Public Sector Investment Loan Bill, there were nine members from the government side to secure passage of both vital Bills. The Prime Minister had thus attained the objective he had set on Monday evening, January 10th, immediately prior to the commencement of the Budget Address by the Minister of Finance.

On that Monday evening, January 10th, as Prime Minister, I had a sense of foreboding that some members of the House could become infected by COVID in addition to Ministers Caesar and King. I suggested that both sides agree to virtual voting, by phone or video. The Leader of the Opposition objected on the ground that such a suggestion was premature and, in his view, unconstitutional/illegal. It is true that the relevant part of Section 41(1) of the Constitution states that "any question proposed for decision in the House shall be determined by a majority of the votes of the members present and voting." Section 41(2) further states that *"a question shall not be regarded as having been validly determined by a vote in the House unless eight members...take part in the voting."*

Opposition Leader Lorraine Friday gave a narrow interpretation of Section 41(1). I accorded the provision a liberal and purposive interpretation in line with the juridically-acknowledged rules of interpretation/construction of the Constitution. Interestingly, the opposition member, Daniel Cummings, representative for West Kingstown, who had been in Trinidad for a year or so for medical purposes, had, hitherto, informally intimated to the Speaker to permit him to participate (debate and vote) in the proceedings of the House from Trinidad, outside the jurisdiction, by a video link; now, he and the Opposition Leader rejected the Prime Minister's suggestion for virtual voting.

It was apparent to me from the very Monday evening (January 10th) that the Opposition was interested in frustrating the passage of the Appropriation Bill if more members of the government tested positive with COVID. In a rhetorical flourish, I assured the House that the Bill would be passed by Friday evening even if it meant bringing the COVID positive members to vote. Of course, I had no intention of so doing; in any event the Speaker would not have permitted it. But I was rolling out a rhetorical decoy for the Opposition to chase me down the proverbial rabbit-hole; I was beginning to conceptualise a possible plan of action, if all the circumstances required and permitted, which I implemented on Friday morning, January 14th. On Monday evening the confluence of circumstances had not yet arrived to put the plan into action but I conceived possibilities, if the circumstances warranted; by the next day (Tuesday January 11th) when two Senators (Francis and Ballah) tested positive for COVID, I sensed realistic probabilities.

It was absolutely clear to me by Wednesday, January 12th, and reconfirmed on Thursday, January 13th, that the Opposition was determined to undermine the principle of representative government by taking advantage of the depletion of the government ranks because of COVID infections. The stark democratic fact of consequence was that on November 5, 2020, the people of St. Vincent and the Grenadines, in free and fair elections, re-elected the ULP for a fifth consecutive term by a margin of nine seats to six. It was entirely unacceptable, and wholly wrong, for six representatives to undermine the authority of nine due to COVID. The large principle of representative government was at stake and I was not going to allow them to get away with it, if it were possible constitutionally. This was especially so in our nation's condition of extreme challenge consequent upon the continued pandemic and the recovery steps in the aftermath of the volcanic eruptions of April 2021.

It is interesting that the Opposition had earlier been insisting that it was of the highest priority for all of its members to speak in the debate. Yet, they absented themselves for absolutely no good reason. In the upshot, only the Leader of the Opposition spoke; he for his allotted four hours. On the government side eight members (the Minister of Finance, Ministers James, Brewster, Caesar, and Peters, Senators Morgan and Baptiste, and the Prime Minister) spoke, in the aggregate, for 14 hours. And both Bills were passed, 9 to 0!

The Opposition was caught entirely unawares on the morning of Friday, January 14th, with the revocation of Ballah's senatorial appointment and the appointment of René Baptiste in his place. On Thursday, January 13th, the NDP spokespersons, including their leading elected members, were gloating on radio that "Ralph did not have the numbers to pass the Appropriation Bill" and that a suspension or postponement of the debate was inevitable. They were metaphorically beating their chests with foolish, infantile utterances such as "NDP run things", "Ralph is cornered", "Ralph has to do our bidding this time". They averred that my suggestion/threat of bringing COVID positive members to the House was an empty non-starter. They did not think out the constitutional possibilities available to the government in the circumstances; they were still chasing me down the proverbial rabbit-hole but I was not there to be found. I was somewhere else: Formulating the action plan under Section 29(2) and 28(a) of the Constitution of St. Vincent and the Grenadines.

The first public response of the NDP confirmed that it had been caught napping and its effort to undermine representative government had failed miserably. The NDP's first response was by way of an inane posting on social media by its Public Relations Officer who made the following two points: First, that the ULP had replaced a young person (Ballah) with an old person who had last served in Parliament in 2010; and secondly, this showed that the ULP had run out of options and was in "crisis mode". Swiftly, users of social medial debunked the NDP's nonsensical posture: It was pointed out accurately that: (i) Ballah's revocation was a temporary, tactical move to pass the Appropriation Bill and he would return shortly as a Senator; (ii) there are two young female senators (Keisal Peters and Ashelle Morgan) who were younger than Ballah; if René Baptiste was "too old" for the House, what about the NDP's failed attempt to foist Kay Bacchus, same age as René Baptiste, on the electorate as a candidate in the 2020 general elections, and in any event, what about the NDP's failed effort to have Bernard Wyllie return as a representative in Marriaqua some 22 years after he was defeated by Girlyn Miguel of the ULP? And far from the ULP being in crisis mode, it was actually on top of its game; instead, it was the NDP and its strategy that were in political tatters.

Indeed, the overwhelming view of the public, including that of stalwart NDP supporters, was that the current leadership of the NDP should be cast aside; they were seen as inept, clumsy, and being repeatedly outflanked by the ULP leadership.

In the actual debate itself, the NDP came with absolutely nothing new to the table. As usual, their only answer to our nation's problems was to sell passports and our country's citizenship to foreigners, including disreputable ones. We have established that this is a terrible idea: Wrong in principle and in fact; and not sustainable.

The ULP wanted the Appropriation Bill to be passed as a matter of urgency because there were monies in it immediately for the poor and the working people that could not be spent unless the Bill's passage was assured. I laid out all the details in this regard and in consonance with the provisions of the Finance Administration Act. The Bill was passed on Friday night, January 14th. By Monday, January 17th, 2022, the Appropriation Bill and the Public Sector Investment Loan Bill had been assented to by the Governor General and published in the Official Gazette. Both the ULP members of the House and the officials in the State administration acted with the urgency that the circumstances of the pandemic and the aftermath of the volcanic eruptions, demanded.

As a footnote, as had been earlier agreed, René Baptiste voluntarily demitted her senatorial post on February 7, 2022; Rochard Ballah was reappointed as Senator and Parliamentary Secretary in the Office of the Prime Minister. On the evening of February 9, 2022, Senator Ballah was on an aircraft as part of the Prime Minister's delegation to attend official business in the United Arab Emirates. Normalcy had returned; the work of the government continued.

Chapter Five

The Mixed Economy: The Private, State, and Cooperative Sectors

The Framework

The mixed economy is central to the philosophy and practice of any advanced social democracy, which the ULP espouses and applies to the context of St. Vincent and the Grenadines. Its 2020 Election Manifesto affirms that:

> The economic approach of the ULP is to cultivate or fashion a tripartite partnership between the private sector (business and labour), the cooperative sector (credit unions and cooperatives), and the State, in a harmonious and integrated manner to ensure optimal benefits for all stakeholders and our people as a whole.
>
> The economic approach is in the quest of building a modern, competitive, many-sided post-colonial economy which is at once local, national, regional, and global. The central desirable outcomes of this economic path and quest are: *Job Creation*; wealth creation; a balanced, open economy of diverse economic pillars; economic growth; fiscal, monetary and financial stability; targeted strategic interventions; economic inclusiveness, equity, and fairness. Each of the above formulations in our economic approach, our economic quest, and central desirable economic outcomes is pregnant with real meaning."

Historically, in the old colonial economy, the amended colonial economy, and even in the post-2001 paradigm shift in quest of building a modern, post-colonial economy, the private sector has been relatively undeveloped and in a largely unwholesome, subservient relationship to monopoly capitalism externally. A brief review of the private sector, historically in St. Vincent and the Grenadines up to 2001 and beyond, is useful for our understanding of its role and place in our country's mixed economy.

The inefficient planter-merchant mode of economic organisation, in partnership with a protective colonial State grounded in abundant cheap labour (unfree and free), subsidies locally and preferential markets externally, low levels of technological or scientific applications, and within a very small domestic market and a limited external one, hardly allowed the private sector to develop. Raw material agricultural production, limited agro-processing, and uncompetitive import-export trade were the central foci of the planter-merchant elite.

The straight-jacketed constitutional colonial order, even after universal adult suffrage in 1951 and a quasi-ministerial system prior to internal self-government in 1969, did not permit or activate alterations in the extant economic arrangements. To be sure, the popularly-elected People's Political Party (PPP) government led by Ebenezer Theodore Joshua (1957-1967) improved somewhat the wages of workers and their labour conditions, and made some advances in education, health, housing, and road construction, but the undeveloped and inadequate/insufficient nature of the private sector of the planter-merchant elite continued.

There were, however, signs that the times were changing: Trade unionism, constitutional, devolution, and populism grounded in elemental democracy were weakening internally the planter-merchant mode of economic organisation; and externally, the growth of monopoly capitalism had no nostalgia for increasingly inefficient, uneconomic, outmoded planter-merchant arrangements. Indeed, the sugar industry collapsed in 1962 from a brutal combination of these internal and external changes.

Nationalist leaders, whether in Joshua's PPP or Milton Cato's St. Vincent Labour Party, were growing impatient with the old order, but a new order was not yet born. Gradually, Milton Cato's Labour Party governments (1967-1972; and 1974-1984) — fifteen years, in office) began to spearhead some alterations, interestingly in compromise with sectors of the old planter-merchant elite. Many inefficient estates were subdivided and sold to small farmers, including some who were estate workers; and other estates (Mt. Bentinck, Grand Sable, Colonarie, San Souci) changed hands — an outsider from humble origins, Basil Balcombe, purchased these estates. The introduction of banana production as a commercial export crop from the mid-1950s and its expansion/consolidation in the 1960s, 1970s, and 1980s, *buttressed by preferential treatment in the British market*, were tailor-made for cultivation on multiple small landholdings.

The alteration of the private sector economic organisation from the planter-merchant model to one increasingly of small farmers, broadened the base, but did strengthen the private sector; it was still undeveloped and fragile. New local players, outside of the old elite, in the mercantile import-export trade similarly did not so much alter the wholesale and retail sector, though the ownership of it was democraticised somewhat. Significant domestic investments were not coming from the domestic private sector or the regional or foreign investors on their own accord. So, the State had to act to provide alterations or amendments to the colonial economy and to propel economic growth.

Thus, the Labour Party government, advised by young economists such as C.I. Martin and Claude Samuel, began to ramp up the role of the State, not only as a facilitator or regulator of the private sector, but also as an owner of means of production. It established an industrial estate at Campden Park and attracted local and foreign investors in light manufacturing. A flagship, in this regard, was its role in the founding of the Eastern Caribbean Group of Companies (ECGC), the owners being Maple Leaf of Canada (40 percent), P.H. Veira — a local investor (40 percent), and the State (20 percent). ECGC began with flour production and expanded, by 1984, into the production of animal feed and rice.

The Labour Party government under Cato established a number of State enterprises and introduced economic initiatives, including St. Vincent Marketing Corporation to market agricultural exports and to run a small supermarket; the National Commercial Bank to provide indigenous banking services in a sector dominated by foreign banks (Barclays' Bank, Bank of Nova Scotia, Royal Bank of Canada, and the Canadian Imperial Bank of Commerce); stone crushing plants for the construction of physical infrastructure including roads; the Diamond Dairy Company to produce milk and juices; the revival of the sugar industry (producing sugar, molasses and rum) in 1979 through State ownership of the sugar factory and rum distillery — the sugar cane was grown largely on the estates formerly owned by Balcombe Investments, purchased by the government, but most of which were leased to small farmers; the active State participation in the arrowroot industry with the passage of the Arrowroot Industry Act; the reclamation of a considerable amount of land seaward in Kingstown for the State and the private sector; the setting up of the legal infrastructure for the offshore finance services industry and the establishment of the Philatelic Bureau;

the founding of the Development Corporation, a one-stop entity for local and foreign investors; and the setting-up of the National Provident
Fund, the precursor to the National Insurance Services.

Further, the Labour government under Milton Cato strengthened
the regulation of private sector activity in a series of legislative measures touching and concerning the following among others: the price
and distribution of goods; the investment in Mustique; the banana
industry; protection of workers' employment; hotel incentives; and the
modernisation of the income tax law.

Moreover, the Labour administration was engaged in a support-
ive mature regionalism with, for example, the establishment of the
Caribbean Development Bank (CDB), the Caribbean Free Trade Area
(CARIFTA), and the Organisation of Eastern Caribbean States (OECS).

Under the New Democratic Party (NDP) governments of James
Mitchell (July, 1984 to October, 2000) and Arnhim Eustace (October,
2000 to March, 2001 – five months), the private sector was extolled
within a neo-liberal paradigm and the State sector in the economy
was substantially rolled back. The NDP government closed the sugar
industry and sold the distillery to the private sector; dismantled the
Marketing Corporation; closed down the Diamond Dairy Company;
reduced the Housing and Land Development Corporation to a debt
collecting agency — the NDP averred that housing was for the private
sector; closed down the stone crushing plants; removed price controls
substantially; and reduced the Development Corporation to a shadow of
its former self.

At the same time, the NDP government under Mitchell leased two-
thirds of Canouan to a foreign investor on extremely generous terms;
placed the government in debt to the tune of almost $200 million in
a sweetheart arrangement with an Italian investor at the Ottley Hall
Marina and Shipyard — a failed project; nearly ran the State-owned National Commercial Bank into the ground; and presided over the exodus
of many foreign investors from the industrial estate at Campden Park.

On the positive side, the NDP government under James Mitchell acquired and distributed to small farmers, though in a haphazard
and sub-optimal manner, the Orange Hill Estates (3,400 acres) from a
Danish group that had purchased the land from an old planter family,
the Barnards; established the National Insurance Services in 1987, three
years after the Labour government had introduced the NIS Bill to the

Parliament shortly before it was voted out of office in July 1984; encouraged the development of tourism services, including cruise tourism — a cruise ship pier was built in 1999; and, with the assistance of the Japanese government, built a small, modern fish market in Kingstown.

The ULP government over the past 21 years has implemented policies to strengthen the private sector, the cooperative sector, and the State sector. In 2001, there were 1,857 employers (businesses) registered at the NIS; in 2019, the last immediate pre-COVID year, the number had increased to 2,347, an increase of 490 private sector employers/businesses or 26 percent more than in 2001; in 2020 this number fell by 1.4 percent to 2,314 employers/businesses. Significant increases in private sector businesses have occurred in the post-2001 period in tourism accommodation, restaurants, construction, education and health services, professional services, service providers in telecommunications, and road transportation. There have been small-to-modest increases in private sector businesses across all other economic activities; there have been no declines in any area of private sector economic activity.

The dominance of the private sector in the economy is evident from the employment numbers. According to *The Population and Housing Census Report of 2012* (the last Census) 69.7 percent of the employed population are engaged in the private sector in four categories: Paid Employees of Private Businesses (42.6 percent); Own-Account Businesses Without Paid Employees (19.2 percent); Paid Employees of Private Homes (4.8 percent); and Own-Account Businesses with Paid Employees (3.1 percent). The State sector accounted for 25.5 percent of the employed population: Central government (21.4 percent); State-Owned Entities (4.1 percent).

The distribution of the employed population by industry indicates the centrality of the private sector in the economy. The industries or economic activities owned exclusively, or almost exclusively, by the private sector engaging, by percentage of the total employed population, are as follows: Wholesale and Retail Trade, 16.9 percent; Agriculture, 11.8 percent; Transportation and Storage, 7.6 percent; Accommodation and Food Services, 7.4 percent; Activities of Households as Employers, 4.8 percent; Professional, Scientific, and Technical Activities, 1.5 percent; Manufacturing, 5.1 percent; Information and Communications, 1.3 percent; Arts, Entertainment, and Recreation, 0.9 percent; Other Service Activities, 2.2 percent; Real Estate Activities, 0.1 percent; Mining and Quarrying, 0.1 percent; Activities of Extra-Territorial Organisations, 0.1 percent; Activities, Not Stated, 1.4 percent. All together these industries or economic activities in which the private sector is dominant account for 60 percent of the total employed population.

The industries or economic activities the private sector, the State sector and the cooperative sector are involved in account for the employed population, in percentages, as follows: Construction, 11.6 percent (largely private sector); Financial and Insurance Services, 1.9 percent (largely private sector, and cooperative credit unions and a building association; but the major bank is largely State-owned). These together account for 13.5 percent of the total employed population.

The State sector is dominant in the following (with percentages of total employed population): Public Administration, Defence and Compulsory Social Security (NIS), 9.7 percent; Administrative and Support Services, 2.9 percent; Education, 9.7 percent; Human Health and Social Work Activities, 3.4 percent; Electricity, Gas, Steam, and Air Conditioning Supply, 0.8 percent; Water Supply, Sewerage, and Waste Management, 0.8 percent. All together these industries in which the State Sector is dominant, employ 27.3 percent of the total employed population.

The dominance of the private sector in the economy is reflected not merely in the number of employees therein, but also in the greater contribution to the Gross Domestic Product and its dominant ownership of the means of production.

The largest contributors to GDP are mainly in the hands of the private sector: Wholesale and Retail, Transportation and Storage, Agriculture and Fisheries, Construction, Hotels and Restaurants (a proxy for Tourism), Real Estate and Renting.

Big contributors to GDP that are largely in State hands are: Public Administration, Education, and Health. Financial Intermediation, a significant GDP contributor, is largely a private sector-owned category, but with a substantial presence of the State and cooperative sectors.

It is noteworthy that 20 percent of the corporate taxpayers (private sector and State) pay 80 percent of the corporate taxes annually. This speaks, importantly, to the dominance of a handful of enterprises in the economy. This is particularly so in the following areas of economic activity: Wholesale and Retail; Air and Sea Transportation; Hotels and Restaurants; Construction; Banking and Insurance; Credit Unions; Telecommunications; Electricity, Water and Solid Waste Management; Manufacturing; and Airports and Seaports.

In our small economy, the State sector inevitably assumes a commanding position in the dominance of critical industries or economic activities such as: Electricity, Water, and Solid Waste Management; the largest single land owner; Airports and Seaports; Education, Health, Defence, Security, and Public Administration; Compulsory Social Security (NIS); and largest shareholder (63 percent ownership — NIS and government), of the biggest commercial bank, Bank of St. Vincent and the Grenadines. The State sector is also the single largest consumer of goods and services and the single largest employer of labour. And, of course, the State possesses huge regulatory powers in the economy and society. Finally, in this regard, one central defining feature of the State is that it has the legitimate monopoly of physical coercion, exercisable in accord with the Constitution and Laws of St. Vincent and the Grenadines.

Under the ULP government (2001-2022 and continuing), the State economic sector has been strengthened in respect of pre-existing State entities and on account of the creation of additional, post-2001 State enterprises. Major advances have been made in the following pre-2001 State enterprises, among others: the St. Vincent Electricity Services Limited (VINLEC), the Central Water and Sewerage Authority (CWSA); the National Insurance Services (NIS); the St. Vincent and the Grenadines Port Authority (SVGPA); the Housing and Land Development Corporation (HLDC); the St. Vincent and the Grenadines Postal Corporation (formerly the Post Office); the Arrowroot Industry Association.

The post-2001 State economic-related enterprises created by or under the ULP government, include: the Bank of St. Vincent and the Grenadines (formerly the National Commercial Bank); the National Lotteries Authority (formerly Lottery); the Agriculture Input Warehouse Company (formerly Input Warehouse); the Argyle International Airport Incorporated; the National Fisheries Marketing Company; the Buildings, Roads, and Bridges Authority (BRAGSA); National Properties Limited; Petro-Caribe (SVG) Limited; the Farmers' Support Company; the National Centre for Technology and Innovation; the Student Loan Company; and the SVG Community College.

Additionally, the following critical promotional or regulatory State agencies embedded in the economy include: the Financial Services Authority (FSA); the Medicinal Cannabis Authority; the SVG Tourism Authority (SVGTA); the National Accreditation Board; Invest SVG; the National Telecommunications Regulatory Commission (NTRC); Sector Skills Development Agency (SSDA); the Directorate of Maritime Administration; the Private Investigations and Security Guards Board; the Commerce and Intellectual Property Office (CIPO); and the SVG Bureau of Standards.

Regional regulatory bodies that serve St. Vincent and the Grenadines authoritatively, include the Eastern Caribbean Central Bank in respect of money and banking; the Eastern Caribbean Civil Aviation Authority as regards civil aviation; the Eastern Caribbean Telecommunications Authority concerning telecommunications; and CARICOM and the OECS regional intra-regional trade.

Further, of course, the State provides overwhelmingly the delivery of services in education, health, security, and public administration through national and regional authorities.

It is useful to highlight the strength and role of a few critical State enterprises such as VINLEC, CWSA, BOSVG, the NIS, SVGPA, and the AIA Incorporated in the economy. The review of these tells a compelling story of the salience and centrality of the State sector in the economy beyond the actual size of the assets or numbers of persons employed, significant as they are.

St. Vincent Electricity Services (VINLEC) and Energy

VINLEC, the State-owned electricity company, has an asset base of nearly EC $300 million. Its principal activities are the generation, transmission and distribution of electricity throughout St. Vincent and the Grenadines as a monopoly provider. Its audited Financial Statements for the year 2020 — the first year of the COVID pandemic — showed a net profit, after tax, of $7.8 million. Its total revenues for 2020 stood at $109.2 million; its retained earnings amounted to $102.8 million; and its return on equity was nearly 6 percent.

In 2020, VINLEC had an installed generating capacity of 38,840 kilowatts (kW) on mainland St. Vincent and an additional 9,641 kW on the Grenadine islands of Bequia, Union Island, Canouan, and Mayreau. It provides a safe and reliable supply of electricity to 46,753 customers (41,870 domestic customers; 4,814 commercial customers, and 23 industrial customers, and 46 others).

In 2020, revenues derived from the domestic customers amounted to $36.89 million; from the commercial customers, $30.5 million; and from the industrial customers, $2.8 million. These revenues came from

72.7 million kilowatt hours (kWh) for domestic customers; 56.3 million kWh for commercial consumers; and 6.9 million kWh for industrial consumers.

The operational expenses of VINLEC for the 2020 financial year amounted to $116.5 million, an increase of $3.7 million over 2018; the main contributor to this increase was the rise in diesel fuel costs; diesel generation provided 85 percent of electricity consumption on an annualised basis.

In 2019, the cost of diesel fuel consumed by VINLEC for electricity generation and transmission amounted to $57.027 million or 49 percent, of the company's operating costs. In 2018, the comparable figures were $54.79 million or 48 percent of operating costs.

For the year 2020, the average price per imperial gallon of fuel consumed by VINLEC decreased to EC $5.74 compared to $7.75 for year 2019. In 2020, diesel provided 85 percent or 129 MWh of power generation; hydro-electricity, 14 percent or 22 MWh; and the remaining 1 MWh from Solar PV. The savings on fuel cost due to hydro-electricity generation in 2020 amounted to EC $7.023 million; and the fuel cost savings arising from solar amounted to EC $0.271 million.

In 2020, VINLEC paid $1.464 million in income tax and declared dividends of $1.0 million. It provided substantial relief by way of a structured moratorium on electricity bills in 2020, and played a vital role in the restoration of electricity in the red and orange zones in the immediate aftermath of the volcanic eruptions in April 2021.

Under the ULP administration since March 2001, phenomenal advances have been made in the supply of electricity to the people of St. Vincent and the Grenadines through VINLEC. In 2001, electricity to households was at 75 percent penetration; by 2012, the household penetration was 90 percent; and by 2020, some 98 percent or 41,870 household consumers. Between 2001 and 2012, electricity as the main source of lighting went up by nearly 35 percent; bear in mind, too, that in 2001 there were 30,558 households, and by 2012 the number of households had increased to 36,829, an absolute increase of 6,271 or 21 percent, although the population as a whole in the 2001-2012 inter-censal period had increased by only 969 persons (an average annual increase of 88). Domestic consumers of VINLEC in 2020 numbered 41,870, a sound near proxy for the number of households in St. Vincent and the Grenadines.

In the period 2001-2012, the greatest increase in public electricity penetration was in the Northern Grenadines, a whopping rise of 106.2 percent, from 1,185 households to 2,444 households, that is from 68 percent of the households in 2001 to 92 percent in 2012. In the Southern Grenadines, public electrification rose by over 50 percent, from 1,000 households in 2001 to 1,511 households in 2012. In 2012, the Southern Grenadines and Kingstown (the capital city area) had the highest rate of public electricity penetration (in excess of 82 percent). And the number of street light installations grew from under 5,000 in 2001 to almost 10,000 in 2020.

Overall, the actual number of customers of all categories increased from 31,615 in December 2001 to 46,753 customers in December 2020, an increase of 15,138 actual customers or 47.9 percent.

Over the past ten years, reliability of electricity improved from a condition of multiple system failures annually to one (1) failure every 20 months. This is a result of 33 kV infrastructure on St. Vincent, and through other measures in the Grenadines.

Total capital investment over the past 20 years amounts to a massive EC $384 million: Up to 2019 from 2001, there was capital spending of $353.9 million; in 2020, capital expenditure amounted to $12.5 million; and in 2021, to $17.3 million. These capital investments, include:

Lowmans Bay Power Plant Phase 1.

Lowmans Bay Power Plant Phase 2: Implemented by VINLEC in-house team. Lowmans Bay Power Plant is installed with diesel capacity to generate 17 MW of electricity – the largest of the power plants in St. Vincent and the Grenadines.

- Electrification of Mayreau in 2003.

- Significant expansion of 33kV transmission system as follows:

- Four additional 33 kV lines: two new lines from Lowmans Bay Plant to Kingstown; and one new line from Cane Hall to the South Rivers Hydroelectric Plant.

- Four new modern indoor 33/11 kV substations at Cane Hall, Lowmans Bay, Kingstown, and South Rivers; and refurbishment of the outdoor substation at Spring Village (Cumberland Hydroelectric Plant).

- Huge upgrades of the Hydro Power Stations at Richmond and South Rivers: Energy output at South Rivers increased by 20 percent.

- Update of control and protective systems at the Cumberland Power Station.

- Reconfiguration of the Transmission and Distribution network to accommodate Argyle International Airport.

- Network expansion to provide electricity to private and public housing and business developments including low-and-middle-income housing throughout St. Vincent and the Grenadines.

- In-house design and implementation of SCADA (Supervisory Control and Data Acquisition). This allows staff to monitor the parameters of all generators and feeders from any part of the world with access to the net. The SCADA system allows remote controls of critical systems; a new switching facility installed at Argyle allows remote switching of the airport from its main feeder to another feeder in the event of a fault on the main feeder.

- Implementation of a comprehensive Geographic Information System (GIS).

- Implementation of a modern information network system.

- Working with the government on renewable energy, especially hydro, solar, and geothermal.

- Significant growth in solar PV installations (Private, Government, VINLEC) starting with a 10 kW pilot project at Cane Hall in 2010 to presently over 3,500 kW installed across St. Vincent and the Grenadines.

- Highest penetration utility-owned solar-battery-diesel hybrid system in the English-speaking Caribbean. The Union Island solar battery system commissioned in 2019 reduces fuel use, when operationalised, on the island by some 30 percent; it is the first of its kind for a utility in the Anglo-Caribbean; it can provide its customers entirely with solar and batteries for 5-8 hours daily. Unfortunately, last year it developed some recurring technical problems that are currently being addressed for a possible permanent solution.

- Accommodation of private grid-connected PV systems.

• Big investments on safety equipment and training and the installation of fire detection systems at all main locations.

In 2020, there was capital expenditure of $12.52 million relating to:

• Enhancing generating capacity at Cane Hall and Canouan ($4.367 million);

• Distribution system expansion and upgrades ($2.679 million);

• Facility and auxiliary asset replacement ($4.531 million);

• Government LED streetlight project ($0.947 million).

In 2021, capital spending amounted to $17.273 million including:

• Cane Hall Expansion Project ($10.0 million);

• Transmission and Distribution ($1.395 million);

• Government LED streetlight project ($0.64 million);

• Customs Service ($0.324 million).

In 2022, VINLEC's planned capital programme is estimated to cost EC $39.9 million. The main items in this 2022 capital programme include: the Solar Photovoltaic and Battery Energy storage System ($15.0 million); the Advanced Metering Infrastructure ($6.0 million); Transmission and Distribution Line Upgrade ($4.6 million); Bequia Capacity expansion ($1.1 million); and replacements to the company's vehicular fleet ($1.6 million).

In 2022, and continuing, the demand for electricity in St. Vincent is to be met by VINLEC's diesel power plants at Lowmans Bay and Cane Hall; the three hydroelectric plants (South Rivers, Cumberland and Richmond); and the PV installations at Cane Hall and Lowmans Bay. The demand in the Grenadines is being met by the diesel plants in Bequia, Union Island, Canouan, and Mayreau, together with the PV and battery storage installations in Union Island and Mayreau. The Lowmans Bay Power Plant will, for the foreseeable future, continue to be VINLEC's main generating station and is expected to produce approximately 47.96 percent of the energy generated by the company. Meanwhile, provision has also been made for the purchase of energy produced by privately-owned photovoltaic systems.

In 2022, VINLEC projects spending $163.7 million comprising capital expenditures of $39.93 million, loan principal repayments of $3.49 million, operational expenditure of $119.0 million (including $18.3 million in depreciation), and finance charges of $1.324 million. Estimated revenues are placed at $123.6 million and a provision for corporation tax of $0.68 million. Net earnings are accordingly projected at $1.59 million. In 2022 VINLEC projects a modest increase in electricity sales of two percent above the projected sales for 2021.

The cost of diesel fuel for the generation of electricity continues to impact the Fuel Surcharge Rate on the customers' electricity bills, and thus the cost of electricity. In 2022, VINLEC is projecting to use 6.91 million imperial gallons of diesel costing approximately $54 million for the generation of electricity; in 2019 the cost of diesel consumed by VINLEC was $57.027 million; and in 2018, it was $54.79 million.

All the capital initiatives VINLEC has been executing are precisely those that were pledged by the ULP in the Election Manifesto of November 2020.

In one area of the provision of renewable energy through the geo-thermal resources of St. Vincent, there has been a setback; it is the ULP government's intention to turn this setback into an advance. The recent history of this is well-known.

The geo-thermal energy initiative of the government and its partners (Emera of Canada, Reykjavik Geothermal (RG), the Caribbean Development Bank, the Department for International Development of the British government, the Inter-American Development Bank, and others) have met with a setback despite some successes or positives. It is established that a geothermal source of sufficiency exists for at least a 10-megawatt plant and possesses the requisite temperature of 250 degrees Celsius. The setback relates to the lack of a sufficient permeability, which could only have been discovered upon the drilling and exploration.

It is important to note that the bulk of the resources expended came from grants of some of our country's "development partners" and equity injection from Emera and RG. Up to when the project had its recorded setback in 2020, the government of St. Vincent and the Grenadines had only spent under EC $1 million on the project, mainly for project management costs.

In going forward on the issue of geothermal energy, the Minister of Finance, Camillo Gonsalves, laid out the framework for our option in his 2022 Budget Address:

> Last year, we promised to continue attempts to turn setbacks into advances, as we seek to sustainably utilise the tremendous geothermal resources of La Soufrière. We are happy to report that we have entered into a Joint Project Development Agreement with Eavor Technologies, a Canadian company, whose proprietary closed-loop geothermal energy extraction system does not require the permeability of traditional extraction. Eavor, at its own cost, is conducting a Front-End Engineering and Design (FEED) study, which will assess the geological data, evaluate the impact of the recent volcanic eruptions, develop preliminary powerplant designs, meet with stakeholders and establish capital cost estimates. By mid-year, Eavor will know whether our La Soufrière site is a feasible location for their closed-loop technology. We are hopeful that this FEED study will yield positive results, and that we can resume our journey to stable, affordable, home-grown baseload power. Mere months after La Soufrière reminded us of its awesome power, it would be apt that we could harness some of that power to provide green energy to the people of St. Vincent and the Grenadines.

In early May 2022, representatives of Eavor visited St. Vincent and the Grenadines for further discussions with the relevant officials of VINLEC, the government, and other stakeholders. There is a realistic prospect that Eavor may be in St. Vincent and the Grenadines in early 2024 to advance practically its geothermal project.

One other principal renewable source of energy is solar. We note VINLEC's pioneering efforts in this regard. In 2021, solar energy generated the equivalent of 3,752 megawatt hours through the end of October, a 5 percent increase over the comparable period in 2020. In 2022, there is a plan to add to solar generation by way of the expansion of solar PV capacity at the Argyle International Airport as part of a $6 million energy efficiency and solar PV plant project, funded by the European Investment Bank. In 2023, the Bequia solar park will be actively pursued in the quest to enhance solar power generation in the Grenadines. There are very generous fiscal incentives for home-owners to purchase solar PV systems.

Meanwhile, VINLEC continues its drive for greater energy efficiency through the near-completion of its programme to convert the streetlights to energy-efficient LED technology with quite encouraging results. By the end of October 2021, energy consumption of the street lights declined from the equivalent of 2,483 mWh to 1,518 mWh, a fall of nearly 40 percent, giving rise to savings of $0.55 million in less than a year.

So, in respect of an increase in the practical use of renewable energy, VINLEC continues to lead the government's drive in the utilisation of hydro and solar energy, and in search of a potential game-changer in geothermal energy. At the same time, VINLEC and the government are in pursuance of energy efficiency on several fronts.

Overall, the government has elaborated a National Energy Policy and a detailed programmatic Plan of Action within the framework of the OECS and CARICOM Policy Frameworks for Renewable and Efficient Energy.

The ULP government keeps under on-going review its National Energy Policy and Detailed Plan to deliver for our people reliable, safe, clean energy at competitive, affordable, prices in all the circumstances. Thus, we continue to pursue principal renewable energy sources and energy efficient initiatives.

Central to the government's energy policy is our government's determination to keep VINLEC as a State-owned entity, never to sell it.

I recall that in the mid-to-late 1990s, there was a mania across the Eastern Caribbean initiated by some veritable ideological prelates of neo-liberalism from the World Bank and the IMF to privatise State-owned electricity companies. Three governments in the OECS succumbed to this irrational, ideological mania, completely inappropriate for our small countries. A fourth, the then NDP government in St. Vincent and the Grenadines accepted that privatisation of VINLEC was the policy to be pursued; it was announced by both Prime Minister James Mitchell and Finance Minister Arnhim Eustace. Fortunately, the ULP was elected to Office in March 2001 and reversed this stance. This, however, did not stop the ideologues of "free enterprise" and "privatisation" from near and far to continue actively their wrong-headed campaign to privatise VINLEC and the CWSA. They are ignorant of that which they are most assured.

For several years into the post-2001 era, some staff members of both the World Bank and the IMF, in their consultations with my government, pushed this privatisation mantra relentlessly. They were never able to answer satisfactorily or at all some straightforward questions, such as: How would the privatisation of VINLEC bring an end to its virtual monopoly in its delivery of safe, reliable, electricity in a *small* country like St. Vincent and the Grenadines? Why does anyone think that a private sector *monopoly* would be more efficient than a State-operated one? Would privatisation of VINLEC not lead to foreign ownership or control of it? Is VINLEC in State-ownership not being run more efficiently than when it was under non-State, foreign ownership hitherto? Are the sources of capital funding for VINLEC's expansion not likely to be cheaper and more reliable if the company is in State hands than in private hands? Where is the evidence that electricity companies in the Caribbean owned by the private sector (whether local or foreign), deliver electricity any safer, more reliably or cheaper than VINLEC? Is a private sector monopoly in electricity more or less likely to accommodate technology change and renewable energy than a State-owned one?

Countries in the Eastern Caribbean that privatised their electricity companies are now regretting the error of their ways. Still, there are the ideologues, in and out of St. Vincent and the Grenadines, and those motivated by self-interest, who still hanker for a "free enterprise", privately-owned VINLEC. This is a wrong idea for St. Vincent and the Grenadines, certainly in the actual, as distinct from any unreal or fanciful, condition of our country.

Meanwhile, the Hugo Chavez Fuel Storage Facility at Lowmans Bay, owned jointly by the governments of St. Vincent and the Grenadines and the Bolivarian Republic of Venezuela, through State-owned companies, continues to play a pivotal role in the delivery of energy products to consumers. Prior to the establishment of this facility under the ULP government, there was storage for diesel and gasoline for just about two-weeks' supply; now, there is storage for in excess of three months' supply.

Currently, in conjunction with VINLEC, the ULP government is pursuing a programme to ensure that every household without electricity is supplied with it; this will take the country from 98 percent penetration to 100 percent electrification of households. Since 2020, this programme has accelerated due to the necessity for online teaching and learning during the time of the COVID pandemic. From the school population, we identify those students whose homes are without electricity and proceed to install it; oft-times the programme requires housing repairs or reconstruction. Consequent upon the volcanic eruptions and the extensive damage to housing infrastructure, the execution of this programme is accorded the highest priority.

The Energy Unit of the government under the Ministry of Energy works closely with VINLEC in the further elaboration and implementation of the government's energy policy.

CWSA: Water and Sewerage

The Central Water and Sewerage Authority (CWSA), a statutory body of the government of St. Vincent and the Grenadines founded over 50 years ago in 1969, is directly responsible for the delivery of water, solid waste and other sanitary services. Its asset base was approximately EC $100 million at December 31, 2020; its annual revenue for 2020 stood at $28.5 million, below pre-COVID revenues of $29.6 million in 2019.

Since 2001, the CWSA, under the proactive leadership of the ULP government has effected the following, among other activities:

• Built out the Windward Water Supply System from Jennings Valley to completion in 2006 at a cost of EC $23 million. This system has enhanced water-delivery immensely to numerous areas (North Central Windward from Byrea Southwards; South Central Windward; and South Windward), and increased water supply by about 30 percent.

• Invested a further $28 million in capital works on water supply between 2006 and 2018, while at the same time, reducing its long-term debt from $29 million in 2006 to $4 million in 2019. This expenditure resulted in increasing island-wide storage after 2006 by 30 percent from 4 million gallons in 2006 to 5.4 million gallons in 2015.

Between 2006 and 2019, the additional storage tanks, as detailed below, were installed:

Majorca (2006)	500,000 gallons at a cost of $2.2 million
Layou (2007)	100,000 gallons at a cost of $400,000
Fancy (2008)	200,000 gallons at a cost of $120,000
Airy Hill, Buccament (2009)	20,000 gallons at a cost of $120,000
Perseverance (Dickson, 2009)	250,000 gallons at a cost of $820,000
Akers (2010)	20,000 gallons at a cost of $100,000
Mamoom (Mt. St. Andrew, 2011)	50,000 gallons at a cost of $190,000
Jack Hill/Rose Hall (2013)	250,000 gallons at a cost of $1.1 million
Belle Isle (2015)	500,000 gallons at a cost of $1.6 million
Sandy Bay (2018)	100,000 gallons at a cost of $250,000

Other capital expenditure initiatives of CWSA since 2006, include:

New Majorca Transmission Main	at a cost of $1.5 million
Geographic Information System Pipeline Mapping	costing $1.2 million
SCADA, Remote Monitoring System	at a cost of $0.5 million
Setting up Water Management Unit	at a cost of $0.1 million
Building Solid Waste Office, Arnos Vale	costing $0.9 million
Modern Technical Operations Building at Montrose	costing $1.3 million
Building Septage Lagoon at Diamond	costing $1.4 million
Truck Loader Equipment Replacement	costing $2.8 million
Garbage Trucks Replacement	costing $2.0 million
Skip Truck Replacement	at a cost of $0.7 million
Installation of Sewerage Treatment Plant, Arnos Vale	costing $0.085 million
Water Treatment Plant at Mamoom	costing $0.135 million
New Dallaway Transmission Main	costing $0.45 million
Water Desalination Plant in Paget Farm	costing $2.0 million

In the years 2020 and 2021, the following major capital projects, among others, were undertaken:

• In 2020, CWSA embarked on a new 250,000 gallon storage tank at Sandy Bay at a cost of $1.5 million.

In 2021, the following works, including others, were done:

• The completion of the Kelbourney water storage tank construction and associated transmission pipeline upgrades.

• The completion of Mt. Wynne/Peter's Hope Water Supply Extension Project to facilitate hotel development in these areas at a cost of $1.0 million.

• The continuation, and subsequent suspension of the $2.0 million Francois Water Supply Intake Project in the aftermath of the April 2021 volcanic eruptions.

For 2022, the CWSA budgeted $6.7 million in capital spending. Significant water supply improvement projects for 2022 include:

• The Golden Vale to Calliaqua transmission pipeline upgrade to improve capacity in the developing tourism, commercial, and industrial belt.

- Planning and Design work on the vital relocation and upgrade of the Kingstown Sewerage outfall pipeline, in conjunction with the modern Port Project in the Rose Place area.

- The continuation of the Francois Water Supply Project in the Vermont Valley to increase resilience in the dry season and to enhance water capacity for new tourism developments in the South and Central Leeward areas.

- Transmission and distribution upgrades on the Montreal system so as to increase supply capacity in the southeast region of St. Vincent.

Arising out of the April 2021 volcanic eruptions are two significant capital projects: (a) The CWSA's engineers have now markedly advanced planning and design work on the further upgrade of its Perseverance source; and (b) even more importantly is the project involving ground water source development at Overland so as to reduce the dependence on surface or river water for the communities north of the Rabacca River, particularly north of Orange Hill. These two major projects are being funded by a soft-loan from the World Bank under the Volcanic Eruption Emergency Package (VEEP) to the government, which delivers it as a grant to CWSA.

Unfortunately, due to the remaining thick deposits of volcanic ash on the slopes of the volcano, and given the fact that the Sandy Bay, Owia and Fancy intakes (all north of Overland) are all situated on the volcano slopes, the communities in these areas will continue to experience repeated cycles of interrupted water supply and restoration each time there is moderate-to-heavy rainfall resulting in lahars. This relatively unstable water supply system, consequent upon the volcanic eruptions, is being buttressed in the short-term by temporary storage and distribution arrangements initiated by the CWSA. The VEEP Overland groundwater project would reduce considerably the dependence of these northeastern communities on the three supply systems (Sandy Bay, Owia, Fancy) on the slopes of the volcano.

The CWSA is a well-run, professional entity that delivers abundant quality water, reliably, at a very low cost to the consumer. Even with the challenges in the northeast of St. Vincent, due to the volcanic eruptions of 2021, it is generally accepted that St. Vincent has, arguably, the best delivery of quality water to its people at the lowest price in the Caribbean. In 2001, quality pipe-borne water was directly available to under

70 percent of the 30,558 households at that time; today, 2022, some 98 percent of the households (some 42,000) have pipe-borne water directly to them. In the Grenadine Islands coverage is practically universal through public-private delivery systems.

In May 2001, garbage (solid waste) collection and disposal outside of Kingstown and its immediate environs were practically non-existent; by the end of 2001, the ULP administration ensured that CWSA delivered this service throughout St. Vincent and the Grenadines.

Due to the continuation of the COVID pandemic and the volcanic eruptions in 2021, the financial performance of the CWSA declined relative to 2020. Still, water and sewerage operations realised a small surplus in 2021 despite the following:

The loss of $0.7 million in revenue from the red and orange zones (the areas closest to and most affected by the volcanic eruptions).

The grant in consumer relief of $0.1 million.

An increase in expenditure of $0.2 million on account of system rehabilitation and restoration in the immediate post-volcanic eruptions period, and the challenges associated with more health and safety protocols because of the pandemic.

In 2021, the Solid Waste Management Unit of the CWSA was further severely impacted by the COVID-19 pandemic: It lost $1.2 million mainly due to the revenue shortfall from environmental cruise ship and stay-over levies as a consequence of the sharp decline in cruise and stay-over tourism; thus, Solid Waste revenues fell by 12 percent.

Despite the revenue shortfalls, CWSA increased its capital spending on plant and equipment renewal in order to maintain critical operation and service levels in the management of solid waste.

In 2021, while there was only a modest increase in receivables on mainland St. Vincent for "solid waste services", the continued non-payment of the environmental fee by Grenadines' consumers caused an increase in solid waste receivables in the Grenadines. In 2018, the CWSA completed a write-off of $1.2 million of uncollected fees in the Grenadines; yet, at the start of 2022, the solid waste receivables in the Grenadines have again risen to $1.0 million. It is wholly unfair to the CWSA and the people of St. Vincent and the Grenadines for this delinquency to continue.

In the aftermath of the 2021 volcanic eruptions, the management and workers of CWSA were heroic in restoring safe water supply to 90 percent of St. Vincent and the Grenadines one week after the first explosive eruption. The CWSA team worked around the clock in their endeavours to serve the people of St. Vincent and the Grenadines.

Over the next ten years, under a ULP administration, the CWSA will focus on: Sanitation and Water supply initiatives; green water and waste water engineering and planning; strengthening its social contract with its consumers and especial target groups such as the over 65-year-olds, including enhancing services at very affordable levels; and lifting management and labour productivity further, ramping up more the utilisation of appropriate technological innovations and enhancing maintenance efficiency. CWSA has a detailed 10-year work programme (2020-2030); much of it was outlined in the ULP's Election Manifesto of 2020.

CWSA does not receive a subsidy from the government for its operations. In the 2022 Estimates a subvention of $1.35 million has been allocated to CWSA to pay for water, solid waste, and other services provided by it to the central government. It is doubtful that there is a better-run water and solid waste entity anywhere in the Caribbean. It is noteworthy that CWSA delivers almost 100 percent of its water to consumers by way of a gravity-fed system; it avoids expensive energy costs associated with pumping water up hill. And almost all of its water reservoirs and supply systems are inter-connected.

The ULP government gives the assurance it will never privatise CWSA. Privatising CWSA is a terrible idea!

Bank of St. Vincent and the Grenadines, Banking, Cooperative Credit Unions

The Bank of St. Vincent and the Grenadines (BOSVG) is currently majority-owned by the government of St. Vincent and the Grenadines (43.13 percent directly by the government and 20 percent by the National Insurance Services — NIS); the other shareholders are the East Caribbean Financial Holding Company of St. Lucia (20 percent), and nationals of St. Vincent and the Grenadines (over 16 percent). Formerly, the BOSVG was known as the National Commercial Bank (NCB) of St. Vincent and the Grenadines.

The NCB was established 45 years ago in 1977 by the former St. Vincent and the Grenadines Labour Party government under the leadership of Robert Milton Cato. It started its initial operations with a stated capital of $14 million; by the end of 2019, the last immediate pre-pandemic year, the shareholders' equity was $125.4 million. As at December 31, 2019, the BOSVG's asset base was $1.127 billion up from $395 million in 2001.

The raw numbers between 2001 and 2019 tell a compelling story of the success of NCB/BOSVG as follows:

Snapshot Of NCB/BOSVG: 2001-2019

OPERATING RESULTS	2001 (EC$)	2019 (EC$)
Net Income	2.2 million	14 million
Total Assets	395.1 million	1.127 billion
Loans and Advances	276.4 million	603 million
Total Deposits	339.3 million	910.3 million
Shareholders' Equity	18.5 million	125.4 million
Capital Adequacy	11.3 percent	26.2 percent
Impaired Loans as a % of all loans	18.0 percent	6.5 percent
Book Value per share	$1.92	$8.35
Earnings per share	$0.22	$0.94

A summary of BOSVG's performance of the last 4-5 years is instructive; the BOSVG has been accelerating its growth performance on loans, deposits, and assets as follows:

Loans BOSVG

2015-2016	2019-2020	Growth Value	Growth Rate
$578.0 million	$641.10 million	$63.10 million	11 percent

Deposits BOSVG

2015-2016	2019-2020	Growth Value	Growth Rate
$651.30 million	$990.30 million	$339.0 million	52 percent

Assets BOSVG

2015-2016	2019-2020	Growth Value	Growth Rate
$889.20 million	$1.214 billion	$314.80 million	35 percent

The comparative performance of the other commercial banks, and other major financial institutions and credit unions in St. Vincent and the Grenadines on loans, deposits, and assets indicates the growing dominance of the BOSVG. These other such institutions are

Imperial Bank of Commerce/First Caribbean International Bank (CIBC/FCIB), Republic Bank, Royal Bank of Trinidad and Tobago (RBTT), St. Vincent Cooperative Bank, St. Vincent Building and Loan Association, Government Employees Credit Union (GECCU), Kingstown Cooperative Credit Union (KCCU), and the St. Vincent and the Grenadines Teachers Cooperative Credit Union (SVGCCU).

LOANS ($ million) Other Banks/Credit Unions

Institutions	2015–2016	2019–2020	Growth Value	Growth Rate
CIBC/FCIB	$131.40	$157.0	$25.60	19 percent
Republic Bank	$357.70	$317.0	$(40.70)	-11 percent
RBTT	$115.80	$93.0	$(22.80)	-20 percent
St. Vincent Cooperative Bank	101.90	$103.90	$2.0	2 percent
St. Vincent Building & Loan	$135.20	$112.20	$(23.0)	-17 percent
GECCU	$123.40	$167.70	$44.30	36 percent
KCCU	$59.70	$80.30	$20.60	35 percent
SVGTCCU	$62.60	$87.40	$24.80	40 percent

Deposits ($ million) Other Banks/Credit Unions

Institutions	2015–2016	2019–2020	Growth Value	Growth Rate
CIBC/FCIB	$381.60	$530.0	$148.40	39 percent
Republic Bank	$377.90	$353.0	$(24.90)	-7 percent
RBTT	$291.20	$192.00	$(99.20)	-34 percent
St. Vincent Co-operative Bank	$164.60	$157.10	$(7.50)	-5 percent
St. Vincent Building & Loan	$116.10	$102.60	$(13.50)	-12 percent
GECCU	$176.80	$259.20	$82.40	47percent

KCCU	$72.70	$99.80	$27.10	37 percent
SVGTCCU	$84.00	$122.00	$38.00	45 percent

Assets ($ Million) Other Banks/Credit Unions

Institutions	2015-2016	2019-2020	Growth Value	Growth Rate
CIBC/FCIB	$426.30	$569.0	$142.70	33 percent
Republic Bank	$450.00	$388.0	$(62.10)	-14 percent
RBTT	$376.90	$226.0	$(150.90)	-40 percent
St. Vincent Co-operative Bank	$188.00	$192.80	$4.80	3 percent
St. Vincent Building & Loan	$172.10	$149.60	$(22.50)	-13 percent
GECCU	$210.40	$314.80	$104.40	50percent
KCCU	$92.0	$122.90	$30.90	34 percent
SVGTCCU	$114.10	$151.60	$37.50	-33 percent

The comparative analysis of the performance of the major financial institutions in St. Vincent and the Grenadines and the salient issues arising therefrom, are evident from the data presented.

In 2001, the ULP government met the NCB in a mess. Among the messy facts were the following:

The stated capital of $18.5 million was hardly sufficient for the bank's stability; and the bank was determined to be severely impacted given the large credit exposures held on the loan portfolio at the time. In particular, credit exposure to Valdattaro Shipyard, an Italian company, and as majority shareholder of CCYY Limited (the company involved in the failed Ottley Hall project), and Union Island Resorts Limited (linked to the Italian investors at Ottley Hall) shackled the bank. In the aggregate, $35 million of their indebtedness to the bank had to be written off. Further, preferred NDP borrowers treated the bank as their veritable "Piggy Bank".

The impaired loans as a percentage of total loans stood at a whopping 18 percent. (The industry standard at the time was 10 percent; the best practice now is 5 percent).

For the two financial years — 1998 and 1999 — the independent Auditors issued qualified financial statements on account of unsatisfactory practices and non-credible or inadequate explanations about audit queries.

The management, supervisory, and credit control systems were deemed wholly unsatisfactory by the Eastern Caribbean Central Bank.

In December 2000, due to the "blacklisting" of St. Vincent and the Grenadines by the Financial Action Task Force (FATF) on account of uncontrolled money laundering and the alleged illegal use of the proceeds of crimes, the major correspondent bank, the Bank of America, severed its corresponding banking relationship with NCB.

In the first 25 years or so of the NCB's operations (1977 to 2001), 17 years of which the bank was under the direction of the NDP government, the capital base of the bank moved from $14 million to almost $19 million, an increase of some 36 percent. (In contrast, it is to be noted that in the subsequent 18 years up to 2019 under the ULP government, the capital base of the bank increased to $125.4 million, a growth of 560 percent).

Swiftly, the ULP government began the process of reforming and strengthening the bank in accordance with a plan devised between the Eastern Caribbean Central Bank and the government itself.

In 2010, in response to the prolonged global economic crisis from September 2008, the liquidity crunch plus under-capitalisation in a small bank, prompted the government sensibly to offload more than half of its NCB debt to the Caribbean Development Bank and to sell 51 percent of the bank's shares, at book value, to the Eastern Caribbean Financial Holding (ECFH) company in St. Lucia. In July 2017, the government repurchased 31 percentage points of what it had sold at a price of $6.96 per share. A mere 2 ½ years later, at the end of December 2019, the book value of the shares was $8.35 per share, representing an appreciation in the value per share of $1.39 or a 20 percent rise. At the time of the government's "buy-back", it sold approximately 17 percent of the bank's shareholding to private individuals, including workers at the bank. The government correctly assessed that a bank is not the same kind of service, like water and electricity, and thus amenable in our circumstances, to a public-private ownership structure. The upshot of all this is that today, the government and the State-run National Insurance Service (NIS) own 63 percent of the bank's shares — the government, 43 percent, the NIS 20 percent. The government (central government and public enterprises) is the bank's largest single customer with loans of just over $100 million in a loan portfolio of $660 million.

Some other highlights of the performance of the NCB-BOSVG since 2001 include:

The asset base of the bank has grown significantly over the last 20 years and crossed the $1 billion mark in 2018 from $395 million in 2001; by 2020, the bank's assets stood at $1.214 billion, the largest of any commercial bank in St. Vincent and the Grenadines.

The bank recorded profits in every year since 2001 with the exception of 2003; in 2003, additional provisioning was made relating to the bad debts from the NDP years. The cumulative profitability of the bank between 2001 and 2020 is over $140 million.

Over the past 10 years, the bank's Capital Adequacy Ratio (CAR) stood over 20 percent, well above the minimum legal requirement of 8 percent set by the Central Bank; at the end of December 2019, the CAR stood at 26.2 percent, slightly above the CAR at the end of 2020.

The book value of the shares increased from $6.96 per share in July 2017 to $8.35 at December 2019.

The correspondent banking relationship with Bank of America was swiftly restored due to appropriate anti-money laundering initiatives and other robust measures against the use of the proceeds of crime: These initiatives and measures included the passage of the Financial Intelligence Unit in 2002; the enactment of a modern Proceeds of Crime and Anti-Money Laundering statute in late 2001; the issuance of supporting regulations and guidance notes to banks, including the NCB; the reform of the menu of legislation for, and the regulation of, offshore finance institutions to meet international standards; and the active strengthening of the relationships between St. Vincent and the Grenadines and relevant international agencies. In 2003, St. Vincent and the Grenadines was removed from the FATF "blacklist". A little later, the government consolidated and strengthened these measures and initiatives, including the passage of the Financial Services Authority (FSA) Act and the setting up of a strong FSA to regulate, in accord with the evolving international standards, the offshore finance sector, insurance companies, and credit unions. Meanwhile, the Eastern Caribbean Central Bank's authority was enhanced and a more robust Banking Act was passed by Parliament, designed, among other things, to strengthen the regulation of commercial banks.

Between 2011 and 2019, the last immediate pre-pandemic year, the government received an aggregate of over $11 million in dividends from the Bank.

Over the six-year period (2015-2020), the government received from the Bank in payments of interest levy and corporate taxes some $43 million.

Over the past 15 years, under the 100 percent house mortgage loans (no deposit) for public servants, the bank loaned over $75 million; this programme remains the best single performing mortgage portfolio with the lowest delinquency rates.

Since the COVID-19 pandemic from March 13, 2020, and continuing, the following highlights of the BOSVG's performance are worthy of note:

In 2020, the Bank recorded a profit, before tax, of $6.4 million, down from $16.2 million in pre-COVID 2019. The main contributing factor to the reduction of profitability was the additional loan loss provisions of $11.5 million allocated mainly to the portion of the portfolio impacted by the pandemic – specifically the loans placed under the loan moratorium programme. At its peak in December 2020, the BOSVG's loan moratorium programme consisted of 798 customers with a total loan value of $97.5 million, representing 15 percent of the total gross loans of $672.3 million.

The 2021 financial performance of the Bank, when assessed independently by the Auditors, is likely to be slightly below the 2020 level, as the pandemic continues to impact adversely. While the overall earnings of the Bank remained relatively healthy, though slightly down from the pre-COVID level, the Bank is anticipating that loan loss provisions attributable to the moratorium loans will remain at the 2020 level, thus impacting the overall profitability. It is, however, expected that over 80 percent of the moratorium loan portfolio will return to normal repayment status by the end of the first quarter in 2022.

Given the increases in loan loss provisions over the 2020 and 2021 periods, coverage ratio, that is, the percentage of loan loss provisions to the total non-performing loans, is likely to have increased from 60.1 percent in 2019 to just over 100 percent by the end of 2021.

The total non-performing loans are estimated at just around 6 percent of total loans — close to "best practice" parameters.

The bank has been modernising its operations and enhancing its efficacious application of information technology. In the October to December 2021 period, the bank has successfully transitioned well over 7,000 of its 12,000 online banking customers to its new state-of-the-art online banking platform; the remaining 5,000 online customers are expected to have been transitioned by the end of March 2022. The bank also partnered with the Central Bank to launch the digital currency, D-Cash in November 2021; to date, over 110 merchants and 153 retail clients are established on the D-Cash platform.

In the latter half of 2021, the BOSVG and CIBC-FCIB announced that the BOSVG has agreed to purchase the CIBC-FCIB operations in St. Vincent and the Grenadines, as part of the sale of that foreign bank's operations in the OECS countries to indigenous banks; BOSVG was the lead bank in these discussions. The purchase agreement, and all matters incidental thereto were approved by the Eastern Caribbean Central Bank before the end of July 2022. Meanwhile, the two entities have been actively engaged in the planning for the full integration of banking business during the second half of 2022.

The purchase of CIBC-FCIB, has made the BOSVG, by far, the largest bank in St. Vincent and the Grenadines. The combined assets of both entities amount to $1.783 billion and dwarfs the size of the assets of Republic Bank ($388 million), RBTT ($226 million), and the savings bank St. Vincent Cooperative Bank ($193 million); the assets of these three last-named banks total, in the aggregate, $807 million. Indeed, when you add to this the assets of the St. Vincent Building and Loan Association ($150 million) and the three largest credit unions, GECCU ($315 million), KCCU ($123 million), and SVGTCCU ($152 million), the combined total assets amount to $1.547 billion, or $236 million less than the integrated assets of the post-purchase expansion of BOSVG.

Similar comparables can be made from the data provided in the tables herein in respect of the loans and deposits of the "new" BOSVG and the other major financial institutions in St. Vincent and the Grenadines. Clearly, this purchase by the BOSVG of CIBC-FCIB presents immense opportunities for BOSVG, and challenges to it and the banking system itself; but these challenges have sensible, appropriate solutions both for the BOSVG and the Eastern Caribbean Central Bank, as regulator.

From very humble beginnings in 1977, the NCB/BOSVG has grown to become the major commercial bank in St. Vincent and the Grenadines. In that entity the State (government and NIS) holds nearly two-thirds of shares. Still, even with an asset-base of $1.783 billion, the "new" BOSVG will be a small bank; thus, its capitalization, its management of credit, the quality of its assets, its liquidity, and its overall management must be optimal for its sustainability. The second largest bank in St. Vincent and the Grenadines is Republic Bank (which purchased the local operations of Bank of Nova Scotia), headquartered in Trinidad and Tobago. Republic Bank with an extensive banking presence throughout the Caribbean, and beyond, has the capacity to provide strong competition to BOSVG. Similarly, the purchase of RBTT's local operations by the First National Bank of St. Lucia, is likely to provide enhanced competition, too. Further, other banking reconfigurations or amalgamations are also possible to alter further the banking landscape. The BOSVG itself may figure in these further potential reconfigurations. In this regard, BOSVG will always act within the interests of its shareholders and the stability of the banking/financial system.

The phenomenal growth of credit unions particularly GECCU, KCCU, and SVGTCCU adds to the competitive mix in respect of loans and deposits. Between 2015-2016 and 2019-2020, these three credit unions saw increases to their deposits, respectively, of 47 percent, 37 percent, and 45 percent. To be sure, the BOSVG and CIBC-FCIB had their deposits grow, respectively, by 52 percent and 39 percent, in the same comparable period while declines in deposits were evident in Scotia Bank/Republic Bank, RBTT, S. Vincent Cooperative Bank, and the Building and Loan Association.

A similar impressive growth in assets and loans of the three major credit unions can be gleaned from the data in the tables presented earlier.

It is likely that the dramatic decline of the RBTT in respect of deposits, loans, and assets in the period 2015/2016-2019/2020 was due largely to the RBTT's policy decision to close the accounts of a large number of customers with small loans and minimal banking transactions. Lots of these customers migrated to the credit unions, and to a lesser extent to BOSVG, and the First St. Vincent Bank, a small indigenous savings bank.

Clearly, the size of the three largest credit unions, among others, and the Friendly Societies required proper regulation. The Cooperatives Division of the Ministry of Social Development had neither the institutional nor technical capacity to regulate them. Thus, the FSA was created to carry out this regulatory and supervisory function.

The indebtedness of the private sector to the BOSVG at the end of September 2021, stood at $531 million; that of the central government was $128 million. The domestic private sector's indebtedness to the entire financial sector in St. Vincent and the Grenadines, exclusive of higher purchase agreements and unregulated money-lenders, is approximately $1.7 billion; the total *domestic* public debt (government and public enterprises) amount to some $525 million; clearly, the government is *not* "crowding out" loans to the private sector. Bear in mind, too, that deposits in the banks, the Building and Loan Association, and the credit unions, at the end of 2021, exceeded $3 billion.

The BOSVG is a vital institution in the drive to build a modern, competitive, many-sided post-colonial economy, fit for purpose in the overall quest for sustainable development in the people's interest.

National Insurance Services and Social Security

The National Insurance Services (NIS) is absolutely vital in the enhancing of social security and socio-economic development, overall, for the people of St. Vincent and the Grenadines. The NIS provides a comprehensive social security benefit package, focusing on pensions, employment injury, disability, sickness, and maternity benefits.

The NIS statute was first introduced in Parliament by the SVG Labour Party government in mid-1984 to build upon the National Provident Fund, but it fell upon the dissolution of Parliament for the July 1984 general elections. The Bill for the NIS was reintroduced and passed in Parliament under the NDP government in 1987. Over the past 21 years, the ULP government has presided over the reform and legislative strengthening of the NIS and its phenomenal expansion. As a result of this, the NIS has been positively transforming the lives of Vincentians through social and income security, economic stability, poverty reduction, human capital development, and health sector strengthening.

A snapshot of the progress of the NIS under the ULP government includes the following:

Enhancing Income and Social Security

The number of active contributors (employees, self-employed and voluntary) increased from 30,385 in 2000 to 42,856 in pre-COVID 2019, declining marginally to 42,749 in 2020, and a further decline in 2021 to 40,968, provisionally; between 2000 and 2019, there was a 41 percent increase in active contributors. The category "active employees" increased from 30,076 in 2000 to 41,191 in pre-COVID 2019, a rise of 37 percent; "active employees" fell marginally in 2020, the first COVID year, to 40,942 and then dropped more markedly in 2021 (second pandemic year and the year of volcanic eruptions) to 39,330; between 2019 and 2021, "active employees" declined by 1,861 or by almost 5 percent. (The NIS estimates that some 15-20 percent of employed persons have not as yet registered at the NIS; thus, the "active contributors" plus 15-20 percent provide a good indication of the number of persons in gainful employment in St. Vincent and the Grenadines.)

The number of pensioners increased from 2,940 in 2000 to 8,240 in 2019, to 9,169 (provisionally) in 2021, an actual increase of 6,229 or 212 percent; between 2019 and 2021, the number of pensioners actually increased by 11 percent, showing that as the NIS system matures, a decline in active contributors does not automatically result in a fall in the number of pensioners.

The average weekly pensions increased from $44.27 in 2000 to $159.71 in 2019 and $168.04 in 2021; between 2000 and 2021, the average weekly pension increased by $123.77 or 280 percent.

The average annual insurable wages increased from $14,374 in 2000 to $23,581 in 2020, an increase of $9,207 or 64 percent.

The number of registered employers at the NIS increased from 1,857 in 2001 to 2,347 in pre-COVID 2019; in 2020, this number declined marginally to 2,314 and more sharply in 2021 to 2,066; between 2020 and 2021, the number of registered employers fell by 248 or by nearly 11 percent – the impact of the pandemic and the volcanic eruptions.

Pensions increased on four occasions under the ULP government: in 2002, between 3-6 percent; in 2005, between 3-6 percent; in 2008, between 4.5 and 9 percent; and in 2012, between 1.5 and 4.5 percent; under the NDP government, for 17 years, pensions increased once.

The funeral grant increased from $3,000 in 2000 to $4,525 in 2015 where it currently remains; and the maternity benefit rose from $400 in 2000 to $660 in 2012, where it still remains.

Contributing to Economic Stability

The asset base of the NIS increased hugely from $218.7 million in 2000 to $494.3 million in 2019; in 2020, the asset base increased to $503 million, and it grew marginally to $505 million in 2021. Between 2000 and 2021, the asset base increased by $286.3 million or 131 percent. The growth in the asset base is commendable for a maturing social security pension fund operating in an extremely challenging economic environment, in a pandemic and at a time of early recovery from the devastating volcanic eruptions of April 2021.

There is regular investment participation by the NIS in government investment securities (mainly bonds and loans) in St. Vincent and the Grenadines, and elsewhere; the returns on these investments strengthen the NIS. The public sector in St. Vincent and the Grenadines owes the NIS at September 30, 2021, $41.4 million by way of borrowings.

The NIS owns 20 percent of the share in the Bank of St. Vincent and the Grenadines, the major commercial bank in our country; dividends from this investment bolsters the NIS.

NIS loaned some $30 million to National Properties Limited, secured by State lands and a government guarantee, to assist in the construction of the Argyle International Airport.

Tackling Poverty and Inequality

In 2019, the NIS paid out $67.976 million in benefits of which $61.465 million were in pensions' payments; in 2021, it paid out $80.524 million in benefits, of which $71.52 million were in pensions. By comparison, in 2001, the total benefits paid out by the NIS amounted to $9.763 million of which $7.494 million were in pensions. In 2001, there were 3,091 pensioners; in 2021, the number had grown to 9,169 pensioners.

The NIS provides two non-contributory pensions: (a) The Non-Contributory Age Pension, initiated in 1997, has paid out nearly $40 million thus far; currently there are over 300 beneficiaries; (b) the Elderly Assistance Benefit, instituted in 2009, has paid out in excess of $5 million thus far to some 180 beneficiaries.

Specific payments for workers displaced through the pandemic. I shall discuss this fully, later.

Building Human Capital

The NIS has loaned in excess of $25 million to the National Student Loan Company to on-lend to Vincentians pursuing university education.

The NIS has spent annually in excess of $400,000 to students who meet particular performance criteria in the CSEC and CAPE Examinations. This programme started in 2005; up to the end of 2020, nearly $6 million has been paid out. This is an innovative incentive programme for students.

Strengthening Health Services

The NIS partnered with the Bank of St. Vincent and the Grenadines to donate a CT-Scan Machine to the Ministry of Health.

It loaned over $7 million towards the construction by the government of a $50 million Modern Medical and Diagnostic Centre (MMDC) at Georgetown; the NIS has donated a top-of-the-line ambulance at a cost of $0.54 million to the MMDC.

The NIS donated $1.0 million to the Ministry of Health to fight the Zika virus.

It contributed $0.75 million in 2020 to assist in the financing of the National Isolation Facility at Argyle as part of the preparation to fight COVID-19.

Promoting the Well-Being of the Elderly

The NIS built two Golden Years' Activity Centres in Cane Grove (2004) and Black Point (2005). It provides over $60,000 annually to assist with the operations of these two Centres. The NIS plans to build a similar Centre in Marriaqua.

Improving Housing Conditions

The NIS granted a particular purpose loan of $10 million to BOSVG to assist in the provision of 100 percent home mortgage financing to central government employees.

The NIS and the Government Employees Cooperative Credit (GECCU) have jointly embarked upon a significant land development initiative at Peter's Hope on 57.2 acres of freehold land (36.6 acres are saleable for housing) for low-and-middle income earners.

Further Property Investment

The NIS owns the so-called "Ju-C" property in Kingstown and has it earmarked for property development of a commercial kind. A similar plan is afoot for a property it owns in Union Island.

The NIS owns the former Anglican Archbishop's residence at Richmond Hill. The central government has agreed to purchase it from the NIS to build a modern Law Court Complex.

The Performance of the NIS at the Time of the Pandemic and Volcanic Eruption

The National Insurance Services (NIS) did not escape the socio-economic shock waves of the pandemic and the recent volcanic eruptions. The NIS' finances were hard hit by a decline in the contribution collections and increased sickness and unemployment benefit payouts. The scope and scale of the impact would depend on the duration and pathways of the pandemic.

Notwithstanding this additional pressure on the costs and financing of social security, coupled with the challenges arising from the pandemic and the volcanic eruptions, the NIS prudently continued its human-centred and inclusive policy measures to safeguard lives and livelihoods. In particular, the NIS extended the Temporary Unemployment Benefits programme for three months in 2021; the programme thus ran from April 2020 to March 31, 2021. The leadership understood the inherent vulnerability and poverty trap of some of its members who seemed to be getting by relatively well prior to the pandemic and the eruptions, but were not adequately covered by existing social protection measures. For instance, although the current social security program of the NIS is comprehensive, it excludes unemployment insurance benefits as part of its legal social security benefits program. Globally, the unemployment insurance is the least developed branch. Global data indicate that only 18.6 per cent of unemployed workers worldwide have effective coverage for unemployment.

The pandemic showed the critical importance of the NIS for mitigating poverty and income inequality in St. Vincent and the Grenadines.

It also revealed the operational and financial resilience of the social security system. In a multi-pronged environment of extreme challenges, the NIS efficaciously delivered the following social security services and measures to promote human-centred and inclusive economic stability:

- The Temporary Unemployment Benefits Programme, which commenced in April 2020 and continued to the end of 2020, was extended for a further three months from January 1, 2021, to March 31, 2021. The NIS paid a further $1.1 million to 1,123 beneficiaries, resulting in $3.0 million total payout to 1,221 beneficiaries under the programme from April 2020 to March 2021.

- The continued administration of the Government Displacement Supplementary Income Support Programme, which ran from April 2020 for that entire year, was also extended from January 1, 2021, to June 30, 2021. In this period, the NIS administered claims to 3,642 persons at the cost of approximately $4.8 million, resulting in total payouts of $10.9 million to 4746 beneficiaries under the programme from April 2020 to June 2021.

- The payment of 1,541 COVID-19 related sickness benefit claims in 2021 at a total monetary amount of $525,000 for 12,603 sickness days. This compared to 28 COVID-19 claims at less than $20,000.00 in 2020. In 2021, an average COVID-19 claim was paid for approximately eight days at a daily cost of $78.00.

- The payment of 41 COVID-19 related funeral grants at a total cost of $181,000.00 compared to none in 2020.

- The payment of $900,000 to 444 non-contributory pensioners in 2021 compared to $1.1 million to 512 in 2020.

- The payment of $70.5 million to 8,721 contributory pensioners in 2021 compared to $64.3 million to 8,109 pensioners in 2020.

- The reinvestment in 2021 of approximately $25 million in the local economy through investment instruments, including deposits and bonds.

- The capital expenditure of approximately $2.0 million in 2020-2021 to local companies to undertake various rehabilitation work at the NIS' Headquarters.

The benefits and services provided by the NIS in 2021 were financed by contributions paid by employers and employees and a proportion of investment income. The estimated contribution collection was $67.7 million 2021 compared to $68.1 million in 2020. The decline in contribution collection was attributable to local labour market challenges relating to the rise in unemployment and underemployment due to the pandemic and the volcanic eruptions. The NIS data show that the total insured population declined by 3.5%, moving from 42,479 active employees in 2020 to 40,968 active employees in 2021. Also, there was a decrease in average weekly insurable wages from $454.00 to $447.80. Additionally, 295 employers indicated that they laid off at least one employee in 2021. Lastly, the number of active employers declined from 2,314 in 2020 to 2,035 in 2021.

Noteworthy is that contributions collections from government and statutory bodies increased by approximately $1.9 million in 2021 relative to 2020. The contribution payments from the private sector declined by about $2.3 million due to layoffs of employees by some private-sector employers, over the same period.

The maturing social security program accounted for the widening of the financing gap between contribution income ($67.7 million) and benefits ($82 million). However, the contribution/benefit gap was financed by investment income. The investment portfolio generated a net financing income of $24 million, representing an annualized yield of 5.4%. The investment yield surpassed the actuarial hurdle rate of 4.5%.

To bolster further its operational efficiency, including reducing costs and improving services quality to its customers, the NIS enhanced its human resources through various capacity building programmes in investments, risk management and corporate governance. In addition, the NIS scaled up its digitization program. To this end, the NIS increased its digital offerings to customers through building on its e-submit software, offering other e-payment options using the Automatic Clearing House channels at local commercial banks and the development of the NIS App as an additional avenue where customers can make inquiries and calculate their pensions under the NIS programme.

While the NIS competently addresses today's challenges, it positions itself to thrive in tomorrow's volatile, uncertain, complex, and ambiguous environment with a clear vision, agility, and the will to act boldly. Accordingly, several priorities are identified to close the financing and coverage gaps, enhance benefit adequacy and comprehensiveness, make the human right to social security a reality for all working

Vincentians and bolster the system's sustainability. The strategic priorities include, but are not limited to, the following:

The NIS's contribution base is broadening through improving efforts in contribution collections and bridging the coverage gaps among the self-employed and informal sector workers. In this regard, the NIS is redoubling its efforts to ensure that employers comply with the NIS Act and pay in their contributions, especially when they deduct the monies from our hardworking employees. The strategies involve moral suasion activities by the Compliance Officers complemented by the strong legal remedies of garnishing bank accounts, placing liens on delinquent employers' real properties, and taking other legal actions at both Magistrate and High Court levels. In the case of the self-employed and informal sector workers, the NIS is intensifying its direct marketing strategies, including hosting symposia, branding some self-employed activities, and forging strategic linkages with self-employed interest groups. Too many of our working Vincentians are still vulnerable to socio-economic shocks because of an absence of social protection in the form of social insurance and social assistance. This "missing middle" certainly creates a challenging vulnerability and poverty trap that cannot be left unresolved by the NIS and the government.

The NIS commenced the second phase of its digital transformation journey to strengthen its operational backbone by further digitizing its processes. In this regard, the NIS engaged Davyn Consulting Firm to develop, implement, customise, and maintain a new national insurance management system at the cost of approximately $4.2 million. This complete digitization process will take 18 months but with modular implementation. This initiative would improve operational efficiency through cost reduction, increased productivity and enhanced service quality and delivery. The modernised system intends to revolutionise the NIS' operations and customers' experience by moving the core social security services from in-line to online. This is a centre-piece of the NIS' administrative efficiency measure to improve financial sustainability.

The pandemic exposed the current social security programme's benefit adequacy and comprehensiveness gap. The current NIS programme has no automatic stabilisation initiative in the event of unemployment risk. Accordingly, the NIS intends to partner with the International Labour Organisation to conduct a feasibility study of introducing an Unemployment Insurance Programme within the NIS' suite of benefit programmes. Currently, only Barbados and Bahamas of the CARICOM states offer this benefit type. However, in 2021, Grenada, St. Lucia and Dominica social security systems have commenced feasibility studies to adopt an Unemployment Insurance Programme.

In its World Social Protection Report 2020-2022, the International Labour Organisation urged governments and social security administrators:

> To take decisive action now about the future of social protection and pursue a high-road policy approach with vigour. Doing so will empower societies to deal with future crises and the challenges posed by demographic change, the evolving world of work, migration, environmental challenges and the existential threat of climate change.

In the context of St. Vincent and the Grenadines, the government and the NIS have made progress in strengthening social protection coverage, but there is room for improvements. The NIS has considered a series of parametric reform measures to strengthen the financial sustainability of the social protection system. However, the unprecedented and unknowable socio-economic challenges brought about by COVID-19 and the volcanic eruptions, propelled the delay in implementing these critical reform measures. Through the advice of the External Actuary, the NIS will implement this tool kit shortly to ensure all working Vincentians and their dependents are well protected against both systemic shocks and ordinary life cycle risks.

In keeping with its longstanding mission of contributing to local economic and social developments, the NIS has earmarked EC$15 million in 2022 to invest in capital projects that create jobs and contribute to building the competitiveness of our local economy.

In contributing effectively to reduce poverty, contain inequality, enhance human capabilities, and foster dignity and solidarity, the NIS must strengthen inter-operability with other social protection partners to eliminate inefficiencies and better serve the vulnerable members of our society. The NIS must lead the way in breaking the administrative silos, and better coordinate with various Ministries and NGOs to strengthen the social protection framework for Vincentians, thereby reinvigorating the social contract.

St. Vincent and the Grenadines Port Authority

The St. Vincent and the Grenadines Port Authority (SVGPA) is a wholly-owned State entity that has its central functions arising first, from its ownership and management of the ports, and secondly, from its regulation of the ports. It is at one and the same time an owner-manager of ports, and the regulatory authority of ports whether or not they are owned by the Port Authority. Under the SVG Port Authority Act 1987, the declared ports are at Kingstown, Bequia, Mustique, and Union Island. Subsequently, ports of entry have been declared at Campden Park, Wallilabou, Chateaubelair, Blue Lagoon, and Canouan. The SVG Port Authority owns and operates the port facilities, which are the main ones, at Kingstown, Campden Park Container Port (98 percent owned), Bequia, Canouan, and Union Island; the Chateaubelair port is owned by the State; the Mustique, Wallilabou, and Blue Lagoon port facilities are owned by the private sector. The SVG Port Authority also owns and operates the Kingstown Cruise Ship and Ferry Berth.

The SVG Port Authority Act provides for the following: The establishment of the Port Authority; and the duties and powers of the Authority. The Act provides, too, for transfer to and investing in the Authority of functions, assets and liabilities of the Port and Marine Department and the former Port Authority established under the Port Authority Act of 1975.

Ports and the SVG Port Authority are vital for a multi-island State like St. Vincent and the Grenadines, which has an open economy for import-export trade. The Campden Park Container Port (CPCP) handles 90 percent of the container cargo entering St. Vincent and the Grenadines; the remainder comes through the Kingstown Port.

The SVG Port Authority has assets of some $150 million and employs slightly over 200 persons. It is a profitable business, but the main ports require substantial modernisation and development; it is necessary and desirable, too, to split the ownership and management of the ports from the regulatory functions of the SVG Port Authority.

The Kingstown port is an ageing port, some 60 years old; it is congested; it is falling apart and demands constant maintenance. The CPCP was built in the 1990s, but it was not built optimally either in terms of the quality of its construction or its size.

The Port Modernisation Project to replace the Kingstown Port, and CPCP, has actually commenced although construction is yet to begin in earnest, but project activities are already being carried out. Actual port construction is expected to start in late 2022. The location of the Modern Port is towards the western end of Kingstown known as Rose Place. In early May 2022, the government signed two contracts: One with the Canadian firm, AECON, to construct the port; and one with the German firm, Selhorn, for the consultancy in overseeing the port's construction. The contracts envisage a three-year construction period.

The Port Modernisation Project (PMP) is estimated to cost over EC $620 million to build and equip a modern container port and associated facilities as the first project phase. The PMP is the second largest infrastructure project ever undertaken in our country, after the Argyle International Airport, which cost some $750 million to construct and equip. It is being fully financed by a soft-loan of slightly over US $110 million by the Caribbean Development Bank (CDB), a grant of US $36 million from the United Kingdom government, US $62 million in soft-loans from a bank in the Republic of China (Taiwan) — a friendly nation — and some US $42 by the Government of St. Vincent and the Grenadines.

In a second phase of this port modernisation, the government intends to construct at the same site a Regional Ferry Berth and a Grenadines Jetty. All the technical and design work has been concluded for this second phase; the additional financing is to be sourced for this phase.

It is planned that the PMP will take three years to complete from the actual start-up of construction. The modern port will be the centre-piece of urban renewal and development in the Rose Place area of Kingstown. The State owns properties in that area on Back Street near to the Milton Cato Memorial Hospital. These properties will form part of the urban renewal and development.

The government has already acted wisely and urgently in compensating the vendors who traded towards the seaward end of the proposed site; it has already built 47 homes (one, two and three bedrooms) at Lowmans Bay to resettle the 51 families affected — two families have opted for compensation; and two others are having, as per their request, houses built for them on their own land elsewhere. In the 51 families, there are 129 persons affected for housing resettlement. Vendors with structures on the site are also being compensated. , are the fishers who operate from the locale at Rose Place; the fishers are being located elsewhere. The government is being generous to all affected persons who are to be relocated. The ULP government has a history of handling such relocations, compensation payments and continued or alternative livelihoods very well and to the satisfaction of all affected persons.

When the PMP is completed, it is in the plans of the government to develop the site of the old Kingstown Port area in a public-private partnership; and one option for the CPCP is to lease it to a private sector entity as an entrepot location; there is a demand for such facilities across the Caribbean.

The government intends to form a State-owned company to own and manage the modern port with possible share ownership from appropriate private sector investors. A separate regulatory authority will be established to regulate all ports, private sector and State-owned.

The State is rightly leading in port modernisation and development in St. Vincent and the Grenadines in the people's interests.

Argyle International Airport Incorporated

The Argyle International Airport Incorporated was established as a wholly-owned State corporation under the Companies Act of St. Vincent and the Grenadines to manage and operate the Argyle International Airport (AIA), which was built by the special-purpose State-owned company, the International Airport Development Agency (IADC). The Airport was opened on February 14, 2017. Domestic, regional, international and private aircraft fly into and out of AIA on a daily and weekly basis. International flights are available to and from Miami, New York, Toronto, and London.

The lands on which the airport (aerodrome, passenger and cargo terminals, and ancillary/supportive facilities) stand are in government hands and the process of transferring them to the AIA Incorporated is underway. There are some 300 employees at AIA Incorporated.

The management of AIA is also responsible for the management of the Jet Airport at Canouan and the smaller airports in Bequia and Union Island; the airport at Mustique is owned and operated by the Mustique Company, but the Immigration, Customs, and Border Security functions are performed by the State authorities. The Directorate of Airport Services in conjunction with the Eastern Caribbean Civil Aviation Authority (ECCAA) regulate civil aviation in our country's jurisdiction. The Air Transport Licensing Board of St. Vincent and the Grenadines, a State authority, licences the aircraft that fly into and out of its jurisdiction, on the advice of ECCAA and the Directorate.

St. Vincent and the Grenadines is the only CARICOM member State that, in the 21st century, built and commenced operations of both an international airport (at Argyle) and a jet airport (at Canouan); both were built by the ULP administration.

Part of the business plan of AIA Incorporated was that the international airport would require a subvention from the central government for the first three years or so. Unfortunately, the pandemic from March 11, 2020, and continuing, and the volcanic eruptions of April 2021 conspired to reduce markedly air traffic into and out of St. Vincent and the Grenadines. Consequently, the central government's subvention continues into the AIA's fifth year of operation. Were it not for the pandemic and the volcanic eruptions, the AIA Incorporated is unlikely to have been in need of the subvention for recurrent expenditure.

Since the opening of AIA, the actualisation of its potential has been made manifest. The opening of AIA has prompted significant investment, domestic and foreign, in hotel and other tourism infrastructure, for example, Sandals/Beaches Hotel, Royal Mill, Black Sands Resorts, the Liming in Bequia, Myah's Luxury Suites, two State-owned hotel projects (Marriott at Mt. Wynne, Holiday Inn Express at Diamond), and the expansion of several boutique/family-owned hotels.

The Argyle International Airport, the tourism investments, the jobs and wealth created are all part and parcel of the building of a post-colonial economy of a sustainable kind.

In Budget 2022, there is a subvention to AIA Incorporated of $6.2 million; capital provision of $5 million to rehabilitate the runway/pavement; and a further provision of $0.337 million for a security scanning machine at AIA. Additionally, for other airports under AIA Incorporated's management, there are allocations in the capital budget for rehabilitation of J.F. Mitchell Airport (Bequia); rehabilitation of Canouan Airport, and a rehabilitation project generally for airports in the Grenadines (Bequia, Canouan, Union Island); the details for these are listed in the Appendix to this volume relating to the capital projects for 2022 by Ministry.

Chapter Six

Conclusion and Further Directions

Managing the Paradigm Shift

The paradigm shift toward the quest to build a modern, competitive, many-sided post-colonial economy has enabled the country, led by the government, to embrace fresh, different, and better ways of thinking and doing things, individually and collectively, in solidarity with each other, rather than to continue with outmoded, wrongheaded, or dead end approaches that fall way short of optimal benefits for the people, individually and collectively.

The paradigm, understood as a comprehensive organising *model* or *theory* with great explanatory power is — in the real world of life, living, and production — akin to a promissory note; the actualisation of the paradigm is essentially the redemption of that promissory note. The achievements in this process of redeeming are necessarily uneven; however, for there to be an overall trajectory of success of the paradigm shift, the unevenness must be within the reality of *combined development of a sustainable kind*; there is, thus, the applicability of a veritable "law" of uneven and combined development common to all historical processes.

The paradigm shift to the construction of a post-colonial economy is not merely to correct anomalies from the outmoded colonial or amended colonial economy. To be sure, the paradigm shift in the real, as distinct from an ideational, world builds upon what existed before and embarks upon a process of transforming it for the better, while at the same time creatively constructing that which is fresh, that which is novel, that which is transformative. Thus, the paradigm shift has two defining dimensions: Transforming lives, living and production, not merely adding in a cumulative way to that which was met but changing it to something different and better as, for example as metaphor, water heated to 100 degrees Celsius becomes transformed into steam; and building completely innovative modalities and realities that were hitherto non-existent or barely existent.

Contradictions abound in the complexities, fluidity and inter-connectedness of constructing a modern, competitive, many-sided post-colonial economy that is at once local, national, regional, and global. The profound changes or alterations in the economic arrangements are inextricably tied up with the political and social processes, as they evolve. These contradictions, complexities and evolutions manifest themselves dialectically through the actions of real flesh and blood individuals in their classes, groups, political affiliations, religious connections, or familial linkages. These changes or alterations, at the centre of the paradigm shift, are required to take place in St. Vincent and the Grenadines through parliamentary means in a competitive political system, and within the framework of a liberal democratic constitutional order.

The political means by which to initiate, continue, ramp up, and consolidate the paradigm shift provide manifold complications. The parliamentary path itself encourages and commands compromises, not so much with the parliamentary opposition, which is frequently obstructionist and instinctively opportunist on all things, but with some of the social forces with which the opposition may have resonance, tribally or programmatically, and with the parallelogram of forces externally, especially those representing monopoly capitalism in the North Atlantic.

Broadly, the compromises to be made with certain domestic social forces are of a different kind or extent to the compromises to be made externally. On the domestic front, the compromises relate principally to two groups: those who support the governing political party and those who oppose. These kinds of compromises are easier to accommodate and are, invariably, in a state of flux; they are also more easily managed on the ground. The compromises externally are more problematic both in the government's accommodations and in its creative resistance. The multi-polar world, international law and practice, and the diverse, competing constituencies within the countries of the North Atlantic afford opportunities for relative autonomy or independence from these countries. Still, given the nature of the economic, security, and historical connections or relations between St. Vincent and the Grenadines and the North Atlantic countries, and the extent of their multiple influences upon our country, our own independence of action is frequently constrained; thus, the requisite of compromises. But compromises ought never to metamorphose into or invite retreat or surrender contrary to our country's core principles and interests. Surely, we ought never "to roll over and play dead." We make pragmatic accommodations or resist creatively as the circumstances admit.

Strategically, the progressive forces in the Caribbean, including St. Vincent and the Grenadines, have tended, since universal adult suffrage and certainly since independence, to make social democratic advances, in some cases of a dramatic kind, whenever they have "negotiated" compromises with the "ancien regime" or major elements thereof in the domestic space. Over the whole sweep of the post-independence period in our region, including St. Vincent and the Grenadines, the tide of history has favoured social democracy beyond that which is moderate or conservative. Indeed, there has been a sufficiency of political and economic space for *advanced* social democracy or a path of socialist orientation, though not of socialism, except of course in the case of Cuba, which is undoubtedly "sui generis".

The weaknesses internally, in the Caribbean, of capitalism, and thus of the national capitalist class, economically and politically, mean that by themselves they are unable to compete with or demand and enforce favourable compromises from the State, unless the political occupants of State authority are ideologically-inclined to surrender to the capitalist class or compromise away other contending interests, especially those of the poor and the working people. But practically, systemic conditions may prompt pragmatic compromises in the interest of all, at least for the time being, until more propitious circumstances arise for further social democratic advances.

The external situation is more problematic for social democratic regimes that are unequivocally anti-imperialist and uncompromisingly wedded to the principles and practices of non-intervention and non-interference in our nation's exercise of sovereignty and independence. The political leadership of governments that adhere to a praxis of advanced social democracy or a path of socialist orientation are required to gauge astutely and soberly the extent and limits of its scope for independent action in an exercise of pristine sovereignty.

Monopoly capitalism and its political representatives externally have shown repeatedly their capacity for retaliation, continuous subterfuge, or even undeclared war against smaller, weaker nations they assess to have gone beyond the tolerable limits set by the monopoly capitalists/imperialists. Still, in today's more complex and multi-polar world, the monopoly capitalists/imperialists have limits to their own actions circumscribed by international law, international institutions of authority, the multi-polar world, coordinated regional action, modern information technology, and certain progressive constituencies within the citadels of the very major monopoly capitalist countries.

In our engagement with monopoly capitalism externally, particularly in the post-pandemic circumstances, we ought to be alert to the warning of Noam Chomsky in an interesting article "We Must Not Let the Masters of Capital Define the Post-COVID World" in his recent book *The Precipice: Neoliberalism, the pandemic and the Urgent Need for Radical Change* (2021):

> We should take a few moments to clarify the stakes for ourselves in the bitter class war taking shape as the post-pandemic world is being forged. The stakes are immense. All are rooted in the suicidal logic of unregulated capitalism and at a deeper level in its very nature. All are becoming more apparent during the neoliberal plagues of the past forty years. The crises have been exacerbated by malignancies that have surfaced as these destructive tendencies took their course. The most ominous are appearing in the most powerful state in human history (the USA) — not a good omen for a world in crisis."

We must be alert also, in our interface with monopoly capitalism, to the lesson taught to the world, recently and repeatedly, by the contrived shortages of important supplies and equipment including elemental commodities such as ventilators to fight the pandemic. The market signals have been clear: there is no profit in preventing a future pandemic or public health disaster; monopoly capitalism awaits a pandemic or disaster, then moves but most selfishly and for maximum profit; the states in monopoly capitalist countries sit for a while on their metaphoric hands and await on Big Pharma to get going. Meanwhile, the small countries in the metropole's hinterland wait helplessly as we are told repeatedly about "supply chain constraints" while people suffer severe illness or death. It is grotesque. It is wicked. It is vaunted neoliberalism at its worst. The global community or nations must be alert to all this and insist on appropriate correctives, now!

Similarly, the current obscenity of manipulated price increases by the huge multi-national corporations in the production and trade in oil, fertiliser, and basic foods result in excessively large and record profits for them, and misery for the peoples of the world, including in St. Vincent and the Grenadines.

More usually, both the internal and external opponents of the political directorate in any progressive government in the Caribbean, including St. Vincent and the Grenadines, use or misuse the political opposition (in and out of Parliament) and civil society entities as battering rams against these social democratic governments in numerous nefarious ways, even in ways blatantly contrary to the interest of the people and the nation.

Two contrived ideological/political issues, centrally, have provided a fragile, quixotic and opportunistic basis for cooperation between the domestic and external opposition to the ULP government: first, the false allegation that the ULP government under the leadership of Prime Minister Ralph Gonsalves is building or intent on building socialism in St. Vincent and the Grenadines; and secondly, the blatant untruth that the ULP government is anti-American and anti-British and is supportive, ideologically, of Cuba, the Bolivarian Republic of Venezuela and other allegedly "rogue" regimes in its foreign policy stances against American and British interests.

These unfounded critiques of the ULP government have been promoted by a backward-looking and anti-national NDP, by neo-liberals and neo-conservatives in this or that American or British administration, and by opportunists and assorted self-seekers among some dubious foreign investors, and the cynical, self-interested promoters of the sale of Vincentian citizenship and passports. The ULP government has had to battle these forces, domestic and external, over the past 21 years in respect of these falsehoods.

The anti-ULP contrivances of an ideological/political nature have arisen, largely, from the ULP government's principled praxis (theory and practice) in its pursuance of advanced social democratic policies and programmes; its quest to construct a modern, competitive, post-colonial economy; its advocacy of the further ennoblement of our authentic, legitimate Caribbean civilisation; its insistent call for the cutting of the umbilical cord with the British monarchy and the Privy Council as the final appellate Court for our country; its leadership in demanding reparations from former European colonisers in respect of native genocide and the enslavement of Africans; its critique of monopoly capitalism and the unfairness of global trade arrangements; its strong opposition to imperialism and neo-colonialism, and their historical/contemporary racist underpinnings; its unwavering commitment to and promotion of the bedrock principles of the Charter of the United Nations inclusive of the precepts touching and concerning the equality of states, sovereignty and independence, territorial integrity, non-interference and non-intervention in the internal affairs of countries, multi-lateralism, the peaceful settlement of disputes, the adherence to international law, and the pursuit of global peace, security, and prosperity for *all*; its pursuance of an independent, principled, yet pragmatic, foreign policy in the interest of St. Vincent and the Grenadines and the Caribbean.

Powerful countries, in a reflex posture, prefer small nations such as St. Vincent and the Grenadines to be permanent members of their political choirs singing routinely, in subservience, from the song-sheet "du-jour" — whatever the mantra of the day. Oft-times the officials/representatives of these powerful countries seek to outdo each other in making wholly unreasonable demands of or judgments about small nations that dare to be independent, noble, questioning, and assertive in their people's interest.

Undermining and Opposing a Progressive, Anti-Imperialist Government

Unfortunately, backward and opportunistic political parties such as the NDP, devoid of clear nationalist principles and keen on pandering to certain powerful developed countries, instinctively provide solace and support for the machinations of imperialism and neo-colonialism. Political parties like the NDP find fertile ground within the domestic political market (inclusive of backward political personages in the Vincentian diaspora) for their anti-national and subservient stances on account of four basic factors: underdeveloped consciousness among the people who have long been fashioned by the incubus ("evil spirit") of colonialism and the effective contemporary mass propaganda of monopoly capitalism and imperialism; the corresponding lack of belief among large sections of former subject peoples that a better alternative path is possible or achievable; an abiding fear resident among too many that bucking the existing global system of monopoly capitalism would be disastrous — so, the mouth becomes muzzled by the food it eats to live; and the backward section of the national bourgeoisie/petit bourgeoisie that control parties like the NDP see their own class interests as bound up inextricably with those of monopoly capitalism, imperialism and neo-colonialism. Indeed, in the latter regard, they are so servile, so slavish, that they actually believe that their space for some "independent" action is far less than the actual situation permits. In short, the "slave" constrains himself/herself in even tighter boundaries than the "master"/"mistress" demarcates.

Following is a list of a few examples of all this confluence or join-der of outlooks or interests between the NDP and imperialism/neo-co-lonialism and against the ULP government:

- In September 2001, on the occasion of the ULP government's first official visit to Cuba, in the immediate aftermath of the terrorist attack on the United States of America on September 11, 2001, the then President of the NDP and Leader of the Opposition, Arnhim Eustace, asserted that his party had no objection to an official visit to Cuba, but he insisted that the timing was wrong. Accordingly, he posed the rhetor-ical question: "What would America say?" and in this regard suggested an association of Cuba with terrorism. It was all nonsensical. Revolu-tionary Cuba has long been a victim, not a perpetrator, of terrorism. In any event, the first country in this world to denounce the terrorist attack on the United States of America was Cuba. My official visit to Cuba went ahead; it was very productive for St. Vincent and the Grena-dines, and there was no adverse comment from the USA.

- The opposition NDP and officials of the U.S. Embassy found themselves in a condition of coordinated political apoplexy on my several visits over the years to Libya, then under Gadhafi's leadership, starting with the visit in August 2001 and in relation to my visit to Iran in 2009. The 2001 visit to Libya was a sub-regional OECS démarche. The delegation included Prime Minister Keith Mitchell of Grenada, Ministers of Government from Dominica, St. Lucia, and St. Kitts-Nev-is; Antigua and Barbuda was represented by the well-known patriot and Africanist, Tim Hector. The delegation of St. Vincent and the Grena-dines included the Director General of Finance and Planning, and the Executive Secretary to the SVG Chamber of Industry and Commerce. The focus of the visit was on finance for development, investment and development banking. My subsequent visits to Libya were of a similar nature or in relation to gatherings of the African Union. Libya con-tributed a relatively small sum of development financing to St. Vincent and the Grenadines, generally, and to the construction of the Argyle International Airport. As regards my 2009 visit to Iran, it is to be noted that Iran was the final leg of a trip that took me on official business to London, Portugal (Madeira and Lisbon), the Vatican (to converse with Pope Benedict VI). On my visit to Iran, I secured some funding for the construction of the Argyle International Airport. University scholar-ships were negotiated, but our Vincentian students did not take them up because the courses were taught in Farsi, the language of 80 million Iranians. Interestingly, neither the NDP nor the American diplomats ever commented on my 10 visits to Taiwan or my far more numerous visits to the USA on official business.

The simplistic, propagandist reasoning of the NDP and the U.S. officials was simple: "Libya and Iran are 'terrorist' states; anyone who visits them is sympathetic to terrorists; the ULP government under Ralph Gonsalves is thus sympathetic to terrorism."

The fact that my government was active in the global fight against terrorism mattered not. How can reasonable persons take some of these critics seriously? So, American diplomats may engage the Libyan and Iranian governments, but the Prime Minister of St. Vincent and the Grenadines cannot? Are Prime Ministers in the Caribbean so gullible, weak or imbecilic that we will fall, willy-nilly, for propaganda or political pressure from others?

• The coordination in 2013 between the opposition NDP and BBC journalists from the Panorama Programme to smear me as receiving corrupt payments from a British investor Dave Ames, who invested in a resort hotel in St. Vincent and the Grenadines. This egregious falsehood first came to my attention when the BBC journalist ambushed me on a regional aircraft as we landed in Barbados as I was transiting en-route to Haiti for a CARICOM Heads of Government meeting. It turned out that this malicious lie first emerged from a prior meeting between top-most officials of the NDP and the BBC journalists. These BBC journalists perhaps thought that I was one of their caricatured "Third World" political leaders, so they bought this canard "hook, line, and sinker". The main journalist and his cameraman actually found out through the airline staff that I was on the flight and booked seats immediately behind my wife and myself. From that advantageous perch they ambushed me with questions as the passengers, including my wife and I, were disembarking. I issued a strong denial that was filmed by them.

Immediately, I went on the offensive. I telephoned an on-air radio programme in St. Vincent and the Grenadines and reported what had transpired. At the CARICOM Summit I raised the matter firmly. CARICOM issued a statement condemning this gutter journalism and reaffirmed confidence in my personal honesty and integrity. I communicated fully and extensively on the matter with the hierarchy of the BBC and made a formal complaint to Lord Patten of the BBC Trustees, the Acting Head of the BBC, and the Head of the Panorama programme. I sent communication, too, to the actual producer of the programme. Dave Ames publicly denied the false allegation; , did the local lawyer, a respected personality whom the journalist had falsely alleged was involved. Meanwhile, persons in the NDP leadership, who had generated the wicked mischief in the first place, were crowing publicly as the announced date for the Panorama programme was drawing near.

The upshot was that the BBC initiated an investigation and found that the Panorama team had breached their journalistic and ethical standards. Among other things, it was discovered that one of the BBC team had paid a security guard at the hotel to lie about the matter. The producer of the programme resigned; the programme was never aired; it was postponed indefinitely. A legitimate part of the Panorama story about the financing of the resort hotel from pension funds in Britain was never ventilated by the BBC. That part of the story was not exciting enough for viewers apparently. It needed something salacious, thus the toxic combination of the NDP, the BBC and others to harm the progressive, socialist-oriented and anti-imperialist ULP government and its leader. I reasonably suspect that the nefarious hands of those foreign business agents who hankered then, and still do now, to sell our passports and citizenship were behind this sordid episode. Perhaps, too, one or more foreign governments were involved.

• Towards the end of 2007, the matter of the pullout from St. Vincent and the Grenadines of the American-owned offshore medical school, the Kingstown Medical College, a part of the parent St. George's Medical School in Grenada, arose. The Kingstown Medical College, established some 25 years earlier, provided for clinical rotations in St. Vincent and the Grenadines and a semester of tutoring for the medical students at St. George's. It was a useful contribution to the economy: Landlords rented apartments; the students, essentially educational tourists, spent money brought into the country; and the Kingstown Medical College provided employment for locals.

The decision to pull out was a straightforward commercial one for the investors in the St. George's Medical School. But the opposition NDP, as usual, got into the act by suggesting that there were political motives for the decision. Incredibly, the NDP alleged that the American government had advised the investors that because of "the growing links" between my government and those of Fidel Castro's Cuba and Hugo Chavez's Venezuela, it was no longer safe or reliable for them to remain in St. Vincent and the Grenadines. The NDP also tossed in the issue of increased criminal activity, but swiftly dropped that one when they realised St. Vincent and the Grenadines was as safe or safer than Grenada from the standpoint of citizen security.

The investors at St. George's then contacted me to indicate they did not have to close the school in St. Vincent and the Grenadines if my government signed another lease agreement for the school compound for at least another 25 years on more generous terms than hitherto, including an exclusivity to them on medical education in St. Vincent and the Grenadines, save and except to permit medical students from the University of the West Indies to use our country's main hospital for limited rotations and internships. The school's negotiator came to St. Vincent and the Grenadines; no mutually satisfactory agreement was concluded. Their insistence on "exclusivity" and other unreasonable demands were unacceptable to my government.

The opposition NDP and officials at the U.S. Embassy in Barbados had a field day against us. The NDP said this was the end of American investment in St. Vincent and the Grenadines and that under the ULP government, St. Vincent and the Grenadines was well on the way to be isolated like "communist Cuba" and "socialist Venezuela". From the sidelines, the U.S. Embassy officials stoked the anti-ULP government fires; some of those officials came to St. Vincent and the Grenadines and told NGOs, journalists, and the business community that they were alarmed at our treatment of American investors at the Kingstown Medical School. Some former landlords got into the drum beat, and more than a few were fanning the flames of hysteria. I met a delegation of the landlords and outlined to them the details of the unreasonableness of the owners of the Medical School. I assured them that after a few months of hardship without tenants, more medical schools were imminent on the horizon.

In reasonably quick time, the Trinity School of Medicine with American investors was established on the same compound as the Kingstown Medical School. This was followed by three others: the St. James School of Medicine, with American investors; the All Saints University with Nigerian, Indian, and Canadian investors; and the American University of St. Vincent and the Grenadines with North American investors. The numbers of students in these four medical schools quadrupled those of the Kingstown Medical College. The NDP went silent with its scaremongering about Cuba, Venezuela and hostility to American investors.

Meanwhile, the relevant U.S. Embassy officials continued to send their largely fictional and rumor-mongering reports to Washington about the situation in St. Vincent and the Grenadines. We know so from Wikileaks!

Let's talk about the Wikileaks' disclosure from the U.S. Embassy in Barbados to the State Department in Washington about the ULP government and Prime Minister Ralph Gonsalves. The misinformation and downright lies were extraordinary. I shudder to think that a serious government like that of the U.S.A. processes these kinds of half-truths and outright falsehoods for decision-making. Among the list of these over the years have been the following:

•   The allegation that the ULP government is hostile to foreign investment. The evidence for this was from conversations with persons such as Jerry George (now deceased), a journalist and NDP partisan, and Ken Boyea, a businessman who resigned from the ULP in the year 2000, formed his own political party that was defeated overwhelmingly in its only electoral outing in 2001, and who remained vehemently opposed to the ULP government, despite pretensions, sometimes, to the contrary when it suited his personal business interests.

The data that contradicted this falsehood mattered not. St. Vincent and the Grenadines has had over the last 20 years the second highest level of foreign direct investment as a proportion of Gross Domestic Product of the countries in the Caribbean and Latin America. We are, however, prudent about the investments and the investors that we welcome.

•   The false allegation that the Prime Minister controls the Director of Public Prosecutions (DPP), an *independent* Office under the constitution, by being Minister of Legal Affairs. Ministerial functions relating to budgets and their presentation to Parliament are quite different than any influence on the exercise of the DPP's sole constitutional discretion as to initiating, taking over, or discontinuing any criminal prosecution. The DPP and all the prosecutors in that Office of the DPP are appointed through the medium of the independent, regional Judicial and Legal Services Commission of the OECS, which Commission is headed by the Chief Justice of the OECS Judiciary.

This false allegation of the Prime Minister's "control" of the DPP was made in the context of the DPP taking over and discontinuing the private criminal complaints brought to the Court by pro-NDP lawyers in 2008 on behalf of two women who made allegations of sexual misconduct against the Prime Minister, which he publicly denied. The matters were investigated by the Police with whom the Prime Minster fully cooperated; the DPP found no credible evidence upon which any prosecution could be pursued. In one of these cases, the lawyers challenged in the High Court the decision of the DPP by way of judicial review. The Judge, a woman jurist of high repute, dismissed the application for judicial review and upheld the DPP's decision. The lawyers appealed to the Court of Appeal; three Appeal Court Judges dismissed the appeal. The very lawyers then initiated the complaint afresh, this time before the President of the Family Court; the President dismissed the complaint as frivolous and vexatious and an abuse of the process of the Courts. The virtual complainant, the woman, publicly dismissed the two lawyers and made it plain that she had not instructed them to bring the complaint afresh. Her new lawyer, on her instructions, discontinued a civil suit that her two original lawyers had initiated in the High Court for damages against Ralph Gonsalves, who had entered a full and robust defence to this suit. One of the original lawyers, now deceased, alleged that a bribe of $40,000 had been paid to the virtual complainant by Ralph Gonsalves. The mother of the complainant asserted that the allegation of any payment was false. The U.S. Embassy staff reported the false allegation of the payment to their superiors in Washington as if it were true. Only rabid NDP partisans in St. Vincent and the Grenadines gave credence to any of these false and contrived allegations.

• The centrepiece of the ULP government's economic policy has been its quest to build a modern, competitive, many-sided post-colonial economy that is at once national, regional and global. Each of those words is pregnant with real meaning; this quest emerges from our historical circumstances and contemporary reality. I had been writing extensively on this subject; indeed, from the time of its formulation, I ensured that its details were presented and analysed by me, as ULP's Political Leader and Prime Minister. The conception and formulation of "the post-colonial economy" were commended by several Caribbean scholars and practitioners, including the former Prime Minister of Barbados, Owen Arthur, now deceased, and Sir Dwight Venner, now deceased, former Governor of the Eastern Caribbean Central Bank;

But this perfectly sensible quest was derided by the staff at the U.S. Embassy in Barbados, as told by Wikileaks, as essentially empty political posturing. If they had taken the time to study the issue rather than making an ill-formed judgement fuelled by instinctive antipathy to someone from a small Caribbean country who has had the temerity to forge an independent sustainable path and to question the anti-people character of imperialism and its big power hegemony grounded in monopoly capitalism.

It was the same instinctive opposition displayed by them to my efforts to build an international airport as part and parcel of our efforts to transform our economy. They questioned its necessity and desirability and the mode of financing its construction. They were so wrapped up with their settled opposition to my government that they remained ignorant of its salience in every material respect. The contributions of Cuba, Venezuela, Libya, and Iran blinded them completely. They, of course, did not see the material contributions of other nations including Taiwan, Mexico, Georgia, Austria, and Trinidad and Tobago. After the airport's construction, my government secured loans from the Export-Import credit facilities from the USA, Britain and Canada to purchase most of the equipment to equip the airport.

• Undoubtedly, there was in the U.S. Embassy in Barbados, certainly from 2001 onwards in the period covered by Wikileaks, an organised effort to smear and report the partisan smears against the ULP government and me as though they were true.

To be sure, the U.S. Embassy staff reported to Washington about my "erudition", "scholarship", and "political skills", but they did so grudgingly amidst an avalanche of misinformation and falsehoods against me.

• Between 2006 and 2013, the U.S. Embassy in Barbados sought to pressure me to reverse a decision made by my government to institute legal proceedings under the Alien Land-Holding Act of 1922, to forfeit 100 acres of beachfront land at Chatham Bay in Union Island — part of St. Vincent and the Grenadines — owned by a group of American investors, including a prominent one who was already involved at Petit St. Vincent. The pressure and threats by the U.S. Embassy were crude, ill-advised, and completely wrong on the facts and the law. The investors known in the law suit as Chatham Bay Club Limited and Chatham Bay Development Corporation Limited had made it clear to the government, through their lawyers, that they were prepared to fight the matter all the way to the Privy Council in London, the final appellate body in our judiciary.

The background to this issue was straightforward. The American investors, defined as "aliens" under the Act that was put in place by the British colonial government in St. Vincent and the Grenadines since 1922, obtained an Alien Landholding Licence from the predecessor government to purchase the land in the late 1980s and did so purchase the land. One of the conditions, pursuant to the Act, was that the investors, by agreement, invest EC $15 million (just over US $5 million) to build a small hotel and restaurant at Chatham Bay. Under the Act, as was stated in the licence, a failure to so fulfil that condition may result in "forfeiture of the land" by the Crown, the government.

The investors never built anything at all on the land; it was left virgin. Up to the end of 2005, the investors did nothing to fulfil the condition in the Alien Landholding Licence. So, in early 2006, I instructed the Attorney-General, on behalf of the government, to institute proceedings in the High Court for forfeiture.

After a spirited trial, the High Court ordered forfeiture on June 27, 2007. In the judgment of Justice Albert Matthew, the mischief the Act sought to avoid was plainly in evidence: A foreign investor simply cannot buy scarce land on the cheap, do nothing to develop it, and later speculate on its sale for a huge profit due to no effort or investment on his part. Land values naturally rise with the State's expenditure on roads, airports, seaports, schools, health facilities, water and sanitation, electricity and telephone services, police and coastguard services, and administrative services generally. And all this the State did in Union Island where Chatham Bay is located.

Additionally, in St. Vincent and the Grenadines there are no capital gains taxes, so the investors were not liable to pay any such taxes on the increased value of the land. Only land taxes of a puny kind were due and payable.

The American investors appealed the decision of the High Court to the Court of Appeal. The stakes were high. The investors brought in a distinguished Queens' Counsel from London to argue the case before the Court of Appeal consisting of three Appeal Court Judges. The Court of Appeal, in a unanimous decision, dismissed the appeal on August 13, 2010, and upheld the forfeiture. An order for legal costs against the investors was made at the High Court, and the Court of Appeal. The investors appealed to the highest court of St. Vincent and the Grenadines, the Privy Council in London. A few days before the final appeal was to be heard before the Privy Council, the English lawyers for the investors intimated to my government's lawyers that they would withdraw the appeal before the Privy Council, if my government would revert to its original 2006-2012 offer of settlement to repay the purchase price of the land from the date of purchase with the usual interest rate at five percent; the investors' lawyers asked if we would also agree that each side bear its own legal costs.

After appropriate consultation and advice, I instructed our lawyers to agree to the proposed terms of the settlement except that interest would run on the principal sum up to the date in January 2006 when the government instituted its legal claim for forfeiture. Accordingly, the appellant investors withdrew the appeal. Clearly, the investors' English lawyers had advised them that they would lose at the Privy Council, so they wanted to cut their losses. For the government's part, I had no interest in leaving the investors empty-handed, even though that is where the law and the facts led. The government's maintenance, unsullied, of its reputation as being investment-friendly was and is a public policy of my government.

The American government could not resist direct pressure and threats against my government and me as Prime Minister. The pressure and threats came to a head on Independence Day, October 27, 2010, two weeks after the Court of Appeal's judgement. The American Ambassador had requested an appointment to see me on that day. I acceded to the request, but I did not know the subject matter she intended to raise.

So, on our nation's 31st anniversary of Independence, after our morning celebrations, I met with the American Ambassador and her two diplomatic colleagues (a senior and a junior diplomat) at the official residence of the Prime MJustice Albert inister.

Immediately, she raised the issue of the American investors' interest, and predicament, in the matter of Chatham Bay. Please note that by then the government had already secured judgments in its favour at both High Court and the Court of Appeal and the matter had started its slow process, as intimated by the investors' lawyers, towards its denouement at the Privy Council. She recounted to me what I had already known: That U.S. Congressmen, Senators, and the State Department were weighing in on the matter and were requesting that my government discontinue the proceedings and leave the American investors with 100 acres of prime beach front land in Union Island. I politely and calmly told her that the facts and the law are on the government's side, and I await confidently any hearing and judgement of the Privy Council.

At this point the accompanying senior diplomat, whom I understood was of Jamaican birth but an American citizen and whom I had never met or heard of, entered the conversation aggressively, threateningly, disrespectfully, and wildly. He was clearly the designated metaphoric "pit bull" for the day. I sensed that immediately and never allowed him to rile me up. He accused my government and me of "expropriating" American investors' property and asserted that America will never allow it to go unpunished. I calmly explained to him that my government stands for, among other things, the right to private property, the rule of law, and the Constitution of St. Vincent and the Grenadines. I advised him that in our country there is no legal category known as "expropriation" of property; thus, we cannot expropriate. I pointed out that a government in St. Vincent and the Grenadines may *purchase* land or *acquire* land under and by virtue of the Constitution and the Land Acquisition Act (which existed from colonial times and which also exists in the USA), and that consequent to acquisition of property, the government is required to pay fair compensation within a reasonable time; or apply to the High Court for forfeiture in circumstances detailed in the Alien Landholding Act. We did the latter and had succeeded in the Courts thus far.

I indicated the terms of a settlement I had proposed to the investors' lawyers from the very beginning, that is to say, payment of the purchase price mentioned in the Deed plus interest at the rate of 5 percent per year from the date of the purchase. I informed the American diplomats that their government was unwisely advising the American investors to be unyielding when they were plainly in the wrong. I told them that the investors' "take it or leave it" offer of sale of the land to the government of US $20 million when they had purchased it for under US $200,000 was absolutely out of the question. I asked them the simple question: Why would my government with High Court and Court of Appeal judgments under its belt for "forfeiture", allow the investors to keep the land, or pay them US $20 million for it?

The senior diplomat kept interrupting me angrily. When I was finished, he was in a veritable uncontrollable rage. He said that all my "nice legal talk" meant nothing to him; he insisted that it was "expropriation" and that it is "the way communist governments behave". He summoned the names of this and that senior Congressman and Senator who may retaliate against St. Vincent and the Grenadines and me; that I did not know what I was getting into by "expropriating" Americans' property; that American visas for Vincentians and my family were in jeopardy; and so he ranted on and on about this or that potential adverse action by the American government against St. Vincent and the Grenadines. I did not take his bait.

I calmly replied that I have no control over what the American government or its representatives may or may not do. I reiterated that our position is entirely reasonable and I await any outcome at the Privy Council. I told them that I am satisfied that reasonable people in the American government would find my government's position compelling. At this juncture, the junior diplomat, who had evidently studied the case well, indicated to the Ambassador that I had presented accurately the facts and the law, as they stood, but he thought that the Privy Council may rule otherwise. I simply said: "Let's see; we believe in the rule of law."

During the discussion, the staff at the Prime Minister's Residence brought us drinks; the Ambassador, the junior diplomat and I indulged; the senior diplomat did not; clearly, he was not thirsty. Two months later, in December 2010, the ULP was re-elected in general elections for its third consecutive term despite hostile external forces being arraigned against it.

• The opposition NDP's collusion with the external sellers of citizenship and passports, Strategic Communications Laboratories (SCL) (the precursor to Cambridge Analytica of Donald Trump fame), and some rich expatriates on Mustique Island (part of St. Vincent and the Grenadines) was evident in the defeat of the reform Constitution proposed by the ULP government in a popular referendum in November 2009. This proposed reform Constitution strengthened immensely popular democracy, individual rights and freedoms; fortified existing independent institutions and proposed the creation of others; reduced the powers of the Prime Minister and strengthened those of the Leader of the Opposition; proposed the removal of the Queen of Britain as our country's titular Head of State, replacing her with a home-grown, non-executive President; and the termination of final appeals to the Privy Council by making the Caribbean Court of Justice the final appellate authority in our judiciary. This matter is discussed at length elsewhere earlier in this book.

• The sinister role of SCL and the substantial external financiers (the passport-citizenship sellers) in support of the NDP and against the ULP in each of the five general elections since the turn of the 21st century (2001, 2005, 2010, 2015, 2020). In 2020, they were joined by "operators" from mainland China, consequent upon the NDP's earlier declaration of ditching Taiwan and embracing the People's Republic of China (PRC). This unsettled the Americans a bit, but they still preferred the pro-U.S. stances of a backward opposition NDP, even though antithetical to the interests of St. Vincent and the Grenadines. The ULP government's independent and principled foreign policy irritates sections of the U.S. establishment who have a neo-liberal and neo-conservative orientation.

In each of these five general elections, the NDP's campaign was financed largely by the external financiers who hanker after the selling of our country's citizenship and passports. Given the fact that the ULP and I are unalterably opposed to selling our sacred patrimony in these respects, these financiers are determined to see my government defeated. In each of the 2010, 2015, and 2020 elections it has been credibly reported that they invested between US $4-$5 million; they paid SCL to run the NDP campaigns and provided on-the-ground support for that party.

In the interesting book, *The Cosmopolites: The Coming of the Global Citizen* (2015), the author, Atossa Araxia Abrahamian, wrote on the issue of the passport/citizenship sales as follows:

> The impact of passport sales in St. Kitts made waves in the normally placid Eastern Caribbean waters. Christian Kalin (who is referred to in Abrahamian's book as "the King of Passports") suddenly had the ear of almost every politician in the region, with the notable exception of the Prime Minister of St. Vincent and the Grenadines, who has loudly and publicly denounced the idea of selling citizenship, saying he (meaning the Prime Minister) has a 'fundamental, philosophical objection' to the concept. These programs, critics argue, undermine the sense of community that ties a country's people together; they're also unfair because they give the rich opportunities and rights unavailable to everyone else.

> 'He's an old far-leftist,' Kalin shrugged, referring to the Caribbean leader. 'He'll never be convinced.' I met with Kalin in St. Kitts one evening after the country held elections. His phones were ringing off the hook. 'We've been working with them for so long that we know where everything is and how everything works,' he told me, excusing himself to take yet another call from a future or former official. 'When the new cabinet can't find something, they call us'.

This quotation is quite telling about the influence and power of these foreign buccaneers in modern garb. Notice, too, the shameless resort of Kalin to standard neo-liberal abuse of an ideological kind to my principled and factually-grounded objection to the selling of our passports and citizenship. The Prime Minister opposes passport-selling simply because is he an "old far-leftist". It is straight out of Cold War propaganda, abuse and falsehood in pursuit of ignoble self-interest.

And so, the war against my government and me continues!

• The NDP's opposition to the ULP government's decision in 2008 to seek a seat as a non-permanent member of the United Nations' Security Council (UNSC) received succour and support from a section of the government of the USA that resented an independent, nationalist, and anti-imperialist voice from the Caribbean. It is an interesting history that ought to be recounted.

Prior to the quest by the government of St. Vincent and the Grenadines for a non-permanent seat on the UNSC, only three member-states of CARICOM had ever sat on the UNSC, namely, Jamaica, Guyana and Trinidad and Tobago; none had done so in the 21st century. The election of St. Vincent and the Grenadines as a non-permanent member of the UNSC in June 2019 for the two-year term spanning January 1, 2020, to December 31, 2021, was historic in that our country was the smallest ever, by geographic size, population and wealth, to sit on the UNSC since the founding of the United Nations in 1945.

The UNSC is the highest decision-making body in the UN; it is accorded the authoritative responsibility on all matters concerning global peace and security. The UNSC comprises 15 members, five of whom are permanent (the USA, China, Russia, Britain, and France), and 10 are non-permanent. The non-permanent members are elected by the United Nations' General Assembly (UNGA) on the basis of a two-thirds majority of all 193 members of the UN. Each non-permanent member of the UNSC serves for two years, and represents one of the designated geographic regions of the world. Two seats are allocated to the Group of Latin America and Caribbean (GRULAC) countries.

So, in 2008 the ULP government decided to put St. Vincent and the Grenadines forward for the election in mid-2009 for a non-permanent seat on the UNSC. Immediately, there was incredulity across several governments of CARICOM and among leading bureaucrats at the CARICOM Secretariat. They considered it an absurdity and an impossible dream. The unimaginative and entirely erroneous view of these governments and regional public servants was that St. Vincent and the Grenadines was too small, too lacking in financial and manpower resources to be so ambitious! This, too, was the received wisdom of the diplomats of the mission of the USA, Britain, Canada, and the European Union headquartered in the Eastern Caribbean. Additionally, the U.S. diplomats were uneasy about the prospects of the anti-imperialist voice of the ULP government at the UNSC; they commenced a whispering campaign against St. Vincent and the Grenadines and expressed derision at "the laughable proposition" of St. Vincent and the Grenadines on the UNSC.

In St. Vincent and the Grenadines, the opposition NDP gave vent to their hostility to the idea of our quest for a non-permanent seat on the UNSC. The NDP's leadership considered the matter a waste of time and resources; they averred that it was all about Ralph's vanity. Ignorant of almost everything about the UNSC and its election process, the NDP's leadership insisted wrongly that the People's Republic of China (PRC) would veto any membership of St. Vincent and the Grenadines because of our diplomatic relations with the Republic of China (ROC-Taiwan). The NDP were in a veritable state of apoplexy about my government's decision on our country's quest to sit on the UNSC.

Contrary to the national interest of our country, the NDP colluded with one of its sister political parties in government in one of the CARICOM-member states to oppose us on this issue; another CARICOM government advanced the erroneous and ideologically jaundiced view in the councils of CARICOM that St. Vincent and the Grenadines is being seen on this matter as "Venezuela's stalking house".

However, many CARICOM governments were apparently unaware of the support that St. Vincent and the Grenadines was quietly building up at the UN for its candidacy to the UNSC on account of the excellent work being done at the UN by the UN Mission of St. Vincent and the Grenadines, headed then by an energetic and visionary Ambassador, Camillo Gonsalves. Several leading countries in Latin America, Africa and Asia, and even a few in Europe, were supporting the candidacy of St. Vincent and the Grenadines to the UNSC.

In the early months of 2009, as the election date for the UNSC approached, my government decided to suspend its quest to a later date; this decision was made contrary to the advice of our UN Mission. We decided to suspend our quest to 2019 for three basic reasons: (i) Three governments in CARICOM were against our quest, two others were unreliable; indeed at least one government had committed itself to vote for our competitor, Colombia. I wanted a fully united CARICOM behind St. Vincent and the Grenadines; (ii) our government's campaign for a root-and-branch reform of our nation's Constitution was on its way to a final denouement at a popular referendum in late 2009 and it demanded our government's overwhelming and undivided political focus; and (iii) our government did not want to contribute to any fracturing of the

vital unity of Latin America and the Caribbean by competing in a bruis-
ing contest with Colombia, even though we were confident of victory in
both the membership of GRULAC and the UNGA.

In withdrawing from the 2009 contest, we formally advanced the
name of St. Vincent and the Grenadines in GRULAC for the 2019
election date for the 2020-2021 term at the UNSC, hoping for an uncon-
tested run, that is, without any competitor from the GRULAC member-State at that time! The only possible drawback to this option was
that we could not be sure that we would be in government in 2019, but
we were focused, as always, on the interests of our nation and the unity
of Latin America and the Caribbean. We decided that over the next 10
years our party and government would do our work to the best of our
ability, in our people's interests, and let the future decide.

Between 2009 and 2019, at home the ULP was re-elected in 2010
and 2015 for its third and fourth terms in government, respectively. Regionally, St. Vincent and the Grenadines and the ULP leadership commended themselves highly and conclusively in the OECS, CARICOM,
the Association of Caribbean States, the Bolivarian Alternative of the
Americas (ALBA), and the Community of States of Latin America and
the Caribbean (CELAC). Internationally, St. Vincent and the Grenadines
strengthened its position among countries in Africa, Asia and Europe,
among small states and in global institutions. At the United Nations, St.
Vincent and the Grenadines continued its phenomenal work in advancing multi-lateralism, the foundation precepts of the UN Charter, global
peace and security for all, and other pressing issues of the day such as
climate change, financing for development, and a reformation of global
institutions, including the UN itself.

Meanwhile, St. Vincent and the Grenadines assumed leadership
positions across a range of regional, hemispheric, and global entities.
In the process, in 2019 St. Vincent and the Grenadines became, prior to
the election for the UNSC seat in June 2019, the President of the highly
influential Economic and Social Council (ECOSOC) of the UN — the
smallest country ever to hold its presidency since its inauguration in
1947 and the second member-State in CARICOM after Jamaica to
have done so. (Haiti held the Presidency of ECOSOC before it became
a member of CARICOM). Camillo Gonsalves' successor as head of
the UN Mission of St. Vincent and the Grenadines, Ambassador Inga
Rhonda King did a magnificent job in steering our country to its seat on
the UNSC, and since then she continues her extraordinary work with a
superb staff comprising mainly of young professionals, 80 percent of

whom are women. As Prime Minister, I provided the lead for the historic candidacy of St. Vincent and the Grenadines to the UNSC.

The date for the election at UNGA for the non-permanent members of the UNSC for the 2020-2021 term was set for June 7, 2019. As that date drew nearer, a section of the President Donald Trump administration in the USA accelerated its search for a suitable competitor in GRULAC against St. Vincent and the Grenadines. By early 2019, St. Vincent and the Grenadines had secured GRULAC's support as its only candidate, but U.S. imperialism was dissatisfied. Quietly and not-so-quietly, it sought to undermine the quest of St. Vincent and the Grenadines. Eventually, it found an ambitious ally on this issue in the newly-elected government in El Salvador.

In the days immediately preceding June 7, 2019, officials from the U.S. State Department and from the U.S. Mission at the UN (but apparently not the acting Head of the Mission) were openly campaigning for El Salvador and against St. Vincent and the Grenadines. St. Vincent and the Grenadines was too independent and too anti-imperialist for the political acolytes of the Trump administration. Both Ambassador King and I were personally told by diplomats of several countries from Latin America and Europe of the lobbying efforts of ials for the candidacy of El Salvador and against St. Vincent and the Grenadines. There is so much more to write on this.

In the upshot of it all, on June 7, 2019, St. Vincent and the Grenadines defeated El Salvador at the UNGA by 185 votes to six, with two abstentions. It was truly historic at so many levels. In the two-year term of St. Vincent and the Grenadines on the UNSC, we worked assiduously for global peace and security for all; we accomplished much. On many occasions, St. Vincent and the Grenadines was at loggerheads with imperialism and hegemonic conduct. This story is yet to be fully told.

Throughout the entire 10-year campaign of St. Vincent and the Grenadines to sit on the UNSC, the NDP actively opposed our government's efforts in this regard. In this, they were at one with imperialism and hegemons. Our country's victory on June 7, 2019, was hailed at home, in our region and globally. The UN Secretary General himself was ecstatic at the achievement of St. Vincent and the Grenadines, and was swiftly congratulatory. It took the NDP over 48 hours after the election of St. Vincent and the Grenadines to offer a mealy-mouthed expression of pride in our country's elevation to the UNSC. Throughout our country's stint on the UNSC, the NDP continued its petty sniping at and opposition to our efforts at the UNSC. The NDP had yet again found itself in imperialism's bed and against our country's interests.

More generally, the NDP has been in opposition to every strategic policy, programme or project initiated by the ULP government in its focused efforts since 2001 to transform the economy and ensure sustainable development for St. Vincent and the Grenadines. Signature strategic initiatives of the ULP government, which the NDP opposed and, in the main, still opposes, include: The Education Revolution; the historic bridge over the Rabacca River; the historic Argyle International Airport; the Geothermal Project for renewable energy; the Modern Medical and Diagnostic Complex at Georgetown; the Housing and Health Revolutions; the Sir Vincent Beache Stadium and the expansion/modernisation of the Arnos Vale Sporting Complex; the modern Parliament and modern Court Complex; the Belle Isle Correctional Facility; the modern Port Project; the State-owned Holiday Inn Express and Marriott Hotels; the Medicinal Cannabis Industry; the privately owned Rainforest Seafood Plant; the extent of the private investment by Sandals Hotel Group in the Beaches Resort; the privately owned and financed Black Sand Resorts; the Owia Fisheries Complex; the temporary secondary schools at Arnos Vale; the Poverty Reduction Programme and the widening/strengthening of the social safety net; the Zero Hunger Trust Fund; the Petro Caribe programme; the establishment of a series of institutions designed to enhance good governance; the Constitutional Reform exercise; legislation designed to protect further the working people; the seeking of reparations for native genocide and the enslavement of African bodies; and the government's progressive, anti-imperialist and anti-hegemonic foreign policy, inclusive of its quest for a non-permanent seat on the UNSC for 2020-2021.

The NDP's drumbeat of backwardness continues against the advanced social democracy and anti-imperialism of the ULP government.

A Note on Compromises

Beyond the in-built tendency of a competitive parliamentary democracy to engender compromises on an ongoing basis, our country's vulnerable condition both predisposes and induces it, generally, towards compromises on purely pragmatic grounds.

At the same time in St. Vincent and the Grenadines, there is the instructive post-independence experience of advancing social democracy, oft-times dramatically in the people's interest in compromises with the "ancien regime". Waves of these compromises have added incremental and cumulative popular advances. But there has not been a conscious attempt by the political leaderships to carve out a paradigm shift until the post-2001 quest to build a modern, competitive, many-sided post-colonial economy, and to defend, unequivocally, our country's sovereignty, independence and national interests.

The construction of the post-colonial economy cannot and does not rule out compromises with internal and external opponents to such a paradigm shift in St. Vincent and the Grenadines. But care and caution are always required; and creative resistance is an appropriate option as the circumstances admit. Compromise in the national interest does not mean compromising our core principles and our developmental trajectory.

First of all, some sections of the population who are benefiting and who stand to benefit even further from this evolving and consolidating paradigm shift, do support an opposition political party, the NDP, which has a distinctly neo-liberal agenda inclusive of its craven proposal of dependency on the selling of passports and citizenship. These sections of the population have to be brought along to embrace the ULP's compelling developmental narrative grounded in the paradigm shift towards the building of a post-colonial economy. The defeat of backwardness, represented by the NDP, can only be achieved over a prolonged period of time through its repeated electoral defeats combined with the deepening and consolidation of the post-colonial economy, the continued electoral successes of the ULP, the lifting of our people's progressive consciousness, and their organised social solidarity through the ULP and like-minded civil society groups.

Further, through sensible accommodation and creative resistance, the progressive social democratic and anti-imperialist ULP government has been able to find a sufficiency of political space to build a mutually-satisfactory relationship of principled coexistence with the political representatives of monopoly capitalism externally.

There is, of course, something in the very nature of compromise, which in particular historical circumstances, may bring redemptive successes over time to the promises inherent in the paradigm shift in the actualisation of the post-colonial economy for sustainable development. Compromises that are designed to carry forward the agenda of *advanced* social democracy and are executed efficaciously, possess within them the dialectic of progressive change in the people's interest.

I began thinking of this idea and its dialectics many years ago when I first read a poem entitled "Private Prayer" by the Vincentian Poet of international renown, Ellsworth "Shake" Keane. It was written in April 1973 for Walter Rodney on the occasion of the publication of his hugely influential book, *How Europe Underdeveloped Africa*, by Bogle-L'Ouverture Publications of London.

Let us quote "Private Prayer" in full:

"To understand
How the whole thing run
I have to ask my parents
And even my daughter and son.
"To understand the form
Of compromise I am
I must in my own voice ask
How the whole thing run.
"To ask
Why I don't dream
In the same language I live in
I must rise up
Among the syllables of my parents
In the land which I am
And form
A whole daughter and a whole son
Out of the compromise
Which I am.
"To understand history
I have to come home."

We in our Caribbean, including St. Vincent and the Grenadines, have been compromised by the fever of our history. Out of our compromises we are in quest to form or build "a whole daughter and a whole son". In so doing, we must ask the question in our own voice, and in our land make our future whole. Understanding how to go about all this we have to turn to our history, to our parents, and for the future, to our children. In the process we have to come home to ourselves "to understand how the whole thing run".

The economic base to form or build "a whole daughter and a whole son" out of the compromises of history which, in part, have made us, requires us to effect the paradigm shift to a post-colonial economy for sustainable development.

Our Caribbean Civilisation

However, by itself, the construction of the modern, competitive, many-sided, post-colonial economy, though necessary, is insufficient to make us "whole". This demands something fundamentally existential, and in our pursuits beyond the pandemic, the volcanic eruptions and Hurricane Elsa, a process of and arrival at respairing, a place of fresh hope. This demands, more than ever, a further ennoblement or development of our unique and uplifting Caribbean civilisation and its magnificent Vincentian component. What then constitutes our Caribbean civilisation?

First, how does one define "civilisation"? Kenneth Clarke, an astute English observer of civilisation wrote a book entitled Civilisations and chose not to define "civilisation"; rather, he provided an offering on "civilised" man. He suggested that, "A civilised man...must feel that he belongs somewhere in space and time; that he consciously looks forward and looks back. And for this purpose it is a great convenience to be able to read and write."

In this sense, therefore, the people of a civilisation must belong to or own their seascape and landscape with a sense of permanence, beyond mere occupation, and with a commitment that goes beyond mere energy and will.

This or that generic definition of civilisation posits that it is "a human society that has a significant level of material and spiritual resources and a relatively complex cultural, political and legal organisation." "Civilisation" is not easily amenable to a generalised definition; in any event, definitions are not so much right or wrong, only more or less useful.

One of the best expositions that I have read on this subject is contained in a perceptive book written by the Mexican Nobel Laureate for Literature, Octavia Paz, under the title *The Labyrinth of Solitude and Other Writings*: Paz wrote:

> Civilisation is a society's style, its way of living and dying. It embraces the erotic and the culinary arts, dancing, and burial; courtesy and curses; work and leisure; rituals and festivals; punishments and rewards; dealings with the dead and with the ghosts who people our dreams; attributes toward women and children, old people,

and strangers, enemies and allies; eternity and the present; the here and now and the beyond. A civilisation is not only a system of values but a world of forms and codes of behaviour, rules and exceptions. It is society's visible side — institutions, monuments, work, things — but it is especially its submerged invisible side: beliefs, desires, fears, repressions, dreams.

...The reality to which we give the name civilisation does not allow of easy definition. It is each society's vision of the world and also its feeling about time; there are nations that are hurrying toward the future, and others whose eyes are fixed on the past.

History, geography, migration, the population mix, landscape, seascape, material production, and contemporary inter-connectedness, and more, help to shape a civilisation; these factors have certainly fashioned our Caribbean civilisation, and its Vincentian component. I have oft-repeated that through the fever of history and the process of creolisation within our especial seascape and landscape, our Caribbean civilisation emerged and coalesced as a metaphoric symphony. We are the songs of the indigenous people (Callinago, Garifuna, Amerindian); we are the rhythm of Africa; we are the melody of Europe; the chords of Asia; and the home-grown lyrics of our Caribbean. Like all symphonies, dissonances do occur, but we have evolved formal institutions and informal mechanisms or codes to correct or mute these dissonances.

Our Caribbean civilisation has arrived at a mature realisation that although we are not better than anyone else, nobody is better than us. Our ownership or permanent sense of belonging to our landscape and seascape grounds us with an enduring solidarity and uplifting values. In us resides "le génie des peuples" ("the genius of the people"), that submerged, imprecise and invisible side that cements, uplifts and even defines us; oft-times it erupts in an undefined or ill-defined sense of celebration that we are "Second to None" — Nulli Secundus/Nulli Secunda, as the Latin Romans once insisted.

Our Caribbean civilisation is of an island or seaboard type. Our Noble Laureate in Poetry, Derek Walcott, holds this as central in his poetic and literary works. In his insightful Nobel Lecture in 1993, "The Antilles: Fragments of Epic Memory", Walcott aptly reports on our Caribbean civilisation in majestic language:

Break a vase, and the love that reassembles the fragments is stronger than that love which took its symmetry for granted when it was whole. The glue that fits the pieces is the sealing of its original shape. It is such a love that reassembles our African and Asiatic fragments, the cracked heirlooms whose restoration shows its white scars. This gathering of broken pieces is the care and pain of the Antilles, and if the pieces are disparate, ill-fitting, they contain more pain than their original sculpture, those icons and sacred vessels taken for granted in their ancestral places. Antillean art is this restoration of our shattered histories, our shards of vocabulary, our archipelago becoming a synonym for pieces broken off from the original continent."

Like all civilisations, our Caribbean civilisation has been built, fundamentally, on labour — the producers — and the contours of the society fashioned by the particular mode of production, inclusive of the social organisation of labour within that mode and the more encompassing social formation. For a full discussion on this specific subject, I refer readers to my book, published in 2019, entitled *The Political Economy of the Labour Movement in St. Vincent and the Grenadines*.

Our Caribbean civilisation finds formal institutional expression through our numerous regional institutions of which the major ones are the Caribbean Community (CARICOM), the Organisation of Eastern Caribbean States (OECS), the Association of Caribbean States (ACS), the Community of States, Latin America and the Caribbean (CELAC), and the Bolivarian Alternative for Our Americas (ALBA), and their allied organisations. These are all works in progress as we establish and consolidate a "mature regionalism" that possesses enormous potential to advance further our civilisation.

In 1992, a decade or so before the signing of the Revised Treaty of Chaguaramas (2001) that established the framework for the Caribbean Single Market and Economy (CSME), and nearly 20 years before the Revised Treaty of Basseterre Establishing an OECS Economic Union (and the subsequent admission to Associate Membership by Martinique and Guadeloupe), the Martinican intellectual, Edouard Glissant, in his *Caribbean Discourse: Selected Essays* stated wisely:

> There is potential in this reality of 'Antillanite' or Caribbeanness. What is missing from the notion of Caribbeanness is the *transition from the shared experience to conscious expression*; the need to transcend the intellectual pretensions dominated by the learned elite and to be grounded in collective affirmation, supported by the activism of the people.
>
> Our Caribbean reality is an option for us. It springs from our national experience, but in our histories has only been an 'ability to survive'." (my emphasis)

At this time of respairing, of the embrace of fresh hope, our Caribbean civilisation, in its formal institutional expressions and more importantly, in its invisible side, has an enlarged role to play, far more than hitherto. Our ideas, beliefs, values, customs, ways of living and dying, our culture, our creative imaginings, our sporting and recreational activities, our religious expressions, our attitudes to work and production, and the totality of "the genius of the people" must become fused, not confused, in our efforts to uplift our civilisation, inclusive of its material base, its material foundation.

It is apt for me to quote at length what I stressed in February 2003 in the Inaugural Lecture in the Distinguished Lecture Series to commemorate the 30th Anniversary of CARICOM, entitled "Our Caribbean Civilisation and its Political Prospects":

> The future of our Caribbean civilisation hinges, in large measure, on our provision of relevant and practical answers to the host of queries, among others, which I have been posing. The answers revolve around us acting together in solidarity, within our respective nations and across the region, in the interest of our own humanisation and the future ennoblement of our Caribbean civilisation. I say all this not for political effect, but with a solemnity and a profound seriousness, informed by a careful comparative study of many years, fashioned on the anvil of experience and forged in the cauldron of political struggle.

> A civilisation, and its prospects, is not to be assessed merely on the basis of the outstanding achievements of individuals within it. But clearly an abundance of individual excellence in various fields of human endeavour is an indicator of the progress of a civilisation. In the Caribbean such individual excellence is extensive. We know the outstanding examples; there is thus no need to recite them here.

> However, the true measure of our Caribbean civilisation is not in the individual efforts of these distinguished persons, but in the community and solidarity of the people, as a whole, in the process of nation building:

>> The ordinary workers in agriculture, industry, fisheries and tourism;

>> The professionalism and extra efforts of health personnel, educators, police officers and social workers;

>> The collective spirit and endeavours of the youths in tackling community problems;

The day-to-day travails of women, and the elderly, in keeping their families together and guiding their off-spring;

The struggles of the poor in addressing their housing needs, with or without state assistance;

The daily grind of ordinary folk in their quest for greater democratic controls on the state administration, and for justice;

The splendid dominance of the West Indies Cricket Team, and the Cuban baseball squad, in their respective sports internationally for nearly two decades;

The near sixty years of tertiary education provided so far by the University of the West Indies, and the two hundred and seventy years of similar work by the University of Havana;

The heroic battles of the Cuban people in defence and promotion of their sovereignty, national independence and internationalism;

The striving of our sportsmen, sportswomen, cultural creators and writers of creative imagination, professionals of all kinds, peasants and workers of excellence;

The building of friendships internationally between peoples and nations; and generally the collective actions of our peoples in the arts, culture, production, architecture, religion, journalism, politics and sports.

All these endeavours, and more, of the civilised whole ennoble us. Contrary actions diminish our civilisation.

Imperialism still views our Caribbean as its backyard. It constantly hankers after hegemony in our region, even though our Caribbean does not possess a strategic centrality as hitherto, and certainly not as important a strategic locale for imperialism as the Far East, Africa, the Middle East, or Latin America. Since imperialism has not been able to secure an integrated Caribbean unequivocally in its own interest, it pursues the neo-colonial option of "divide and rule"; in this latter regard it has been quite successful, particularly in its policies towards the Bolivarian Republic of Venezuela and other flashpoints around the world, but not quite so much on Cuba.

I have come to accept that my dream for a political union of the Caribbean is unlikely to be achieved in the foreseeable future, but meaningful modalities of "mature regionalism" are being achieved, with great possibilities for further enhancement. This is central to our government's ongoing quest to build a modern, competitive, many-sided post-colonial economy that is at once national, regional and global.

The further extant challenges of an exceptional nature from the COVID pandemic, the volcanic eruptions and Hurricane Elsa over the past two years make it more urgent than ever to accelerate, strategically, the paradigm shift of building a post-colonial economy of a special type to engender or facilitate sustainable development. We do not conceive these exceptional challenges as a crisis since for us a crisis is a condition in which the principals are innocent of the extent of the condition *and* have no credible path, policies, or programmes to meet successfully these extraordinary challenges. We are *not* innocent of the extent of the dislocation, disruptions, despondency and, in some sections of the population, even despair; and we have a clear and credible framework and accompanying policies/programmes for the way forward.

A Note on Management and Leadership

In the circumstances of a paradigm shift and exceptional challenges, not of our own making, there are problems touching and concerning the sequencing of the transformative measures and the creative initiatives required to support issues of immediate livelihoods, production, training/retraining, and specially targeted avenues of employment for those adversely affected by the paradigm shift and/or the instant exceptional challenges. These considerations entered the design of Budget 2022 and the policies/programmes therein. Given, too, the importance of the State administration in driving the economic acceleration through both its facilitation/regulation of private sector initiatives and the public sector investment programme, the quality of public management has to be at the most optimal level, practicable. This, too, is a critical consideration in Budget 2022 and the rollout of the capital programme.

In all this, I reiterate, the question of political leadership is vital. I have written extensively on this subject in various publications. It is a matter that is at the core of our process of respairing, recovery, and rebuilding. At the same time, people as a whole, or the overwhelming majority of them, must be in solidarity with each other, and the political leadership of the government has to be in communion with the people, always. This is a complicated process in a competitive multi-party democracy and a veritable tower of babble, frequently uninformed and poisoned with the bile of personal ambition, a jaundiced partisan political agenda, fuelled by a complaints industry propagated on various social media platforms.

Still, a clearly-articulated, compelling developmental narrative, quality leadership, quality government's programme, and a steady, truthful communication of our accomplishments and difficulties tend to silence nay-sayers, save and except those on the fringes with anti-national negativism who are of no real political moment. Indeed, the difficult circumstances provide opportunities galore to advance further our people-centred vision and our Caribbean civilisation, the post-colonial economy, sustainable development, targeted strategic interventions, mature regionalism, and internationalist solidarity — the seven central pillars for our path forward.

The Immediate Material Priorities Ahead: At a Glance

The priority outcomes at the most optimal levels in our respairing, recovery and transformation have been established in our preceding narratives: Job Creation and Wealth Creation; Poverty Reduction, Zero Hunger and Proper Nourishment; Equity and Equality; Low Inflation; the Deepening and Broadening of the Education, Health and Wellness, and Housing Revolutions; Fiscal, Monetary, and Financial Stability; Justice and Citizen Security; Good Governance, an Alive Constitutionalism, and Democratic Participation; Water, Sanitation, Electricity, Telecommunications; Climate Change Mitigation and Adaptation; Actions against Desertification, Land Degradation and Drought; Marine Resources and the Blue Economy; Airports and Seaports; Roads and Bridges; Air, Sea, and Road Transport; Sports and Culture; Empowerment of People Especially Marginalised Groups; our Caribbean Civilisation and Mature Regionalism; Internationalist Solidarity.

In the period between 2022 and the end of 2025 (the remainder of the ULP's 5th consecutive term in office) the following are the immediately actionable priority projects and programmes to deliver ongoing transformation for the better:

• The construction of 270 houses and repair of 1,000 houses consequent on the volcanic eruptions of 2021.

• The roll-out of the Volcanic Emergency Project (VEEP) of $118 million and other budgeted programmes to address the immediacy of recovery from the volcanic eruptions, including abundant social safety net supports.

- Implementing the massive array of budgeted projects and programmes to address efficaciously the COVID pandemic.

- The private and public sector investments in hotels and tourism including: Sandals/Beaches Resort at Buccament; Royal Mill at Ratho Mill; Black Sands Hotel Development at Peter's Hope; and the State-financed hotels — Holiday Inn Express at Diamond and the Marriott Hotel at Mt. Wynne.

- The EC $630 million Modern Port Project (Construction and Equipment) at Rose Place.

- The construction of the Modern Parliament and Modern Court Complex Projects.

- The construction of the US $85 million Acute Referral Hospital at Arnos Vale.

- The Rollout of the Plans for the Modern City at Arnos Vale.

- The EC $46 million CDB Government of St. Vincent and the Grenadines School Rebuilding and Rehabilitation Project.

- The Caribbean Digital Transformation Programme (CARDTP) of EC $80.65 million.

- The Human Service Delivery Project (Special Needs and Tech-Voc Education, among other elements) of EC $27.7 million.

- The Projects and Programmes on Agriculture, Fisheries, Forestry, the Blue and Green Economy as detailed in Budget 2022.

- The EC $94.8 million in 34 projects in Transport and Works, especially those on Roads, Buildings, River and Sea Defences, including at Sandy Bay.

- Airports rehabilitation at Argyle and in the Grenadines.

- Projects on Renewable Energy (Solar and Geothermal).

- Rehabilitation/repair of roads and government buildings (schools, police stations, clinics, hospitals, court rooms, prisons, and so forth).

- Building out further Sports, Community, and Cultural facilities.

- Specially-targeted interventions for the poor, vulnerable groups, women, youths, farmers, fisherfolk, small entrepreneurs.

- More efficient delivery of all recurrent expenditure programmes as budgeted.

- Deepening mature regionalism and expanding diplomatic presence overseas.

A Note on Symbols and the Process of Respairing

Symbols, and symbolism of a positive kind are reflective of the ideational and material condition of a nation; they have an important role in galvanising the evolution of our people's consciousness for uplifting purposes.

First, it is surely more necessary and desirable now than at any time since 2002 for our nation to embrace the naming of more national heroes to join the Right Excellent Joseph Chatoyer in this exclusive pantheon.

The Advisory Committee on National Heroes under the Chairmanship of René Baptiste has recommended that George Augustus Mc Intosh, Ebenezer Theodore Joshua, Robert Milton Cato, and John Pamenos Eustace be elevated to the office and status of National Hero. I am strongly advocating that we get on with it at this time. I suggest, too, a further assessment for the possible elevation of one or more of our heroic women.

Second, we ought to cease accepting any of the traditional colonial awards (Knighthoods, CMGs, OBEs, MBEs and the like), save and except any such awards for the Governor General, Her Majesty's representative in St. Vincent and the Grenadines. I realise that there is, logically, a problematic issue since the people of St. Vincent and the Grenadines, in a popular referendum on November 25, 2009, reaffirmed the constitutional and political legitimacy of the British sovereign as our country's Head of State. Indeed, by the affirmative vote in a popular referendum, the people endorsed Her Majesty as Head of State, Queen of St. Vincent and the Grenadines. Thus, her various honours may be viewed, however uncomfortably, as the national honours of our country. But, if the truth be told, it is becoming more and more difficult to get our deserving citizens to accept these British Honours. For example, none of the distinguished health professionals, on account of their work during the pandemic, gave permission for their names to be forwarded to Her Majesty for any of the awards of Commander of Order of St. Michael and St. George (CMG), Commander of the British Empire (CBE), Order of the British Empire (OBE), or Member of the British Empire (MBE). Each of these deserving candidates for a national award specifically rejected the idea of being offered "a colonial award". One esteemed medical practitioner, a proposed awardee, joked, "If Renwick Rose (anti-colonial and anti-imperialist fighter of St. Vincent and the Grenadines) advises me to accept, I may consider it."

As Prime Minister, in recent years I have had reason to note that the only enthusiasm is for knighthoods. Many men seem to enjoy the recognition of the prefix "Sir" and the formal accolade "Lady" for their wives. Indeed, a few years ago, in my process of consultation on the award of some honours, I thought that a CMG may be appropriate for a particular deserving citizen. The Governor General concurred, so I invited this gentleman to visit me to discuss the matter. In rejecting the CMG, he asked plaintively, "What would they call my wife?" He insisted on a knighthood and nothing else; a knighthood was not on offer. This gentleman went to his grave without being suitably honoured. I have noted, too, that many women have a very strong preference to being called "Dame", the title of a "female knighthood".

I am personally unenthused about these "colonial honours" or their assumed "national" status since the referendum of 2009; indeed, I am opposed to them. I get involved only because I am duty-bound as Prime Minister to advise on the particular awards. Needless to say, I have personally rejected more than once, any suggestion, proposal, or recommendation for me "to be knighted".

Unfortunately, the people of St. Vincent and the Grenadines rejected the "reformed Constitution" in the popular referendum of November 2009 in which it was proposed that the British monarch be replaced by a home-grown non-executive President elected by a wholly representative National Assembly. By their rejection, the people have placed me, as their Prime Minister, in the invidious position to be engaged in an annual awards exercise for which I have absolutely no appetite. To be sure, I respect Her Majesty and her family personally as human beings "in service" and as representatives of the British Crown; but I am philosophically constrained to accept Her Majesty as our Head of State, even though I am obliged to do so constitutionally and legally. I am truly pained about this.

Fortunately, the ULP government has been able to alter the Oath of Allegiance. Hitherto, it was to "Her Majesty, her heirs, and successors" that allegiance was sworn; now it is to "the people of St. Vincent and the Grenadines". This alteration was made possible because the Oath of Allegiance to Her Majesty does not appear in the Constitution of St. Vincent and the Grenadines, entrenched or otherwise; thus, we were able, by an Act of Parliament, to effect the statutory change. We may reasonably do the same with a national system of honours. We ought to do so, despite the political and constitutional reaffirmation, through referendum, of Her Majesty as the Sovereign Lady of St. Vincent and the Grenadines.

In our respairing and recovery, we ought to carry the symbolic process of decolonisation further. Our streets, villages, and facilities are chock-full with names of colonialists and members of the planter-merchant elite of the colonial era, including Murray's Road, and Murray's Village (named after the colonial Administrator Gideon Murray in the early 20th century); Victoria Park (after Queen Victoria); streets in Kingstown such as Higginson, Egmont, and Grenville; Redemption Sharpes (called after the planter Sharpe — no relation to the fighter against slavery; the place was called simply "Redemption", hitherto); Mt. Bentinck (after Governor Bentinck); and so forth.

I am not for rewriting historical facts; I simply want our symbols to reflect our nation, our people, our aspirations, our respairing. There are far more appropriate and glorious names for us to embrace from our local, national, regional, and global spaces. We can make this name-changing a meaningful national campaign. And we do not need to make the changes all at once; we do so over time, but we do so determinedly, with purpose, and without rancour.

It may be useful, too, for us to give consideration, legislatively, to introduce a category of distinguished persons who do not rise to the status of "a National Hero" but whose contribution to our nation's well-being has been significant and legendary. Perhaps the category could be called simply, "Legend". A process similar to that for the elevation of a person to the category of a National Hero could be put in place for a "Legend". And I prefer our Legends to be deceased persons, just like our National Heroes. Indeed, I do not think that the name of anyone who is alive ought to be put on any public facility. Living persons have the potential of embarrassing the nation; dead ones cannot.

In this wide-ranging process of conscientization of our citizenry, decolonisation of the mind and respairing, we ought, in a bi-partisan political effort, to address yet again in a referendum the national democratic question of replacing the British monarch in our Constitution with a home-grown, non-executive President as Head of State. Indeed, recently on July 25, 2022, in Parliament I raised this bundle of issues for public consideration.

Respairing and the Genius of Our People

In every civilisation, including our Caribbean civilisation and its Vincentian component, there are several dialectically interconnected sides: the material — the economic order — upon which rests the basis and sustenance of civilisation (life, living, and production); the formal institutions, through which interests are articulated and aggregated, decisions made and implemented, rules and conflicts adjudicated, and the outcomes communicated; the civic, a swathe of non-governmental activities engaging individuals and groups; the religious, the beliefs and practices beyond, though linked to, the temporal and the secular; the anthropological, which constitutes the informal but structured bundles of ways of living and treating with death; the cultural and sporting through which the people express themselves, as the case may be, on matters creative, artistic, athletic, and entertaining; and a fluid space in the people's consciousness awash with possibilities beyond the ordinary, regular, normal, usual. It is this fluid space from which the genius of our people manifests itself and flourishes. It is this existential spirit and yearning from which we must draw, individually and collectively, in our respairing; it is that which encompasses a social individualism and solidarity beyond an atomised individualism.

This genius of our people prompts the recognition that we are all on the dangerous, metaphoric road to Jericho; we have to look out for one another; we cannot be like the priest, the Levite, or the lawyer who passes the wounded and the robbed: we must be like the Good Samaritan who ably helps to the best of his/her ability. This fluid space of the people's genius contains, upliftingly, an instinctive social solidarity and critical thought; that space, too, possesses debilitating, backward instincts and uncritical thinking wedded to pristine individualism and empty rationalisation to fit pre-conceived prejudices as distinct from critical, scientific reasoning. I discussed these issues at some length in a monograph entitled *The Atomised Individual, the Social Individual, and the COVID Vaccine*, and published in 2021.

In our respairing, and beyond the dislocations and despondency arising from the pandemic, the volcanic eruptions and the hurricane, and in our recovery and building back stronger and better, we must draw out, from our people's genius, new and more productive attitudes to work, study, production, management, and leadership. Workers, students, producers, managers, and leaders of all types and at all levels are required in this period of respair and recovery to lift ourselves, more than ever, to higher heights of endeavour and accomplishment. This is easier said than done; there is no one blueprint; there is trial and error in a messy, uplifting process, but there are certainly particular elements, requisites, or ingredients that engender new, orderly, and productive attitudes to take us beyond the episodic hit and miss.

Some of the ingredients, elements or requisites in this regard are generally well-known and widely acknowledged; others, not quite so. Let us thus begin by clearing the decks: First, no society, no civilisation has ever progressed on the basis of laziness, pleasure, leisure, and "nice time"; on the other hand, hard and smart work at all levels, from ground floor to top managerial posts, in communion and interaction with each other and nature and by the application of the best or most appropriate technology, is the basic foundation for the material advancement of the society.

At the same time, there must always be just economic rewards for labour as is emphasised in the Preamble to the Constitution of St. Vincent and the Grenadines. The principle of equity at the work place manifests itself in fairness, not necessarily equality, in wages, salaries, allowances, and retirement benefits; it involves transparent opportunities for promotion and training, non-discrimination on the basis of established constitutional criteria, and reasonably acceptable conditions of work, generally. The equitable principle of fairness applies in relation to owners of capital, technology, and other means of production, including labour and its social organisation (objects of labour, means of labour, and labour itself).

At this stage of the development of St. Vincent and the Grenadines, an efficacious application is required, too, of the principle, "from each according to his ability, to each according go to his work." Inevitably, the practical application of this principle at the workplace delivers an inequality of incomes, but in the society at large it ought never to result in an inequality in the distribution of power and an inequality of opportunities to access public goods (publicly financed or subsidised education, health, housing, electricity, water, sanitation, telecommunications, sports, culture, security, administrative or other services provided by the State). Necessarily, too, the application of this principle at the workplace demands appropriate social safety nets in the society at large since the extent of workplace inequities must be muted or lessened to ensure minimum acceptable standards of life and living, through social solidarity, so as to strengthen social cohesion in pursuit of sustainable development for all.

It is necessary and desirable that discipline and orderliness in work, management, leadership, and productivity be accorded a premium at the workplace. Senseless bickering, infantile complaining, the over-emphasis on rights and the disregard of obligations and confusion, have no place in the process of respairing; neither do time-wasting, learned helplessness and childish divisiveness of a personal, political, religious, or other type. All must be fully respected regardless of sex, sexual orientation, status, role in the social organisation of labour, age, beliefs, political affiliation or otherwise. Violence, criminality and dishonesty are to be eschewed; back-biting, scurrility, falsehoods, and misrepresentations are to be banished. A fresh civic culture at the workplace and in the society at large, purposed to the further development of our society and civilisation, is to be fashioned out of the people's genius for lifting their game when required to do so.

The outcomes of the process of respairing and recovery must be seen practicably to include new or additional jobs, inclusive of quality jobs, enhanced opportunities, improved living standards, poverty reduction, the ending of under-nourishment and hunger, citizen security, improved delivery of public goods, and quality time for leisure from necessary and desirable work.

In the process of respairing and recovery, the social state, in partnership with the private and cooperative sectors and civil society, must strive to ensure the achievement, not only of the narrowly defined economic outcomes, but also the marked reduction of inequality and the enhancement of participatory good governance. Over the past 21 years much has been achieved in these respects, but much more is still to be done. Undoubtedly, for example, there has been a huge enhancement, indeed a veritable seismic shift, towards the equality of access to the basic, quality public goods of education, health, social security, housing, water, electricity, telecommunications, the delivery of justice, and so forth, but there are still unfinished tasks. These accomplishments of the ULP government, its compelling developmental narrative, and its quality leadership place it in the best position to chart the course of respairing and recovery beyond the pandemic, the volcanic eruptions and impactful climate change.

Recently, I was reading a fascinating and illuminating book entitled *The Dawn of Everything – A New History of Humanity* (2021) by David Graeber and David Wengrow, in which appears this relevant and persuasive pronouncement:

> The ultimate question of human history...is not our equal access to material resources (land, calories, means of production), much though these things are obviously important, but our equal capacity to contribute to decisions about how to live together. Of course, to exercise that capacity implies that there should be something meaningful to decide in the first place.

In our respairing and recovery, a central consideration must always be "our equal capacity to contribute to decisions about how to live together." We thus must pose the serious questions for appropriate policy answers. Trivia and sideshows may be entertaining, but they are not the substantial issues of life, living and production, together now and for the future. The decisions having been crafted through established democratic processes, inclusive of public discussions or consultations, and authoritatively determined through the apparatuses of the democratic State, we implement them and follow them.

From their extensive anthropological and historical research, Graeber and Wengrow contend that three basis forms of social liberty are played out, centrally, across human civilisations: The freedom to move away or relocate from one's surroundings; the freedom to ignore or disobey commands issued by others; and the freedom to shape entirely new social realities, or shift back and forth between different ones. The exercise of each of these freedoms has consequences for the individuals, the society, and the civilisation. If one stays, moves or relocates, it is imperative that one stays in organic connection with our St. Vincent and the Grenadines; similarly, atomised individualism, as distinct from social individualism, undermines social solidarity that is so critical for social cohesion and society's progress; and in shaping new realities, together, we ought always to emphasise progress, not regression.

In the continuing aftermath of the pandemic, the volcanic eruptions, Hurricane Elsa, our nation's historical legacies, and contemporary challenges, the process of respairing and recovery demands that we answer *authoritatively* the queries posed by the necessary and desirable quest to shape or continue to shape a fresh bundle of social realties.

This is what Budget 2022 in St. Vincent and the Grenadines and this commentary is about.

There are, of course, those who scoff at large strategic ideas, concepts or frameworks within which to locate public policies and programmatic details for sustainable development. Invariably, those very persons, unknowingly, articulate unformed, ill-formed, bad, or even dangerous, ideas that cannot pass the simplest tests of reasonable scrutiny.

Some 130 years ago, the Cuban revolutionary and patriot, José Marti, definitively addressed this question in an extraordinary essay entitled "Our America" (1891), thus:

> These are not times for going to bed in a sleeping cap...without our weapons for a pillow, weapons of the mind, which vanquish all others. Trenches of ideas are worth more than trenches of stone. A cloud of ideas is a thing no armoured prow can smash through. A vital idea set ablaze before the world at the right moment can, like the mystic banner of the last judgment, stop a fleet of battleships.... We can no longer be a nation of fluttering leaves, spending our lives in the air, our treetop crowned in flowers, humming or creaking, caressed by the caprices of sunlight or thrashed and felled by tempests. The trees must form ranks to block the seven-league giant. It is the hour of reckoning and of marching in unison."

We, the people of St. Vincent and the Grenadines, must be in the active arena, meaningfully, not in facile mischief-making and infantile contrariness, but brimful with creative, practical and achievable ideas beyond the trifling or the banal, to lift St. Vincent and the Grenadines higher and to carry out our respective tasks optimally, in solidarity, marching in unison at this the hour of reckoning; to so march in our quest to respair our condition and to recover beyond the pandemic, the volcanic eruptions, Hurricane Elsa, the myriad challenges arising from our national condition and the global political economy.

Over the sweep of our country's post-independence history, drawing on our earlier antecedents, our people have utilised the material, formal, informal, visible and invisible aspects of our civilisation to build ourselves a functional society at a high level of human development and civilisation. In the process, we have marshalled sensibly our instruments of sovereignty and independence to make our lives better in every material particular. And we have, especially at our most challenging times, relied on the collective genius resident in our people to take us beyond what most casual observers who know not us well, thought practical or achievable.

Over the years this collective genius of our people, and the talented individuals among us, have ensured that we have not only survived, but thrived against seemingly insurmountable odds. Our resilience and creativity in life, living, and production have been a marvel to others. Time and again we have demonstrated it. At this most difficult confluence of circumstances (the pandemic, the volcanic eruptions, Hurricane Elsa, global turmoil, and more) and their consequences, we must summon yet again that collective genius and embrace our fresh hopefulness, not helplessness, respairing and not despairing. With our stronger material base, our education revolution, our good governance apparatuses, our technological advances, our enhanced infrastructure, our regional and global solidarity, and more, the collective genius of our people will find even greater scope and opportunities for us to overcome the enormity of our extant challenges and forge ahead in our collective interests.

Our people's collective genius has improvised home-made tools; fashioned beautiful music from steel drums; built lovely houses with abundant local material with the hands and brains of skilled carpenters and masons; produced tasty, nutritious foods and a selective cuisine of quality; ploughed our lands, traversed our seas, welcomed visitors, and traded in goods and services, in the building of our economy; danced, laughed, and entertained; displayed our sporting prowess, worshipped our God joyously in prayer and song; cared for our young, the elderly, and the infirm; and buried our dead with touching solemnity. Teachers have taught, leaders have led, parents have parented, our elderly have guided, our young have grown magnificently, our public servants have served, our nurses and doctors have tended the sick, the police and jurists have helped to keep the peace, our farmers and fisherfolk have farmed and fished productively for our food and for exportso our workers have kept the wheels of industry turning, and our prophets have prophesised of the Second Coming and God's amazing grace. Amidst all of this, our women have been exemplary as mothers, as partners, as producers; our rocks, our glue that holds us together, as women simply and profoundly, as history-makers.

To be sure not all persons of and in these categories have performed as well; indeed, some have fallen way short of what is required of them. But we ought never to make perfection the enemy of the good even as we strive to be better, to be the best that we can in all the circumstances. Overall, there has been a good score sheet, with some exceptional performances, oft-times from unsung social individuals.

The quality endeavours at the workplace have to be more than matched within the family and the society at large. A nurturing family in which the children's welfare is paramount is central to our respairing. In the society-at-large, good neighbourliness in every material particular is more than ever required for our advancement. Our robust, competitive politics, too, must not descend into intolerance, hatred, and self-centred divisiveness.

Frankly, the opposition NDP has abandoned any sense of responsibility and constructiveness. It traffics in anger, bile, falsehoods, and mispresentations fuelled by a seemingly unquenchable thirst for power. Its emptiness of policy and programme propels it inevitably to scurrilous "ad hominem" attacks against the leaders of government and their supporters. The opposition's long sojourn in the political wilderness (21 years and counting, five successive electoral defeats) has caused it to lose focus and has made it susceptible to an array of internet crazies who are as ill-informed as they are hankering for personal glory, government jobs, diplomatic postings, and status. Every ordinary complaint, any spurious disaffection or contrived injurious affectation is raised aloft as a "cause célébre" of mighty proportions only to collapse swiftly under the weight of its own triviality or the exposure of the unvarnished truth. The modern telecommunications platforms of social media, YouTube, Instagram and so forth, amplify this malignant tower of babble among the occupants of the opposition's echo chamber, to the amusement and sometimes dismay of dispassionate ear-witnesses and eye-witnesses.

Still, the more balanced tribal NDP vote, and more than a pocketful of others in their ranks who are prepared to listen, have to be patiently informed of the dangers of the NDP's current anti-national path and its plan to sell out the country to foreign purchasers of our country's existential patrimony, its citizenship, and its passports that are the outward signs of the inward grace of our treasured, highly-valued citizenship. This is but the tip of the dangerous political iceberg of the NDP's vaunted neo-liberalism, its austerity programmes, its advocacy of an open sesame sale of our country to disreputable foreigners, and its alliances with some of the most backward, hegemonic political forces on earth, including the current Republican Party in the USA. It is the fate of our country to respair while still carrying the heavy political baggage of the opposition NDP. In time, as our nation respairs fully, the NDP will disappear as a serious political force; the people will condemn it to irrelevance or worse. To be sure, the NDP will linger on as it prolongs its political goodbye, but it is doomed, sooner rather than later, unless it undergoes a metamorphosis; but they seem incapable of running anything new, different and better.

What is the role of the Christian churches in St. Vincent and the Grenadines at this time of respair beyond our current travails from the amalgam of exogenous forces, not of our making? Our country consists nominally, and overwhelmingly so, of Christian believers. Our nation's Constitution begins with a preambular affirmation that we are "a nation founded on the belief in the supremacy of God and the freedom and dignity of man (and woman)".

The religious or "churchical" lay of the land is as follows: The Anglican Church, hitherto supremely dominant, recorded a member-ship of only 14 percent of the population in the last Census (2012); the Methodists still hold their own at 9 percent; the Roman Catholics are a steadily declining religious force at 6 percent; together they constitute 29 percent of the population who adhere to baptism by a sprinkling of water on the baby's forehead. In the ascendancy are all those who are "born again" with full immersion, water baptism of cognitive souls: Pentecostals, 29 percent of the population; Seventh Day Adventists, 13 percent; Evangelicals, 9 percent; and Spiritual Baptists, 9 percent, are the major denominations in this reshaped religious landscape. Of these broad religious groups, there is internal doctrinal coherence, more or less, in the following: Anglicans, Methodists, Roman Catholics, the lead-ing Pentecostal sub-groups, such as the Pentecostal Assembly of the West Indies (PAWI); the Seventh Day Adventist Church; the New Tes-tament Church of God and the Evangelical Church of the West Indies, among the broad group of Evangelicals; and the belonger churches to the Archdiocese and Primacy of the Spiritual Baptists.

Among the Pentecostals, Evangelicals and Spiritual Baptists there are also dozens of independent, single pastor-owned churches, often with links to an external entity providing funding and other supports. This organisational fluidity/independence and doctrinal diversity prompt much confusion in religious offerings. Perhaps the more inter-nally consistent numerically of the smaller churches are denominations such as the Thusians (a breakaway group from the larger, more influ-ential Seventh Day Adventists), and the Ancient Churchical Order of Nyabinghi (a Rastafari grouping).

On the vital matter of the COVID vaccine and the related issue of the requirement for frontline and strategic public sector employees to be vaccinated, there was broad, but relatively muted support from the Anglicans, Methodists, and Roman Catholics (these three churches and the Salvation Army constitute the St. Vincent and the Grenadines Christian Council), the Seventh Day Adventists, PAWI, and some Evangelicals. Even among some pastors in some of these churches there was no real cohesion. Among others, confusion reigned supreme: Yes to the Vaccine; "Yes, but", to the vaccine; anti-vaxxers; anti-vaxxers, "but"; pro-vaccine requirement; anti-vaccine requirement; and every conceivable position in-between. It has not been the Christian churches' finest hour! On display among the leading church men and women was high principle; but among some others, objective observers witnessed demagoguery, cowardice, opportunism, and ignorance; the more demagogic, opportunistic, cowardly, and ignorant the posture, the more loudly, invariably, was the invocation of God's name in defence.

I worry deeply about the direction of some of the Christian churches in St. Vincent and the Grenadines in their commentaries on divisive, or not so divisive public issues. Added to all this is the public cynicism that greets the almost daily-minted apostles, prophets and prophetesses; sometimes it appears that a spouse becomes a prophet or prophetess through holy matrimony. In my innocence I have always conceived of these lofty elevations as demonstrably divine callings from God, with appropriate validations. In this matter, my innocence has been shattered.

Still, the central purpose of Christian teachings is the redemption of sinners, that is to say, the redeeming of all of us. Redeeming embodies hope, faith, and love; redeeming is akin to respairing. So, despite the confused and confusing cacophony of voices from the Christian Church about the pandemic and the vaccine, there is a huge role, nay, existential mission for the Church to embrace in our process of respairing. I expect them to take a fresh guard and fulfil their central calling not only in private prayer, but also in their responsible public mission where it greatly matters. As far as is humanly practicable, the Church and the government ought to work in tandem in the mammoth task of mobilising the entire society to respair beyond the extant challenges of life, living and production in quest of sustainable development.

Similarly, the government must be in partnership with civil society, organised business, and organised labour. It is unfortunate that in small societies like ours, differences on this or that matter swiftly become seemingly unbridgeable chasms; petty politicking, personality clashes, personal vanities, and a lack of a full understanding of the perils at hand oft-times intervene to complicate matters. Chasms, of course, cannot be traversed by baby steps; inexorably such an approach results in a descent into the widening gorge. The crossing of the chasms has to be effected boldly in communion with the people as a whole.

Neither organised business nor organised labour ought ever to conceive as their role or function to alter, or to conspire with others to bring about a change, alteration, neutering, or obstruction of government. That right belongs to the people as a whole through general elections. Any trade union leadership that pits itself in perpetual opposition to the government, particularly a Labour government like that of the ULP, short-changes the interests of the union membership and society as a whole. In time, the union membership will realise that their leadership is engaged in useless vanity and senseless bickering when a constructive partnership is preferred, especially with a Labour government. To be sure, be critical if you have to, but be measured and mature.

The leadership of any public sector union who espouses a petty-bourgeois quest for an "aristocracy of labour" among government employees is destined to find itself in a cul-de-sac, isolated from its members and the rest of the working people at large. Rather, it is in the interest of the membership of the public sector unions to insist that their leaderships work collaboratively with the Labour government, particularly at this time of extraordinary challenges not of our own making. They will find the ULP government willing to meet them more than halfway along the journey of respairing. Indeed, the ULP government is way ahead of most of these union leaders in promoting, advancing, defending, and securing gains for the working people and the nation as a whole.

In late 2001, some 4,000 "frontline" or "strategic" employees of the State (permanent secretaries, heads of central government departments, teachers, police officers, health personnel, customs and immigration officers, employees of the Port Authority and Argyle International Airport Incorporated) were required by law to take the COVID vaccine as an incident of their employment. Their failure or refusal to do so meant an abandonment by them of their office or job. Approximately 250 of them who failed or refused to meet the requirement, were assessed ineligible for one of two possible exemptions ("medical" or "religious"); thus, such employees chose to vacate their offices or jobs.

At the time of writing this (July 2022) most of these vacancies have been filled by temporary employees or persons on assignments; some posts have been filled permanently. The government, as employer, has announced, as a matter of policy, that, *all things being equal,* the vacant positions may be available to be filled by the employees who abandoned their posts provided they either comply with the statutory vaccine requirement or an amended regime (testing, mask-wearing, specified protocols) occasioned by an altered epidemiological condition in the country. Clearly, the window has narrowed or is narrowing for those employees to be re-employed; it cannot be reasonably expected that the State authorities will continue to wait way beyond any further requirement deadline that had been originally set at mid-December 2021. The government has been generous and fully proportionate in its accommodation of the relevant employers, but many are adamant that they will not take the vaccine or even a COVID test. The public sector unions and some employees are currently testing the constitutionality/ legality of the government's actions on this public health and safety matter. The government awaits the response of the individual former employees to its invitation to reapply for their jobs under the recently amended regime announced in late July 2022.

I am deeply disappointed that some employees of the State — a small minority — failed or refused to comply with a completely reasonable vaccine requirement of late 2021 that the government is fully satisfied easily passes constitutional/legal muster in every material respect. My government holds no rancour towards these employees; we continue to be keen to engage them reasonably and sensibly during the pandemic and after. That, too, is part of respairing and recovery. Indeed, the government is metaphorically bending over backwards to accommodate these former employees in the hope and reasonable expectation that the valued former employees will act reasonably in our nation's continued effort to protect health and save lives in a context of the still ongoing COVID pandemic and public health emergency.

More than ever the leadership of the ULP government must accomplish the quality leadership task of not merely inspiring the people, but drawing out of them their genius, their goodness and their nobility; and to draw out such genius, goodness and nobility the people may not as yet know that they possess. This task is achieved by articulating a compelling developmental narrative, by elaborating targeted strategic initiatives to suit the times, and by the doing of the mighty deeds required. Time in this enterprise is always of the essence; yet, the strategic path and the programmatic details within that path must be pursued with steadfastness and creativity, with a patience and a calm in the people's sustainable interests in all the circumstances.

In the process of respairing the role of young people, sports and culture are critical. Sporting and cultural expressions are always avenues through which to bolster our people's spirit in the returning of hope so as to uplift further our endeavours of solidarity and sustainable development. They are particularly helpful in mobilising young people toward desired ends. This has been so since the time of ancient Greece; it has been also our Caribbean and Vincentian experience. These expressions are of inestimable value.

There are troubling signs that the pressures of COVID and the aftermath of the volcanic eruptions are having strenuous psycho-social impacts of a negative kind on children, young persons, and adults, including government employees who chose to abandon their jobs on account of their failure or refusal to take the COVID vaccine as required by law. Our health professionals and those from PAHO and UNICEF were predicting all this. As a consequence, they have rolled out a number of interventions at both the centre and in the communities to assist in combatting these psycho-social travails and disorientations. But it appears as though these interventions, thus far, have not arrested adequately or sufficiently these challenges. This is an ongoing exercise of varying correctives.

Anecdotal and persuasive evidence suggests that children and students in early childhood, primary and secondary schools are experiencing more anti-social behavioural problems than hitherto. More school fights are taking place, and some teachers are having a difficult time coping with these behavioural challenges. Further, young adults, especially males but also females, are becoming more aggressive than usual and are lacking elemental social restraint. Facebook and other social media platforms are exacerbating these disturbing tendencies. So far this year, seven months into 2022, there have been 20 or so homicides nationwide and two significant cocaine hauls in the northeast of St. Vincent. The Police are reporting increased restlessness among motorists and citizens generally, though the actual crime rate has declined.

There is no breakdown of law and order, but there are troubling signs to watch carefully and arrest sensibly, not by coercion or incarceration but by appropriate psycho-social interventions, quality parenting, quality school leadership, quality teaching, religious mentoring, family and community solidarity, and national unity around achievable goals of sustainable development. The Police, the Prosecutors, the Prison Officers, the Magistrates, and the Judges need to grasp what is happening and respond accordingly in ways to facilitate respairing, solidarity, and caring. Obviously, the social and coercive responses to hardened criminals are of a different nature; but we must all understand what is happening. I do not think that I am over-stating the case.

Clearly, much of this relates to the difficult socio-economic condition arising from the pandemic and the volcanic eruptions; but the material uplift is easier to achieve than the connected psycho-social challenges to be lessened or resolved. Huge State investments have been made in broadening and strengthening the social safety nets; employment is picking up and the housing reconstruction is very much on its way. Budget 2022 makes ample provisions for all these areas, and more, but the work is to be done effectively on the ground.

In all these and more, the pace of implementation needs to be quickened. Time is not on anybody's side. And the public and private capital investment programmes demand the swiftest possible implementations. No lethargy is acceptable.

I worry greatly about the educational deficits that may be on the horizon if appropriate correctives are not undertaken robustly, compellingly and swiftly. Due to the COVID pandemic, our students have lost nearly one year of face-to-face instructional time. Although our government purchased 30,000 tablets to facilitate online teaching and learning in the early childhood, primary, secondary, and post-secondary institutions, the results have not been uniformly successful. Our educators, parents and students need to realise this, and we all must put in an herculean effort with sensible, practical educational policies/ programmes to ensure that we do not have a near-insoluble educational and socio-economic problem of massive proportions within five to seven years or so.

Globally, UNICEF has been raising the alarm about what it calls a potential "generational catastrophe", given the pandemic's disastrous effect on students' education. In developed and developing countries the early data so far indicates that scores and proficiencies in Mathematics, Language, and Science have fallen significantly. On the basis of the Caribbean Primary Exit Assessment (CPEA) at primary schools and the CSEC and CAPE examinations (for fifth formers at secondary schools, and college students respectively) in 2021, this decline has not yet been observed in St. Vincent and the Grenadines. Educators, however, suspect that the educational deficit is being accumulated below the levels of CPEA in the primarily schools, below CSEC in secondary schools, and for new student intakes in the post-secondary college in the next two or so years. All this requires urgent attention. Budget 2022 addressees these and related issues but the real work must be done in the classrooms accordingly.

As difficult, uncertain times unfold, selfish and criminally-minded persons will take advantage of some gullible or even desperate persons; the prospect of human trafficking is real. As Prime Minister, in the first week in February 2022, I sounded the warning about some nasty people at home and abroad in England who were recruiting mainly young women to go to England to work as "baby sitters". It is an illegal, wicked, craven, exploitative scheme! Nothing good will come of it for these young women and some young men. Thus far, anecdotal evidence suggests that it is a trickle of persons who are being trafficked; it must not become a flood. I have instructed the Commissioner of Police to investigate; and he has so directed the Trafficking-in-Persons Unit (TIPU) of the Police Force to act swiftly in this regard. I have personally spoken to the British High Commissioner in Barbados on this matter; and I have discussed the matter fully with the High Commissioner of St. Vincent and the Grenadines to the United Kingdom. The authorities in both the United Kingdom and St. Vincent and the Grenadines are collaborating on this issue.

I am concerned, too, that there are dangers that the opioid crisis in the USA may spill over into our Caribbean, our St. Vincent and the Grenadines. Overdose deaths (OD) caused by opioid drugs are now more than 100,000 in the USA. We have noted, for example, the way a Big Pharma company has successfully pushed OxyContin, referred to by alert medical observers as "an addictive cash-cow painkiller", into "blue-collar" America.

Recently, the *Lancet*, a prestigious and authoritative British medical journal, addressed this issue, thus:

> The risk of global spread (of opioids) is greater...where corporations look for new markets, but are left to self-regulate. To manage pain, greed must be managed as well.

It does appear that some pharmaceutical enterprises in the USA are in partnership with Chinese manufacturers in this dangerous trade. Increasing numbers of Americans are turning to a relatively low-priced synthetic opioid known as fentanyl, often used as a general anesthetic. Fentanyl is reputed to be much more potent than heroin — just 3ml will kill an average man; overdosing is thus easy. Almost all of the illegal fentanyl is made, it is alleged, by the chemists in China. Loads of money are being made in this deathly trade.

Some addicts are lacing cocaine with fentanyl; this way of getting "a high" is increasing;, the overdose deaths. In New York City in 2015, only 17 of that city's overdose deaths were from cocaine mixed with fentanyl; in 2019, the number jumped to 183. I have been advised, too, that another popular admixture in some circles is marijuana and fentanyl. This dangerous cocktail is of particular relevance to us in the Caribbean.

Once these forms of addiction are taking place in the USA on the scale described, it is only a matter of time before they arrive in deadly numbers in our Caribbean, our St. Vincent and the Grenadines, particularly if the psycho-social circumstances are propitious in their joinder with money-making. Our nation's Advisory Council on the Misuse of Drugs must be very alert to the real possibilities for harm, especially to youths and young adults who may be craving cheap experimentation in drugs. Even one death in this regard would be a tragedy, additional to our existing challenges.

Unfortunately, there has been a slow uptake on the vaccine designed to combat COVID-19. Less than 40 percent of our country's population and less than one-half of the age groups, 12-years and above, have been fully vaccinated against COVID. Although, our country was never closed due to the pandemic — other countries closed down on us — we have had restrictions fashioned to limit the pandemic's spread. Obviously, a higher rate of vaccination will assist in loosening further the limited restrictions in place and open up fully all the spaces for enhanced economic, social, cultural, sporting, religious, and political activities.

Fortunately, the overwhelming number of front-line and strategic public sector employees took the vaccine as required by law for their jobs; the numbers ranged from over 92 percent in some employment categories to statistically 100 percent in others. I am advised that the earlier omicron variant provided temporary immunity, too, to significant numbers of persons who contracted it. But as time passes the temporary immunity from the vaccine or the COVID infection is being lost. So, I urge the taking of the vaccine or the booster.

The government has set a target of 70 percent vaccination for the over-12-year-old segments of our population that number some 80,000 persons. Despite the non-achievement of this goal, the country held a fully-fledged Carnival in June-July 2022 for the first time since 2019. The people's need for a "release" to be provided by this cultural/musical festival was viewed as part of their respairing. The government was keen to have the Carnival, but it depended clearly on an improved favourable epidemiological condition in the country. As at June 04, 2022, there were 120 or so active cases, and seven hospitalisations, five of whom were unvaccinated; there were 108 COVID-related deaths since the start of the pandemic on March 11, 2020 — there were two such deaths recently in early June 2022, the first since February 2022.

The pandemic has made problematic some real life-and-death choices in the health system by the medical doctors. Among the queries they are required daily to answer in practical ways, consistent with the Hippocratic Oath and their professionalism are: Should a COVID patient who fails or refuses to take the vaccine be accorded a limited hospital bed in preference to another ill person who would normally have received the bed space? In marginal cases, where does the medical doctor come down with his/her decision? To what extent does the health system or the hospitals become focused on the COVID patients to the detriment of other patients with other life-threatening conditions? Where is the line drawn and who draws the line, the attending physician or the Medical Director of the hospital?

Amidst our optimism for respairing and recovery in 2022 and beyond, we ought never to minimise the extant challenges and potential dangers around the corner. Facts, clarity of thought, and clear-sighted policy directions are the way to go. This is not the time for folly or sideshows. This is serious business for serious people!

Over the past near-54 years as a political activist in our Caribbean, through varied times and seasons inclusive of 28 years as a parliamentary representative, 21 years thus far as Prime Minister, I know what it is to meet daunting challenges and not flinch or grow weary. In the Book of Chronicles in the Hebrew Bible, it was said of Issachar, one of the leaders of the Twelve Tribes of Israel, simply that he knew the times and he acted accordingly; this guidance commends itself to me as we face a time of respair in our challenging journey to recover and rebuild consequent upon the pandemic, the volcanic eruptions, the debilitating vagaries of climate change, and the ill winds of a harsh, unequal globalisation affecting adversely a small, multi-island State like St. Vincent and the Grenadines, racked as it is, too, by historical legacies of underdevelopment.

I have been accorded an especial responsibility as Prime Minister, certainly for a time like this; it is a very challenging time to have a pivotal role in the central arena of political activism. In 1910, Theodore Roosevelt, one of the USA's robust, activist Presidents, delivered his celebrated speech in Paris, France, entitled "Man in the Arena", part of which resonates with me. Devoid of any arch-imperialist bombast or commentary, for which he was well-known, Roosevelt, in addressing leadership, declared:

> It is not the critic who counts; not the man who points out how the strong man stumbles, or where the doer of deeds could have done them better. The credit belongs to the man who is actually in the arena, whose face is marred by dust and sweat and blood; who strives valiantly; who errs, who comes short again and again, because there is no effort without error and shortcoming; but who does actually strive to do the deeds; who knows great enthusiasms, the great devotions; who spends himself in a worthy cause; who at the best knows in the end the triumph of high achievement, and who at the worst, if he fails, at least fails while daring greatly, so that his place shall never be with those cold and timid souls who neither know victory nor defeat.

Metaphorically, in cricketing terms, the ULP government, since 2001 and continuing, has put huge scores and mighty achievements "on the tins", on the scoreboard. They are there for all to see. Our government, over the last 21 years, has altered life, living and production immeasurably for the better for Vincentians of all walks of life, but especially so for the poor, the working people, the farmers, the fisherfolk, the children, the young people, the elderly, the women, the vulnerable and marginalised groups. In the process, we have been faithful to the Constitution, the law and good governance. We have enriched our Caribbean civilisation in myriad ways; we have more than played our part in strengthening a mature regionalism and we have been in international solidarity with our global family of nations in pursuit of peace, security and prosperity, for all. We have what it takes to lead successfully at this hour of our reckoning in communion with our people for sustainable development.

Fresh challenges have been upon us: the national budgets for the years 2020 and 2021, inclusive of the specific supplementaries targeting the pandemic and the volcanic eruptions; and now Budget 2022 is rolled out for a time like this. We put our markers down decisively, boldly and comprehensively to meet efficaciously the extant and prospective challenges.

In our respairing and recovery, we remind ourselves of the poetic teaching of Daniel Williams, a Vincentian poet of the highest quality, in his "We are the Cenotaphs", that of all time "only the future is ours to desecrate." In learning from our history, as "Shake" Keane advises, we must "come home" to ourselves. So, today, we are enjoined to respair, to recover, to rebuild; in that committed way we shall avoid the desecration of our future!

Bibliography/References

Abrahamian, Atossa Araxia, *The Cosmopolites – The Coming of the Global Citizen*
(Columbia Global Reports, New York, 2015)

Banerjee, Abhijit V and Duflo, Esther, *Good Economics for Hard Times* (Public Affairs,
Hachette Book Group, New York, 2019)

Beckford, George, *Persistent Poverty: Underdevelopment in Plantation Economies
of the Third World* (Oxford University Press, UK, 1972;
republished by University of the "West Indies Press, Jamaica, 1999)

Beckles, Hilary, *How Britain Underdeveloped the Caribbean — A Reparations Response
to Europe's Legacy of Plunder* (University of the West Indies Press, Jamaica, 2021)

Best, Lloyd, "A Model of Pure Plantation Economy" Social and Economic Studies,
Volume 87, No. 3, September 1968

Brewster, Havelock and Thomas, C.Y., *The Dynamics of West Indian Economic Integration*
(Institute of Social and Economic Research, UWI, Jamaica, 1967)

Chomsky, Noam, *The Precipice: Neoliberalism, the pandemic and the Urgent Need
for Radical Change* (Penguin Books, Random House, U.K., 2021)

Clarke, Kenneth, *Civilisations* (Penguin Books, Harmondsworth, 1969)

Demas, William, *The Economics of Development in Small Countries with Special Reference
to the Caribbean* (Mc Gill University Press, Montreal, 1965;
Republished by UWI Press, Jamaica, 2009)

Eastern Caribbean Central Bank. *Eight-Point Growth and Stabilisation Plan,*
(ECCB, St, Kitts, 2008)

Friedman, Milton, "The Social Responsibility of Business is to Increase
Its Profits"(New York Times Magazine, September 13, 1970).

Garvey, Amy Jacques (ed), *Philosophy and Opinions of Marcus Garvey*
(originally published in 1923; republished by Routledge, USA, 1977)

Girvan, Norman, *Foreign Capital and Economic Underdevelopment in Jamaica*
(ISER, UWI, Jamaica, 1972)

Gonsalves, Camillo, *Globalised, Climatised, Stigmatised* (Strategy Forum Inc.,
St. Vincent and the Grenadines, 2019)

— —, "Rising from the Ashes to the Challenges" (Budget Address 2022
to Parliament on January 10, 2022, Government of St. Vincent & the Grenadines)

Gonsalves, Ralph, *The Non-Capitalist Path to Development: Africa and the Caribbean*
(One Caribbean Publishers, London, 1981)

— —, *History and the Future: A Caribbean Perspective* (Great Works Depot,
St. Vincent and the Grenadines, 1994)

— —, *The Politics of Our Caribbean Civilisation: Essays and Speeches*
(Great Works Deport, St. Vincent and the Grenadines, 2001)

— —, *The Making of the Comrade: The Political Journey of Ralph Gonsalves*
(Strategy Forum Inc., St. Vincent and the Grenadines, 2010)

— —, *Our Caribbean Civilisation and Its Political Prospects*
(Strategy Forum Inc; St. Vincent and the Grenadines, 2014)

— —, *The Case for Caribbean Reparatory Justice*
(Strategy Forum Inc., St. Vincent and the Grenadines, 2017)

— —, *The Political Economy of the Labour Movement in St. Vincent
and the Grenadines* (Strategy Forum, Inc., St. Vincent and the Grenadines, 2019)

— —, "Budget Address 2003" (Delivered to Parliament on
December 02, 2002; Government Printery, St. Vincent and the Grenadines)

Gordon, Robert, *The Rise and Fall of American Growth* (Princeton University Press,
NJ, 2016)

Government of St. Vincent and
the Grenadines, *Estimates of Revenue and Expenditure for 2022 – With Projections
for 2023 and 2024* (Government Printery, St. Vincent and the Grenadines, 2022)

Graeber, David and Wengrow, David, *The Dawn of Everything: A New History of Humanity* (Allen Lane, London, 2021)

Keane, Ellsworth "Shake", "Private Prayer" in "Shake" Keane: *The Angel Horn – Collected Poems* (House of Nehesi Publishers, St. Martin, 2005)

Kuhn, Thomas, *The Structure of Scientific Revolutions* (Chicago University Press, USA, 1962)

Lewis, Arthur, *Labour Movement in the West Indies: The Birth of a Workers Movement* (Victor Gollancz Ltd and the Fabian Society, 1939; republished by New Beacon Books, London, 1977)

— —, *Economic Development With Unlimited Supplies of Labour* (The Manchester School, Manchester University, UK, 1954)

— —, *The Principles of Economic Planning* (originally published 1949; republished by Routledge, UK, 2010)

— —, *The Theory of Economic Growth* (originally published in 1955; republished by Routeldge, UK, 2003)

— —, *Development Planning: The Essentials of Economic Policy* (Harper and Row, USA, 1966)

— —, *Tropical Development 1880 – 1913: Studies in Economic Progress* (North Western University Press, Evanston Ill., 1971)

— —, *Growth Fluctuations 1870 – 1913* (George Allen and Unwin, London, 1978)

Lincoln, Abraham, Quoted in Theodore Roosevelt: Address on the "New Nationalism" (August 11, 1910) in Craig Fehrman (ed.): *The Best Presidential Writing, From 1789 to The Present* (Simon and Schuster, NY, 2020)

Lucas, Robert E (Jr.), "On the Mechanics of Economic Development", *Journal of Monetary Economics* 22, No. 1, 1988

Madison, James, *The Federalist Papers* (No. 1, November 22, 1787) in Craig Fehrman (ed.), op. cit.

Marti, José, *Our America* (originally published in El Partido, Mexico City, January 20, 1891)

Marx, Karl, *The Eighteenth Brumaire of Louis Napoleon* (original English edition published in 1869; published in Marx, Karl and Frederick Engels: *Selected Works* (Lawrence and Wishart, London, 1950)

Mc Millan, William M, *Warning from the West Indies: A Tract for Africa and the Empire* (Penguin, Harmondsworth, 1938)

Millette, James, *Society and Politics in Colonial Trinidad* (originally published in 1970; republished by Zed Books, UK)

Moyne Commission, "West Indian Royal Commission, 1938 – 1939" (Report by Lord Moyne, Command Paper 6607, HMSO, London, 1945)

Paz, Octavio, *The Labyrinth of Solitude and Other Writings* (Grove Press, USA, 1989)

Piketty, Thomas, *Capital in the Twenty-First Century* (Harvard University Press, Cambridge, MA, 2013)

— —, *Time for Socialism — Dispatches From A World on Fire, 2016 – 2021* (Yale University Press, USA, 2021)

Rodney, Walter, *How Europe Underdeveloped Africa* (Bogle — L'Ouverture Publications, London, 1973)

Romer, Paul, "Increasing Returns and Long Term Growth", *Journal of Political Economy* 94, No. 5, 1986.

Roosevelt, Theodore, "State of the Union Address, 1901" in Craig Fehrman, op. cit.

— —, "Man in the Arena" (Speech formally called "Citizenship in a Republic", delivered on April 23, 1910, at Sorbonne, France, available widely on the Internet)

Schumacher, Ernst, *Small is Beautiful: A Study of Economics As If People Mattered* (Massachusetts Institute of Technology, MA, USA, 1973)

Scott, Cleve Mc Donald, *The Politics of Crown Colony Government: Land, Labour and Politics in Colonial State*, St. Vincent and the Grenadines, 1883 to 1937

(PhD Thesis, UWI, Barbados)

Smith, Godfrey, *The Assassination of Maurice Bishop* (Ian Randle Publishers, Kingston, Jamaica, 2020)

Solow, Robert M., "A Contribution to the Theory of Economic Growth", *Quarterly Journal of Economics* 70, No. 1, 1956.

Spinelli, Joseph, *Land Use and Population in St. Vincent, 1763 – 1960 — A Contribution to the Study of Economics and Demographic Change in a Small West Indian Island* (Ph.D Thesis, University of Florida, 1973)

Unity Labour Party, Election Manifesto 2015

— —, Election Manifesto 2020

United Nations, *17 Sustainable Goals* (UN Publications, 2015)

Walcott, Derek, "The Antilles: Fragments of Epic Memory", Nobel Lecture 1992 (The Nobel Foundation, Harper – Collins, NY, 1992)

World Bank, *The Growth Report: Strategies for Sustained Growth and Inclusive Development* (Commission on Growth and Development Chaired by Professor Michael Spence; World Bank Publications, 2008)

Index

A

Made in the USA
Middletown, DE
25 September 2022

11106945R00168